Becoming an Early Years Teacher

Becoming an Early Years Teacher

Edited by Jessica Johnson

Open University Press

Open University Press
McGraw-Hill Education
McGraw-Hill House
Shoppenhangers Road
Maidenhead
Berkshire
England
SL6 2QL

email: enquiries@openup.co.uk
world wide web: www.openup.co.uk

and Two Penn Plaza, New York, NY 10121–289, USA

First published 2014

A catalogue record of this book is available from the British Library

ISBN-13: 978–0–33–526444–5 (pb)
ISBN-10: 0–33–526444–1 (pb)
eISBN: 978–0–33–526445–2

Library of Congress Cataloging-in-Publication Data
CIP data applied for

Typesetting and e-book compilations by
RefineCatch Limited, Bungay, Suffolk

Praise for this book

"Authoritative, scholarly and grounded in practice, this is surely destined to become the must-have practical handbook for all those seeking Early Years Teacher status."

Geoff Taggart, Lecturer in Early Years, University of Reading, UK

"Becoming and Early Years Teacher will prove valuable to all those working in the early years sector, and is an accessible and user friendly resource that promotes increased professional responsibility. Theoretical underpinning and the use of case studies, activities and links to observed practice, provide thought provoking material which recognises the importance of partnership working with families and wider community organisations. Emphasis is placed on the importance of reflection to question values and beliefs and to continually evaluate and challenge practice.

This book aims to support inspirational practice that will enhance positive learning opportunities for all early years' children."

Soraya Goni, HE Award Leader Childhood Studies, Kirklees College, UK

"I am delighted to recommend this comprehensive, challenging and accessible power-pack of a book, which deserves to become essential reading for all Early Years Teachers in training and equally for those engaged in studying on Early Childhood Studies degrees. The team of contributors bring a wealth of both professional and academic knowledge and experience to their chapters and overall the book promotes critical thinking and reflexive practice. Whilst explicitly addressing the standards for Early Years Teacher Status the book avoids taking an instrumentalist approach and explores a range of perspectives and tensions related to professionalism within the early childhood world."

Penny Holland, Early Childhood Consultant

"This book provides essential, well-articulated, thought-provoking guidance for students working towards Early Years Teacher Status. Throughout the chapters, for each of the eight standards there are strong themes encouraging reflection, reflective practice, leadership and a commitment that in-depth knowledge of theory is closely linked to practice. Scenarios are presented to encourage extension of thought and knowledge whilst ensuring adherence to the statutory and non-statutory framework for the Early Years Foundation Stage. This approach helps to ensure that the students work towards leading continuous improvement in practice so that babies and young children experience their learning and development through play and individual care needs. This is a very good book that I would recommend to all Early Years Teacher Status students."

Tricia Johnson, EYT Assessor, Buckinghamshire New University, UK

To Tina Corr, Programme Administrator, Kingston Early Years Partnership (KEYP), delivering Early Years Professional Status and Early Years Teacher pathways at Kingston University, London Metropolitan University, Reading University, and Buckinghamshire New University, 2011–13.

Your wise, efficient, resilient administration provided a consistent hub for:

- marketing and recruitment
- induction and pathway delivery
- collaborative communication
- quality assurance
- assessment and moderation
- ongoing data collection
- managing budgets
- celebrating success
- and, repeatedly, managing change.

Being able to 'go to Tina' enabled staff to develop programmes smoothly and candidates/ trainees to commit, engage and gain Early Years Professional Status or Early Years Teacher Status. The contents of this book have arisen from our experiences. Thank you for 'being there.'

Contents

Notes on contributors   xi
Acknowledgements   xiv

Introduction: who's teaching who?   1
JESSICA JOHNSON

1 Professionalism in early years   4
   DARYL MAISEY

2 The Early Years Teacher role: play and playful pedagogy that
   inspire babies, children and a new generation of professionals   17
   DENISE SALTER AND YASMIN MUKADAM

3 Building and sustaining relationships: Early Years teaching with
   babies, young children and parents   34
   KELLY COOPER AND VICKY MUMMERY

4 Curious engagement: creating learning opportunities within the
   Early Years Foundation Stage   50
   JESSICA JOHNSON

5 Adapting education and care to respond to the strengths and needs
   of all children: reflections on practice by senior professionals in
   early years   72
   LALITHA SIVALINGAM AND FIONA DEARMAN

6 More than just a Post-it! Making accurate and productive use
   of assessment   92
   HELEN SUTHERLAND AND ANGIE MAXEY

7 A safe environment: safeguarding and promoting the welfare of children   116
   JO ELSEY

8   Early Years Teachers as influential leaders   136
    JOANNE McKIBBIN AND GEMMA PAWSON

9   A unique Early Years Teacher: presenting my evidence for assessment   153
    JESSICA JOHNSON

Appendix: Teachers' Standards (Early Years) 2013   172
References   176
Index   187

Notes on contributors

Kelly Cooper is currently a Principal Lecturer at London Metropolitan University with responsibility for the Early Years Teacher Programme. Kelly holds both a BA (Hons) and MA in Early Years and has a special interest in working with children from birth to three. Kelly has worked in the Early Years sector since 1997 in various roles, including as early years practitioner, early years manager and volunteer in a hospice in Romania for children with complex needs and HIV. Kelly has taught on EYPS/EYTS since 2007. She has been involved in developing accessible teaching routes for work-based learning students, acknowledging diversity.

Fiona Dearman, with extensive experience as an Early Years Teacher, is currently Head of Centre and Head Teacher of a Children's Centre nursery, deeply committed to working with children and their families. She supports the continuing professional development of her staff team, as they enhance 'learning through play' for children and families within their local community. Fiona welcomes students from surrounding universities, colleges and schools in the Centre, as well as sharing her experiences as a guest speaker at times within BA (Hons) Early Years programmes at Kingston University.

Jo Elsey is Director of Studies, Early Years, University of Reading. With a background in Local Authority workforce development, she runs the Early Years Professional Status/Early Years Initial Teacher Training programmes. With a specific concern in relation to safeguarding and child protection issues, she is consistently looking for ways to enhance learning for early years practitioners in this field.

Jessica Johnson is Kingston Early Years Partnership Programme Manager for the delivery of Early Years Professional Status/Early Years Teacher pathways across the four universities represented by the authors here. Starting her professional career in paediatric nursing and health visiting, Jessica's ongoing interest in building positive relationships has developed across disciplines over time in childminding, in the voluntary sector, children's services and education. Her tutor career has followed the development of Sector-endorsed Foundation Degrees, BA (Hons) 'top-ups' and Early

Years Professional/Early Years Teacher routes. Facilitation of the Kingston and Richmond Early Years Professional Status Network enables her to engage with the ongoing challenges of professional identity within early years.

Daryl Maisey, as Associate Professor and a Senior Manager within the School of Education, Kingston University, draws on her Director of Studies, Early Years expertise to develop staff and student academic programmes. She leads the Masters-level Early Years programmes. Extensive nursery education experience still drives her commitment to enhance professionalism, with additional research interests in relation to Special Educational Needs and safeguarding. Current research relates to the impact of learning from Serious Case Reviews.

Angela Maxey is the Children's Centre Manager of Norbiton Children's Centre. She is a qualified EYP and teacher (QTS) and has a wide range of experience in working with children in various capacities from school settings to early years environments. At present, her role includes working with parents to share her knowledge of child development and the impact of early positive interactions for pre-school children.

Joanne McKibbin is a Senior Lecturer at Kingston University, specializing in Early Years Education and Leadership in Practice. She has extensive experience in the early years and social care fields as a practitioner, manager, lecturer and trainer. Joanne has been responsible for developing and managing early years provision and leading large staff teams. Her research interests include exploring emotional resilience and how this impacts on children's development and well-being, the quality of safeguarding training and effective supervision of the Early Years workforce.

Yasmin Mukadam is a Senior Lecturer in early years education at Kingston University. She is the university Early Years Liaison Officer, monitoring quality and parity of early years provision across nine collaborative Further Education partner colleges. Yasmin is responsible for enhancing employer engagement through the widening participation agenda. She is responsible for the mentor training delivery for both work-based and university mentors. She continues to work with key Local Authority representatives to support workforce development. Her research interests are the impact of higher education on practitioners' pedagogical practice, management and leadership, mentoring and coaching as support mechanisms, and children's development within the early years, particularly social, emotional and language development.

Vicky Mummery is a Principal Lecturer at London Metropolitan University. Before going to university, she taught in Further Education for four years, teaching students from entry level through to Foundation degree. Vicky qualified as a level 3 Early Years Practitioner in 1997, and has since completed her BA (Hons) in Early Childhood and MA in Education. She has held various roles from practitioner to manager across a range of settings for children from birth to five.

Gemma Pawson is a Senior Lecturer in early years and leadership at Kingston University, where she is the Programme Leader for the Foundation Degree in Early

Years; Leadership and Management, and the Foundation Degree in Special Educational Needs and Inclusive Practice. Her research interests focus upon issues relating to the life stories (narratives) of parents who have accessed training provision within a children's centre; this includes the exploration of methodologies that actively promote the voice of the parent. Other areas of interest include the development of reflective practice and value-based leadership. Gemma has worked in a variety of settings across the early years sector during her career as an early years practitioner. This includes a senior leadership role within a large Phase One children's centre, where she was responsible for developing a culture of learning for staff, children, families and the local community. Gemma has also worked in the FE sector where she coordinated a range of early years programmes and was a tutor on the Sector-endorsed Foundation degree.

Denise Salter is a tutor on the Early Years Professional Status programmes at Buckinghamshire New University. With a background in teaching on Sector-endorsed Early Years Foundation Degrees, she brings expertise in early child development and learning linked to practice.

Lalitha Sivalingam has been in the role of Programme Leader for the Early Years Professional Status/Early Years Teacher, Graduate Entry Pathway at Kingston University since 2008. Her current role involves teaching on the programme and acting as an assessor and internal verifier for the National College for Teaching and Leadership. Lalitha qualified as a teacher from the Institute of Education in Singapore and has experience of managing and running her own playgroup for 14 years. Research interests are the impact of higher education on practitioners' pedagogical practice, the role of Early Years Professionals and Early Years Teachers in raising the quality of early years education and childcare.

Helen Sutherland is a Senior Lecturer in Early Years Education at Kingston University. She is currently programme leader for the Early Years Professional Status (EYPS)/ Early Years Teacher Graduate Practitioner Pathway and teaches on a range of early years courses at the university. She is the lead for the Kingston University partnership with the EU TODDLER Project working with eight European partners, sharing, examining and developing different approaches to support toddlers' learning. She has a wide range of experience in working in different early years' environments and post-compulsory education.

Acknowledgements

Kingston Early Years Partnership (KEYP) – Kingston University as Prime Organization, with delivery partners, London Metropolitan University, the University of Reading and Buckinghamshire New University – developed specifically to deliver Early Years Professional Status programmes from 2010. The contents of this book have emerged as a result of constructive collaboration between the administrators, Early Years teams, their colleagues, and the many Early Years Professionals and, now, Early Years Teachers, with whom it is has been a privilege to work. Thank you all for being willing to rise to the challenges of rapid change.

Specific thanks are due to the driving forces that started KEYP: Anne Rawlings, Daryl Maisey and Andy Hudson, School of Education, Kingston University, and Penny Holland, then at London Metropolitan University.

Inspiration in Early Years always comes from the babies, children and families we meet, thank you those who have allowed us to share experiences within these pages.

Likewise to those employers and settings who share our commitment to ongoing training. For direct involvement we are grateful to Norbiton Children's Centre, Surbiton Children's Centre, Early Years Professionals – Karen Hankin, Ulla Usenko, Sue Ingram, Bex Halden, Rheanne Bernard, Michael Cowley – and our Kingston and Richmond Early Years Professional Network, jointly co-ordinated by Neil Blumsom and Claire Grayson.

Introduction

Who's teaching who?
Jessica Johnson

> A new professional space has emerged in the early years and wider children's workforce occupied by an holistic leadership professional – an advocate for young children.
>
> (Lumsden 2012: 314)

Welcome on our journey through the contents of this book, as we discover learning and teaching opportunities with babies, young children, families, colleagues and other professionals across a range of early years provision. Lumsden, in the quote above, recognizes the impact of the emergent role of the Early Years Professional, with Early Years Professional Status (EYPS), as truly 'change agents' (CWDC 2006). So, as specialists of child development from birth to age 5, can Early Years Teachers, with Early Years Teacher Status, continue to be 'holistic leadership professionals' and 'advocates for young children' and their families?

The contributors to this text have all been actively engaged in the delivery of Early Years Professional and Early Years Teacher programmes – whether based in university or early years settings. Candidates and trainees, currently on pathways for both awards, plus Early Years Professionals who have already achieved the Status, have also shared their experiences, adding specific content to Chapters 4, 6 and 9. There is always more scope to enable children, families and other professionals to share and influence the impact of practice. Maybe you will enable that through trying out some of the ideas presented in the following chapters.

Early Years Initial Teacher Training (EYITT) programmes, as from September 2014, are due to be delivered through individual Initial Teacher Training providers, working closely with early years employers. All routes will equip trainees to demonstrate competencies for assessment against the eight Teachers' Standards (Early Years) 2013, laid out in the Appendix. Remember, though, most of your practice will holistically encompass more than one Standard. Throughout this book, the Standards that are specifically addressed are shown in bold in a box at the start of chapters, with Chapter 9 covering assessment of each Standard in turn. However, the text has been written to promote critical thinking and reflection at graduate level about current early years provision in England, so it can engage graduate leaders in practice as well as undergraduate and post-graduate students on Early Childhood Studies, Foundation Degree and BA (Hons) 'top-up' routes.

Overview of the book

The chapters are organized to allow engagement in the broad field of practice first. Daryl Maisey, in Chapter 1, poses the challenge of engaging with the tensions of early years professionalism as you create your own identity as an Early Years Teacher. This is the time to start your own reflective journal, recognizing personal and professional values and beliefs, and follow how these develop through study and experience. Chapter 2 by Denise Salter and Yasmin Mukadam and Chapter 3 by Vicky Mummery and Kelly Cooper, both with links to Standards 1 and 2, then combine the 'seminal' (established) underpinning theories with current research to enable critical analysis of early years practice today, including playful pedagogy and attachment. Why are we doing what we are doing with babies, young children and families? While editing this book, I found myself challenged as I read each chapter, identifying areas of interest to follow through. Do use the Reference section at the end of the book to further guide your studies, as the team of authors introduce you to key texts, academic journals, legislation, reports and a range of organizational web-sites, while modelling Harvard referencing!

Chapter 4 by Jessica Johnson aims to bridge the theory and research of the previous chapters with the creation of daily learning opportunities within the Early Years Foundation Stage (EYFS) (DfE 2012) and the 'educational continuum of expectations, curricula and teaching of Key Stages 1 and 2' (Standard 3). In each chapter, clearly labelled Activities and Reflection points encourage you to value and develop your own pedagogical practices, including recognition of early reading and early mathematics.

Lalitha Sivalingam and Fiona Dearman, in Chapter 5, use interview techniques to enable other professionals to share how a range of services can support care and education to meet diverse needs (Standard 5). This collaborative approach may encourage you, even by using their questions as templates, to arrange informal meetings with other specialists. As an Early Years Teacher, with babies and young children under 5 years, you can identify needs and initiate multi-agency working to benefit your children and families. A potential audit tool is introduced as an aid.

The practicalities of observation (Standard 4), planning and assessment (Standard 6) are then covered in detail in Chapter 6, which includes a range of templates and exemplars to use. Helen Sutherland and Angie Maxey draw on first-hand experience within a Children's Centre nursery, allowing you to engage with children, colleagues, families and Health Visitors. Possible ways to address the Two Year Check (NCB 2012) and the Early Years Foundation Stage Profiles (STA 2013) (Standard 6) are described.

Safeguarding children and child protection will underpin all aspects of your work as an Early Years Teacher. Chapter 7 by Jo Elsey enables you to critically analyse personal responsibilities as well as how you lead and support others through recruitment, training and emotional engagement with children, families, colleagues and other professionals (Standard 7).

The different styles of leadership, then shared in Chapter 8, acknowledge the reality of the varied environments you may find yourself in across early years. There is certainly no 'one-size-fits-all' approach. Gemma Pawson and Jo McKibbin encourage you to venture out and find what is best for your team, as well as reminding you that you need to be responsible for your own continuing professional development (Standard 8).

You will be bringing personal and professional knowledge and experience to your assessment process for Early Years Teacher. Chapter 9 aims to help you identify how to produce strong, unique evidence for each of the eight Teachers' Standards (Early Years) 2013. This chapter is more directly related to Early Years Initial Teacher Training (EYITT) trainees, together with their mentors in practice. As each EYITT provider will have their own assessment procedures, you are encouraged to be proactive in the way you present your expertise – a true graduate-level reflective practitioner. Management of placement experiences, including observation in a Key Stage 1 setting, and assessment, are explored.

Above all, the structure outlined here will enable you to select key material, reflect, learn and hopefully be inspired to create positive learning opportunities with babies, young children, families, colleagues and others in your wider community. Let's see who really does teach who, for the enjoyment and achievement of all.

1

Professionalism in early years

Daryl Maisey

Professionalism in early years involves risk and uncertainty, whether internally or externally imposed, within a constantly changing context.

(Daryl Maisey)

Chapter objectives

By the end of this chapter you should be able to:

- have knowledge and an understanding of the key debates, tensions and discussions on the development of an early years 'profession';
- define your own identity in relation to care and education within the early years profession;
- appreciate the impact of your own personal values and beliefs on your professional behaviour and responsibilities as an Early Years Teacher;
- identify how reflection and being reflexive can support your professional role.

Link with Teachers' Standards (Early Years) 2013

S8

Introduction

When we try and explain to others what we mean by being a 'professional' in early years, it becomes apparent that this is a term that is almost impossible to define. The more that we try and 'unpick' the word, the more complex the definition of being a 'professional' appears to become. You may then wonder why it is that we have dedicated a chapter to looking at what it means to be a professional in early years. In terms of your role as an Early Years Teacher, there are certain expectations of practice, behaviour and attitude that people refer to as your 'professional responsibility'. As such, it is important that you have knowledge and understanding of the key debates, tensions and discussions on the early years 'profession' and what this may mean for you in determining your 'professional identity'. In this chapter we will explore the historical emergence of early years teaching as a profession and we will look at some of the arguments that have influenced how this has developed. We will examine some of the tensions that exist between care and education and explore how collaborative working between practitioners is supporting the movement towards society's recognition of the early years as a professional stage of education. Finally, we will begin to look at the attributes and characteristics of a professional and how these may be interpreted as you work towards your 'professional status'.

The interplay between the emergence of early years as a recognized stage of education (Deparment for Employment and Skills 2000) and the need for it to be recognized as a 'profession' is very complex. In addition, to define 'professionalism' is itself problematic and subject to much debate (Eraut 1992). When we look historically we can see that the first recognized and established profession of medicine was defined by the need for specialized knowledge and an agreed set of principles underpinning practice. At that time, much of this knowledge was gained through appropriately designed but imposed university education programmes. This created a situation where, very simply put, individuals entering a profession were told, 'This is what you need to do and these are the skills you need to do it.' Schön (1983/1991) considered this approach to be the required 'technical rationality' of professions based on scientific and standardized knowledge. However, while this might be applied in general to some existing professions, research by Oberhuemer and Scheryer (2008) into early childhood professionalization strategies across Europe identified no agreement on the 'technical' competencies required by practitioners and therefore stated there was a resultant discourse that further complicated what it meant to be a professional within early years. With the introduction of the first Early Years Professional Standards (DCSF and CWDC 2008), or the set of 'specialized knowledge', you can now see how professionalism in early years began to position itself alongside other recognized professional sectors of education. However, the introduction of professional standards was not welcomed by all in early years and the following discusses some of the difficulties and tensions that arose.

In sociological theory, professionalism is perceived as being largely dependent upon restricted access to exclusive knowledge and accredited practice within a particular field (Lloyd and Hallet 2010). In early years, this would mean providing evidence to meet the requirements of the professional standards and being judged, through observation, on whether you are able to translate these into practice. However, it is argued that this perspective of being a professional cannot be achieved without the support and engagement of the government and the general public (Macdonald 1995). Indeed, some have argued that the introduction and subsequent development of the statutory Early Years Foundation Stage (EYFS) curriculum (Department for

Employment and Skills 2000; DCSF 2008a; DfE 2012) has enabled delivery of a consistent set of principles that underpin perceived effective practice in settings. As a result of this initiative, early years practitioners are now responsible for delivering this agreed curriculum. Reference is made to this accountability in the Teachers' Standards (Early Years) preamble: 'Early Years Teachers make the education and care of babies and children their first concern. They are accountable for achieving the highest possible standards in their professional practice and conduct' (NCTL 2013b: 2).

The 'specialised and capability knowledge and skills' as discussed before can now be measured against inspection criteria (Ofsted 2012), thus reassuring the general public of the effectiveness of the provision. Some have also argued that this has contributed in part to public recognition of early years as an accountable profession aligned with practice in subsequent Key Stages. However, the resultant dilemma facing early years practitioners is whether the prescribed curriculum with measurable outcomes may erode professionalism to 'technician status' (Osgood 2006a, 2006b, 2006c) and restrict the 'personal' within the 'professional'. In other words, once an individual has met the Standards, does that determine their right to be called a professional? Does the number of early years teachers then determine whether the early years workforce as a whole can be considered a profession? Does being accountable for the delivery of the EYFS determine the 'professional' label?

In other areas of the children's workforce there has been a shift in focus from professional autonomy to a technical and systems-driven process that has resulted in challenging and conflicting outcomes:

> A dominant theme in the criticisms of current practice [in social work] is the skew in priorities that has developed between the demands of the management and inspection processes and professionals' ability to exercise their professional judgment and act in the best interests of the child.
>
> (Munro 2010: 5)

Moss (2010: 12) agrees with this concern and argues that 'the task of the educator as technician is to apply prescribed human technologies of proven effectiveness ("what works") to produce predetermined outcomes' and, it could be argued, that this is not possible within the complex field of early years. Certainly the early years workforce consists of a vast number and diverse range of roles such as child-minders, teachers, teaching assistants, family support officers, learning support assistants, children centre managers, key persons, room leaders and nursery nurses to name but a few, which is unique to this phase of education. The nature of each role differs significantly in terms of practice requirements, context and the need to address the child's care and well-being as well as their learning. To further complicate the situation, the field covers the state-maintained, private, voluntary and independent sectors with distinctive and individualistic requirements within each. Consider then whether we can define 'professional practice' within early years or whether this is more complex than we originally thought.

To help us make sense of what is happening, we look to current studies into the professionalization of the early year's workforce. However, these seem to be dominated by work emanating from America and Australia. As these contain contextual bias, we could argue that they may not be appropriate to our current systems in the UK (Miller and Cable 2011). While an interesting point, this presents and augments the problematic undertaking when trying to establish what constitutes the 'professional' within the early year's field in England. In light of all these factors and arguments, attempting to define the 'professional' would appear to oversimplify the very knowledge and skills that are unique to the context and community within which the practitioner may be employed. The provision of a collective agreement on what is meant by 'professional practice and conduct' (Miller and Cable 2011) in this field may still be found to be impossible, irrational and, as some might argue, irresponsible. However, having raised so many tensions and questions, let us examine more fully the debates concerning qualification, or competency, requirements.

Exploring a competence-based approach to professionalism

In general, definitions and research into professions adhere to a common understanding that a graduate qualification and on-going post-graduate learning requirements underpin a professionally regarded status (Oakeshott 1989; Downie 1990; Vanderstraeten 2007). Certainly the limited early years research in this area appears to concur that there is a positive correlation between higher levels of practitioner qualifications and the quality of provision that contributes to recognized professionalization (Sylva et al. 2004; Fukkink and Lont 2007). However, I would suggest that it would be foolish to consider an appropriate qualification as automatically providing the 'right' to be a professional. Likewise, having a professional status would indicate that the early years provision in the school or setting of employment, could then, undoubtedly, be regarded as effective (Brock 2006; Early et al. 2007). While examining the nature of qualifications as potentially underpinning the emergence of professionalism in the field of early years, it is apparent that this could also be highly controversial.

In England, there currently exists a dichotomy of training between practitioners in the early years' private, voluntary and independent (PVI) sectors and those in the state-maintained sector. Members of staff in the maintained sector such as the Foundation Stage and Key Stage 1 teachers have a minimum workforce entry requirement of graduate level 6, with support staff predominantly at level 3 or equivalent. Conversely, staff members in the PVI sector have a minimum requirement of level 3 with a possible graduate level 6 employed within the setting, though this is currently not statutory. Undoubtedly this raises questions of comparability, equity and parity of practice expectations. Clearly this anomaly in the basic competency requirements of an early years practitioner serves to intensify the debate about the holistic 'professionalization' of the early years workforce. If the question of 'professionalism' is related to the acquisition of a graduate 'status', construed as meeting the threshold requirements of competences, it would appear that, in current practice, recognition of professionalism in early years under this guise may be more rapid in some areas of the field than others (Ofsted 2012). Moss (2006) agrees and also cautions that issues of differences between employment terms and inter-sectorial divisions relating to adult/child ratios, salaries, training opportunities and inspections may also impact upon discussions concerning the 'professional role' across the early years workforce. Interestingly, in Australia, there has been a shift in raising the status of those working in non-school early years contexts by locating qualifications within a 'teacher identities' framework, thus promoting equality in pay, conditions and 'professional' standing within the community (Burton and Lyons 2000). The introduction of the Early Years Teacher Status (2013) may therefore be seen by some as the catalyst towards a socially accepted model of professionalism in early years. Arguably it could be considered that early years practitioners should actively embrace such a movement towards locating their identity within this arena. Indeed, the need to belong to a recognized profession may empower the individual and may lead to the realization of a professional voice within a new and emerging professional organization.

This aspect of professionalism as belonging to a unified, recognized body is important for us to consider. In order to enable an individual's professional views and opinions to be represented, Friedson (1994) advocated the need for a strong 'group identity' within a professional field, in order to enhance employment status, pay and conditions. At present, in early years, once a practitioner has gained graduate status, there is no established professional body to which they can belong. In a small-scale research project undertaken by Lloyd and Hallet in 2010, it was found that 'the aspiring early years professionals' views on belonging to a professional group highlighted their need for a collective professional identity in "a cohesive group", with a clear "identification" and "a sense of belonging", and a group characterised by a "shared vision and understanding"' (2010: 83). Certainly through work undertaken in the Early Years Department at Kingston University a successful network of early years practitioners with graduate status was established in collaboration with three Local Authorities. The resultant sharing of best practice began to emerge and the group developed a collective identity that empowered positive influences in the early years field (Conference paper, March 2011). I certainly believe that collective, professional recognition of the knowledge, skills and effective practice of those working with very young and vulnerable children can be achieved.

Organizational theory attempts to clarify aspects of collective practice in terms of structure, control, culture and conflict that influence, explicitly and implicitly, the individuals within it (Vanderstraeten 2007). The debate considers the tensions that exist between the 'shared' organization as a 'powerful body' and the individual's need to exercise autonomy; yet one does not exist without the other. In early years there is currently little evidence to suggest that there is an emergence of an organization that is either recognized or influential in determining changes to policy or practice (Osgood 2006a, 2006b, 2006c). Maybe the very nature of early years and the diversity of provision do compound the complexities of having a single organization that would effectively represent each professional within the field. However, having worked with early years practitioners for some years, I have seen evidence of a collegiate ethos of practice emerging. Practitioners who may previously have worked in isolation are beginning to recognize the positive impact of shared knowledge, skills and expertise across and between settings. Oberhuemer's proposed 'democratic professionalism' (2005: 13) founded upon relationships, collaborations, alliances and cooperative practices between practitioners may make the recognition of professionalism in early years not only feasible but also a reality.

Reflection 1.1: Being a professional

How would you describe a 'profession'?

How would you define the word 'professional'?

Do you think that meeting 'competency standards' defines a 'professional'?

The role of reflection in professionalism

Examining the complexities of Oberhuemer's (2005) 'democratic professionalism' it is evident that the role of the individual practitioner greatly influences its success and this is heavily influenced by factors affecting the 'personal within the professional'. Arguably contentious, it could be considered that professionalism in early years is inextricably linked with the unique ability of individual practitioners to understand their position within the overarching philosophy of early years. In other words, we need to give consideration to our understanding of what it means to be a professional and what contribution we might make in gaining social recognition of early years as a profession.

Schön (1983/1991) identified some of the complexities of the interrelation between the knowledge and skills required for a 'profession' and the need to be 'reflective' in order to address the unpredictable nature and uniqueness of practice problems and challenges. He added that the technical 'know-how' may not equip practitioners to manage interventions appropriately and suggested that this approach also ignored the socio-cultural dimensions of practice which would be more effectively addressed through an adaptable or 'artful' competence. Reflection is certainly considered by more recent researchers to be an important aspect of professionalism (Dunn et al. 2008; Urban 2008), though agreement on how reflection is applied in practice is still to be reached. The arguments consider that reflection can take many forms, such as reflection of the self within a disciplinary context, reflection of intention, and reflection before, during and after an action.

The need to be adaptable and reflective is certainly an issue within early year's practice, which we have already identified, does not have clearly defined roles and expectations, and is constantly responding to meet the demands of a rapidly changing policy field (DfE 2012; NCTL 2013b). However, in the 'emerging professionalization' of the early years field there is agreement that there is not only a requirement for practitioners to have reflective capabilities but also the need to move beyond this to becoming reflexive: challenging assumptions and questioning the underlying knowledge base (Kuisma and Sandberg 2008). Being self-reflective requires practitioners to examine their position within the establishment whereas being reflexive requires practitioners to question that very establishment. Practitioners need to consider whether they are, '*doing things right* as well as *doing the right things*' (Peeters and Vandenbroeck, cited in Miller and Cable 2011: 7).

In early years it is suggested that the changing field is an opportunity for practitioners to scrutinize and challenge assumptions and beliefs in order to construct their own professionalism. Dalli and Urban state that 'professionalism can be understood as a discourse as much as a phenomenon: as something that is constantly under reconstruction' (2008: 132). The opportunity and the potential for practitioners to be reflective, reflexive, to co-construct new knowledge and engage in transforming the early years field could be an actuality. Professionalism is about embracing complexity and uncertainty (Moss 2010) and early years is uniquely positioned to exert influence in establishing a 'professional' voice within the field of education.

Reflection 1.2: 'Reflection' and 'reflexive'?

How would you describe 'reflection'?

How might reflection support your professional role?

How would you describe what is meant by being 'reflexive'?

How might being 'reflexive' support your professional role?

Historical relationship between care and education affecting professionalism

A limiting factor when considering the 'strength' of the voice may be perceived as the female-gendered nature of the workforce. Research undertaken in Denmark (Jensen and Hansen 2003) found that men opted to work with older children despite pay and conditions being comparable across the workforce, regardless of the children's age. This suggested that the predominantly female workforce (in line with England at 98 per cent) was not explained by pay and conditions alone but was indicative of how society viewed the work. Underpinning the existing demographics of early years education is the historical and contextual evolution of the current workforce. Examining the profiles of students entering training in early years, Penn (2000) concluded that there was a consensus of the trainees' perspective identifying not the acquisition and application of specialized knowledge about how children learn and develop but an acceptance that they were building on 'natural' everyday interactions and experience.

Current practice indicates that the prejudices of working with young children that historically required few qualifications and had low status, compounded by an acceptance of no career progression, may still be apparent (Colley 2006; Cooke and Lawton 2008; Moss 2010). One of the most debated and challenging discourses is the knowledge and skills set required of early years practitioners that embrace both the care and education of the very young. Traditionally there has been an uncomfortable and uncompromising dilemma between demands of ensuring that very young children are physically, socially and emotionally healthy as well as being 'educated'. Moss describes the need for educators of young children to 'work with an ethics of care and the ethics of an encounter' (2010: 15). The issue under debate here is whether care and education can or should be separated as care is perceived to be an 'assumed role' and as such is not recognized as a professional requirement and consequently is 'accorded a low economic value' (McKie et al. 2002: 903); whereas education is considered a recognized 'competence' consisting of knowledge transfer and the technical skills required for effective teaching and learning. In my experience I would suggest that it is ludicrous to assume that one would exist without the other.

Certainly when discussing the safeguarding of young and vulnerable children there is a consensus that it is a requirement of all those employed within the children's workforce to take responsibility for a child's care, health and well-being above all else (Ofsted 2008; Munro 2010; NCTL 2013b). It is therefore intriguing that early years practitioners may need to 'justify' the care of very young children as being a discrete activity not within their 'professional competency'. Currently this is not the case with medical staff who carry out such 'care' within their own recognized 'profession' with little controversy in terms of whether it is a professionally recognized competence requiring an expected level of training and qualification. Indeed, Howe (2002) examined the assessment regime of health care practitioners which he found contained elements to ensure that they actually demonstrated a caring attitude towards patients. Some argue, however, that in early years, 'the provision of care is seen as part of a "taken for granted" assemblage of lower skills which acts as a platform upon which the higher skills of professionalism can be built' (Taggart 2011: 87). Certainly the examination of what constitutes 'care' within the early years field appears to be inextricably linked to relational and nurturing pedagogy (Scheiwe and Willekens 2009), in particular, the engagement of emotions. Moyles agrees: 'To be an early years practitioner carries the expectation that you will like all of the children all of the time and respond to them as unique individuals: in this way, operating from the emotions is positively expected by society' (2001: 83).

Interestingly, research undertaken by Hargreaves (2000) concluded that practitioners working with very young children engaged at a higher level of emotional intensity than their peers working with older children. This investment of 'emotional labour' was perceived to be the measure by which the practitioners found their work 'rewarding'. In addition, evidence cited by Day (2004) found that qualities such as caring, loving and passion were characteristics of early years practitioners deemed to be excellent in practice. This supports the convincing argument that 'professionalism' in early years is not just about qualifications but about attitude, disposition, commitment, motivation and passion (Moyles 2001: Brock 2006).

Research from neuroscience (Kotulak 1996) clearly shows that positive emotional engagement between an adult and a very young child is significant in establishing 'patterning' within the child's brain that will affect their future strategies for coping effectively and efficiently in different situations. There would appear to be little evidence to suggest that separating emotional engagement through the care aspect of working with young children is either in the best interests of the child or the wider family and professional community. As Taggart states, '"Passion" in the context of school teaching, nursing or ministry does not appear to undermine professional status; it is simply evidence of moral vocation' (2011: 93). The importance of caring within early years education does not appear to be disputed but rather it is the perceived 'professional' standing afforded to the practice of care.

Many of the 'professional traits' mentioned earlier appear to be inextricably linked to relational pedagogy. Daily practice in early years requires practitioners to engage in complex relationships involving parents, carers, children, colleagues and other professionals. When considering the wider implications of how these are interpreted as being professional it is interesting to note how challenging it is to discuss and define the 'boundaries' of acceptable 'professional practice' between individuals. Even the use of controversial terminology excites debate. Page (2011) introduces the term 'professional love' to describe the relationship that could exist between a young child and a practitioner. She provokes debate by asking whether mothers want professional carers to love their children while maintaining an assumption that this may not be the choice of the practitioner but an expectation of professional practice.

Likewise, Frowe (2005) introduces and discusses the concept of 'professional trust', asserting that individual education practitioners engage in different relationships within their practice that involve an element of trust. The parent has 'trust' that the professional has the knowledge to act in their child's best interest. The practitioner has 'trust' in the organization that has created the professional standards and the curriculum. Frowe argues that 'trust is an essential component of what it means to be a professional' (2005: 38) and this affects the way professionals make judgements. He asserts that to be a professional requires the ability not to simply follow instructions but also to exercise professional judgement within each particular and individually situated context and this requires 'trust'.

The professionalization of early years needs to address historical perceptions, to challenge and realign misconceptions about the justified need for care and to gain parity with society's acceptance of education as a profession regardless of whether the practitioner works with a 4-year-old or a 14-year-old. The age of the child does not determine whether they need care but how that care might meet their particular needs in their particular context. There needs to be a concerted effort to raise awareness of the influential factors that may be affecting society's perceptions of the importance of care within the early years field. Certainly Bottery identifies tensions between the values of 'efficiency, effectiveness and economy [that] become the criteria of success, whilst other values like care, trust and equity are increasingly perceived as second-order values' (2006: 103). A realignment of early years education that highlights the importance of care and emotional engagement may serve to reposition and value the field as an essential aspect of the education continuum. Subsequently this may act as a catalyst for the conceptualization of professional identity for those practitioners in early years. Perhaps there is the need for trust.

Reflection 1.3: Professional identity

What are your reflections on the aspect of 'care' in education?

In your opinion, which characteristics define a 'good teacher'?

How might these reflections impact on your own 'professional identity'?

Recognizing the personal in the professional: the place of values and beliefs

Having made the decision to enter the early years field you will undergo, or have undergone, some basic education to prepare you with knowledge and expectations of practice. During this time you will probably be engaged in working closely with your peers, attending the same teaching and learning experiences. However, despite having similar exposure you will not complete this preparatory education with the same knowledge and expectations of practice as that of your peers. As an individual you will have gained different understandings, depending upon how you have interpreted, responded, reacted and construed meaning. This is the 'personal within the professional'. Oakeshott (1989) captures this phenomenon when he describes the need for professionals to recognize two components of knowledge, 'information' (impersonal facts) and 'judgement' (that cannot be taught). He argues that judgement 'only appears slowly as a sort of by-product of the acquisition of information' (1989: 60) and that it is always affected by our own values and beliefs.

The person that we have become has been constructed by the complex interplay of many different factors such as family, culture, environment and experiences. The professional we want to become will also be constructed by the interplay of such factors. Recognizing why we behave, respond and react in the way we do will enable us to be aware that we should not impose our own judgements on others. Beliefs can be so strong that we rarely question them but rather accept them as truths. As these beliefs have developed, they may have been examined and contested but they may have also been affirmed and reaffirmed until they become, in our individualized context, a certainty. These beliefs are so strong that, when they are challenged, we often experience a physiological response (usually aggressiveness or anxiety) and feel uncomfortable in the situation. However, we will normally defend our position.

Our values are about what we perceive to be important to us and these can change as our interactions, experiences and significance attached to individuals and context alter. Values govern the way in which we choose to live our lives and these undoubtedly affect the way we perceive our 'professionalism'. While we may recognize that values and beliefs are individual to each person, we also need to acknowledge that they affect the way we behave towards others and how they behave towards us. They are not discrete entities but are interrelated (Figure 1.1).

If we accept that our values and beliefs affect our attitudes and behaviours, then one of the challenges of being a 'professional' is to recognize the 'personal' when making decisions in practice. An awareness of factors influencing the way in which we perceive different situations, people and contexts enables us to make more informed and rational judgements. However, to recognize these influences requires a heightened level of self-critical reflection and analysis (Schön 1983/1991).

Frowe (2005) advocates Oakeshott's (1989) model as he explains the differences between knowledge and judgement that require an element of 'trust' that the professional will make the right decisions:

> [N]ow the practitioner can reflect on what they know and consider its significance, identify the salient principles that are relevant to a particular situation, evaluate

alternative strategies and, importantly, make decisions in situations that are novel or unexpected where the information available underdetermines any one correct course of action. When faced with such a situation the professional is called upon to draw on their knowledge and experience to make a judgement about what ought to be done.

(Frowe 2005: 45)

When discussing the meaning of being a professional, consider how judgements in practice are made and whether there is a need to recognize the personal. Alternatively some might argue that being a professional means to put aside the personal. Consider your position in this debate.

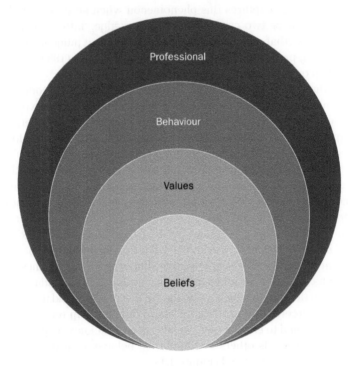

Figure 1.1 Professional behaviour, values and beliefs.

Reflection 1.4: Values and beliefs

What are my values and beliefs?

Do I consider that these affect my 'professional identity'? Why?

Should I remain aware of personal influences when making decisions in practice? Why?

Conclusion

The emergence of political and social 'competence-based focus' in early years education has raised numerous issues and dilemmas for those practitioners seeking recognition and acknowledgement for the work undertaken with young children in line with colleagues working with older children (OECD 2001; DfES 2005; CWDC 2007; NCTL 2013b).

Research, legislation and theorists agree that early years is an important phase of education in its own right and should be afforded 'professional' recognition (Miller and Cable 2011). However, the historical emergence and interface between early years care and education have complicated the deliberations. While there appears to have been a 'shift 'of approach from a 'maternal discourse' to a 'technician discourse', challenges still remain in terms of addressing on-going legislative reviews, evolving roles and changes in responsibilities, which are compounded by the diversity of the field (Ball 1994; Colley 2006). In addition, the political, social and professional expectations of the early years' role fail to address conditions of employment with little reward other than job satisfaction (OECD 2001). Under some recognized 'models' of professionalism early years education struggles to be acknowledged. However, models that suggest empowering early years practitioners to directly influence their emerging 'professionalism' present an opportunity for change and acceptance (Moss 2006).

Evidence of imposed standards of effective practice threatens to undermine the autonomy of individual practitioners while providing a recognizable and measurable framework for society to hold accountable, as in other established professions. The need for a recognized structure versus the need for flexibility, in order to meet the demands of diverse service users, compounds the debate and the tension continues to be discussed (Osgood 2006a, 2006b, 2006c). However, it is recommended that those involved with developing and delivering early years initial and on-going training need to establish an ethos of the reflective and reflexive practitioner in order to empower the individual practitioner to 'shape' the future of the professional workforce. As Moss states: 'To be a professional means being able to construct knowledge from diverse sources, involving awareness of paradigmatic plurality, curiosity and border crossing, and acknowledging that knowledge is always partial, perspectival and provisional' (2010: 15).

An awareness of factors affecting professional attributes and decision making continues to influence the personal within the professional, and early years practitioners need to be aware that they are responsible for the move towards professional recognition within society (Brock 2006).

In conclusion, professionalism in early years involves risk and uncertainty, whether internally or externally imposed, within a constantly changing context. It is with courageous integrity that we can assert that professionalism in early years will be acknowledged and appropriately rewarded. Quality practice, high expectations, perseverance and passion are inextricably linked to the move towards recognition as a profession (Moyles 2001). The current uncertainty of rapid policy change in England can be unnerving for the early years sector whose very 'professionalism' is emerging in the context of societal recognition. However, historically rooted and prejudiced interpretations need to be challenged in order for a 're-envision of the workforce . . . and scope for contestation and change' (Moss 2006: 30) to be realized.

It is an exciting time to be entering the early years field with opportunities to engage in debate and redress the balance. To be part of the pioneering movement to establish early years as a recognized profession alongside other education phases and to be one of the 'professionals' influencing the work of others in the field, is challenging but also motivating. Moreover, I would argue, it is a privilege.

2

The Early Years Teacher role

Play and playful pedagogy that inspire babies, children and a new generation of professionals

Denise Salter and Yasmin Mukadam

> Early years pedagogical practice involves supporting children's learning through play in ways that are responsive to children's interests and motivations.
>
> (Neaum 2013: 120)

Chapter objectives

By the end of this chapter you should be able to:

- examine a range of theoretical perspectives about play and playful pedagogy;
- reflect on and evaluate the effectiveness of your early years provision in relation to the Early Years Foundation Stage (EYFS) (DfE 2012) and the above theories;
- make informed choices that shape and support good practice in relation to care, learning and teaching strategies with babies, young children, families and colleagues;
- identify opportunities to take responsibility for leading practice (NCTL 2013b: S8.5).

Link with Teachers' Standards (Early Years) 2013

S1 S2 S3 S4 S8

Introduction

This chapter invites you to reflect on the importance of play to children's learning and development, considering challenges related to curriculum. It also provides you with the opportunity to further examine theoretical perspectives, with the aim of providing you with strategies to further develop your pedagogic role as an Early Years Teacher. It starts with a gentle reminder that young children are born with a breath-taking desire to grow and learn. From the moment a child is born, they are on a quest to make sense of their world and to become part of the wider world, by continually striving to develop new skills, competences and understandings. If a young child is allowed to take the lead and control the tempo, then with a little help from caring adults who really know and understand them, they will engage in playful and industrious ways to achieve this; for children do not see this as work or play, as in childhood there is no distinction.

The ambiguities of play as a concept when related to a play-based curriculum

Play is the way in which children absorb the rich culture they are immersed in; it allows them ownership as well as providing an outlet for making sense of the world and their role and involvement within it, therefore, it encompasses every aspect of the child's being from the impact of their first movements, ways of communicating, feelings, thoughts, and interactions with others, to developing a sense of belonging. It is, for the child the most natural way of being a young human. Hence it is the way in which practitioners harness children's natural desires and dispositions to learn that is paramount.

Therefore, as an Early Years Teacher, it is essential that you understand the value of play to children's learning and development and recognize and reflect on the complexities associated with such a commonly used term, a term that has been firmly embedded for over two hundred years into early childhood education philosophy. According to Nutbrown et al. (2008), pioneers like Rousseau, Froebel, Steiner, Dewey and Isaacs helped to lay strong foundations for seeing play as central to children's learning and development, as well as recognizing the importance of training for those who worked with young children.

However, this strongly defended philosophy within early years education on the importance of play to young children's learning and development is problematic, because the word 'play' can be used to mean different things. Further complications arise when considering the history and the constantly evolving foundations that rein-force the importance of play as a teaching vehicle for learning and development; for example:

- Theories and ideologies have been discussed in different eras and cultures where perceptions of what constitutes childhood may have differed;
- Play has been examined from a range of perspectives including psychological theories, sociological studies and educational principles.

According to Wood (2013), this has led to recognition of childhood as a distinct phase, it has also led to play being examined in different ways to promote and support learning. The picture that emerges is messy; there is no clear definition of play; it is simply a white elephant, valuable but burdensome, and, as Bruce (1991) recommends, should be used as an umbrella term. However, early years practitioners are influenced by EYFS (DfE 2012) which promotes the use of play as providing the right foundations for future progress through school, and sees it as one of the three characteristics of effective teaching and learning, be it rather brief, 'Play and exploring: children investigate and experience things, and "have a go"' (DfE 2012: 28).

Hence practitioners are expected to engage in a pedagogy or art of teaching that encourages purposeful play and learning and the Early Years Teacher role is to inspire, motivate, challenge, and model good practice. This requires a range of complex pedagogic (teaching) skills, and, according to many authors (Canning 2011; Rogers 2011; Palaiologou 2013; Wood 2013), there is, currently, no cohesive pedagogical base to guide practitioners on ways to use play as a vehicle that truly enhances babies' and children's learning and development.

The picture, then, appears muddled regarding the value of play, with no clear definition of play and no unified framework to support the pedagogic role of the adult. Further challenges become apparent when viewed in relation to recent policy documents. Powell's analysis of policy statements on play (2008, cited in Rogers 2011: 8) suggests that while they appear to promote play, the actual statements are often vague with little explanation of why it should be supported. In reality, play appears as an instrumental tool to meet learning outcomes and targets; and practitioners have been encouraged to view play as a medium for learning and preparation for adulthood; as is apparent in EYFS (DfE 2012) which promotes the purpose of teaching and learning to ensure school readiness. Take, for example, the following statement:

> Each area of learning and development must be implemented through planned, purposeful play and through a mix of adult-led and child-initiated activity. Play is essential for children's development, building their confidence as they learn to explore, to think about problems, and relate to others.
>
> (DfE 2012: 6)

It could be argued that children's play, when chosen by them, is naturally purposeful and the challenge comes for those supporting children's play as to when, how, and if they should participate in such play, as well as how they might plan adult-directed activities that build on those experiences. The next extract from the same section claims that:

> Children learn by leading their own play, and by taking part in play which is guided by adults. There is an ongoing judgement to be made by practitioners about the balance between activities led by children, and activities led or guided by adults. Practitioners must respond to each child's emerging needs and interests, guiding their development through warm, positive interaction.
>
> (DfE 2012: 6)

So, at this point, tensions between the need to provide planned, purposeful and instructive play as well as supporting children to engage in meaningful and intrinsically motivating play activities occur. As Rogers (2011: 6) states, this could have the potential to create a work/play divide as practitioners endeavour to evidence measurable learning outcomes and prepare children for formal schooling: 'As children grow older, and as their development allows, it is expected that the balance will gradually shift towards more activities led by adults, to help children prepare for more formal learning, ready for Year 1.'

The 'school readiness' or 'readiness for school' agenda which, has according to Whitbread and Bingham (2011) become more frequently used in government rhetoric is important to reflect on; what might this tell us about the perceptions of childhood and where might the child's voice be heard? Early Years Teachers need to be aware of such rhetoric and consider the potential implications for the quality of children's early learning experiences. Indeed, as Whitbread and Bingham state, while it is a frequently used term, there is little clarity on what it actually means and what exactly young children should be prepared for. However, as Papatheodorou and Potts (2013) remind us, it is important to be aware of the requirement for school readiness as to ignore it may well disadvantage some children.

Values, beliefs and a shared vision

There are, then, many pedagogic challenges in providing a play-based curriculum, not least because of the tensions and ambiguities mentioned in the first part of this chapter. However, this awareness informs and shapes the pedagogic role, as Moyles et al. (2002: 5) state: 'Pedagogy encompasses both what practitioners actually do and think and the principles, theories, perceptions and challenges that inform and shape it.' There is no doubt that play does support children's natural desire to learn; however, it is not enough to acknowledge the centrality of play in early years practice. It is also essential, as Moyles et al. (2002) point out, to really explore what you as an Early Years Teacher do in your pedagogic role in relation to what you think, avoiding the potential mismatch between the two, highlighted by McInnes et al. (2011). As an Early Years Teacher you need to be able to clearly articulate to others why play is important; in other words, you need to have a clear vision before you can challenge, motivate and inspire others.

Reflection 2.1: Play . . . or not play

A simple but effective method is to list what is not play and then what is play. Look at your list – how did you come to those decisions?

How might your own experiences and memories have influenced your decisions?

Personal experiences will have informed your current views and values regarding play; these often prompt emotive (subjective) responses rather than logical analysis because our own memories are often vivid – we have been there and because of these vivid memories we know that play experiences will be remembered, recreated and made sense of; hence creating a history for the child (Canning 2011). Therefore, it is important that you are aware of these as they are deeply rooted in your cultural values. It is these values that influence the way in which you engage with children, the environments you provide and the hidden messages that children pick up on about the values you place on play. These hidden messages or cues are used by children to distinguish between play and not play activities which, according to McInnes et al. (2011), can be environmental, for example, location of activity, or adult involvement, and emotional, such as choice and the voluntary nature of the activity.

Ideas, values and beliefs are not developed in isolation, consolidation often occurs when we share views with others; hence look to other practitioners and ask them to list what is/is not play and to identify what may have influenced their decisions. These discussions are extremely valuable as they can lead to an increased awareness, which, according to Moyles et al. (2002), helps to identify what play is in early childhood education, and how it can be developed by practitioners. Play and playful pedagogy are clearly whole setting issues, and with the effective leadership of an Early Years Teacher who frames and encourages open discussion and reflection on practice, a truly empowering and playful environment for young children can be created.

Theoretical perspectives on play and play pedagogy

Selecting from the vast array of material available on play has indeed been challenging; however, in many ways that reflects the strong beliefs of many that play is valuable to children's early learning. But before we embark on theories that are associated with the benefits of play, it is important that you hold on to your values and beliefs as these will have influenced your current views on the value of play to children's learning and development. Similarly your values and beliefs will also influence how you connect with past and current thinking, regarding play.

Reflection 2.2: Linking theory to practice

As you examine the following theories introduced in this chapter:

- think about how the ideas presented have influenced current practice on how to support children's learning and development;
- consider how their ideas may further shape your own practice.

Keep your own journal account, reflecting on how theoretical insight may help you to articulate clearly the benefits of play on children's learning and development, leading others.

While play has historically been seen as a natural behaviour that benefits children's all-round development, the quest to identify Garvey's (1991) three categories – what play is, what play does, along with what it means to children – has substantially grown in recent times as a result of increased government intervention. This began in 1997, when the then Conservative government introduced free part-time places for three terms after a child's fourth birthday. With this investment came the need for accountability and a national curriculum for the under-fives emerged. The period between 1997 and 2012 saw an unprecedented focus on early years; with four changes to the Early

Years Foundation Stage during this time. With each revision the struggle to justify and make visible the benefits of play to young children's learning and development has become more apparent, and as Goouch (2010) points out, this was always going to be difficult where settings are required to demonstrate measurable outcomes related to school readiness in terms of literacy and numeracy.

Kwon (2002) identifies free play, individualism, developmentalism and the child-centred perspectives of the adult educator, as deeply embedded traditions in Britain's early years education. These values were further reinforced by Piaget's work, which was hugely influential during the 1970s and 1980s. Piaget emphasized the centrality of children being active in their learning, through such things as discovery and exploratory play and child-centred learning. Piaget felt that children were driven to seek a state of balance or equilibrium where ideas matched actual experiences. He saw children as intrinsically motivated to make sense of their world by striving to eliminate uncertainty; it was this process that Piaget felt helped children to acquire new knowledge. Piaget also believed that children pass naturally through an ordered sequence of developmental age-related stages, which Wood (2013) identifies as: immature to mature, simple to complex and concrete to abstract, with critical periods where the child is ready to move onto to the next level. By combining these two aspects, one can see how Piaget saw play activity as a means of supporting children's ability to take on new information through the practical actions of exploration and discovery, allowing children opportunities to explore clusters of ideas (schema) through repetitive actions.

This places the child as a leader of their own learning with the adult acting as a facilitator rather than providing direct instruction. For Piaget, play simply provided activity that helped a child to take on new information; and the play activity became more complex as the child developed. This link to development was documented in his play stages:

- 0–2 years: sensorimotor stage – children explore and experiment using all their senses.
- 2–6 years: symbolic stage – translating experiences to symbols, for example, a wooden spoon might represent a microphone.
- 6 years and upwards: games with rules – begin to understand social concepts, co-operation and competition.

These categories have been refined and much of his work has been tested with the result that he underestimated children's abilities. As Donaldson (1978), among many, has argued, the tests used did not make human sense to young children; equally linking development to ages and stages is not helpful as progress is often uneven, and Piaget did not take into consideration the wider social context in which the child was embedded. However, as Broadhead and Burt (2012) caution, the EYFS (DfE 2012) still tends to reflect an individual developmental model.

As an Early Years Teacher you need to be aware that your role is not, as Piaget might suggest, about always following the child's lead; nor is it just about providing direct instruction in preparation for school; it is far more complex and requires an understanding of the importance of expanding and enriching the content of play activities. The significance of expanding and enriching play experiences for children began to be examined from a broad range of perspectives when Vygotsky's socio-cultural theory started to influence research and practice from the mid-1990s. Viewing the child as part of a complex social and cultural world provides a more useful lens through which to examine the benefits of play to children's learning and development; for children do not learn and develop in isolation, they are shaped by the social and cultural context into which they are born, and by considering the importance of relationships and interdependence with others as a way of making meaning out of their experiences, one begins to see how play activities have the potential for young children to find out more about themselves, their culture, social roles and relationships.

Vygotsky saw play as a means for social interaction and the leading source of development in pre-school years; because when a child is involved in a make-believe or role play situation, they are not simply operating at their current level of development, they are playing beyond their level, as the role often requires more mature skills. Bodrova (2008) uses the example of a boy who was asked to be the lookout as part of a play scenario, it was observed that he remained at his post and concentrated for a lot longer than when the teacher had asked him to sit still and pay attention. However, while Vygotsky saw this way of playing as a leading activity for young children, it is important, as Wood (2013) points out, to clarify that leading in this context refers to the processes and social situations involved in developing existing ways of thinking into more complex forms of intellectual functioning.

While Vygotsky's definition of play is limited to dramatic or make-believe play, it is seen as a more holistic perspective, in that he considered opportunities for imaginary play can promote cognitive, emotional and social development. This is evident in Vygotsky's three components of real play, where:

- children create an imaginary situation;
- children take on and act out roles;
- children follow a set of rules determined by specific roles.

(Bodrova 2008: 359)

Vygotsky felt this type of play was driven by a cultural-historical experience, meaning beliefs, cultures, customs, values and skills are transferred from one generation to the next, and through imaginary play children learn the thought processes and behaviours specific to their culture or society. Therefore, imaginary play is not totally spontaneous as rules are required; rules that stem from the imaginary situation, for example if the child is playing the role of the baby, then she is bound by the rules of baby behaviour. This point is important because it shows that imaginary play scenarios require forward planning, involving self-regulation as an essential skill to enable play partners to constantly monitor each other's conformity with the rules (Bodrova 2008).

Vygotsky undoubtedly saw this type of play as pivotal to children's learning and development, as, according to Bodrova (2008), he cited this as one of the social contexts responsible for creating young children's 'zone of proximal development' (ZPD), a term you are probably familiar with. Subsequent studies supported Vygotsky's theory showing that when young children play in this way they are using mental skills above the skills seen in other activities.

This understanding is vital in your role as an Early Years Teacher as it may help you to reflect on the importance of providing open-ended environments/resources that encourage imaginary play where opportunities for higher mental skills (attention, concentration, problem solving and symbolizing) are provided. Equally, you may reflect on this in relation to the balance between adult- and child-initiated activities. Interestingly Vygotsky maintained that for pre-school and kindergarten children (up to about the age of 7), the quality of their play is a better predictor of later educational achievement than the mastery of academic skills. However, Bodrova and Leong's (2007) research, which replicated a study carried out 60 years ago, found children's make-believe play between the ages of 4 and 5 was generally of a lower level more associated with toddlers. These studies revealed very few new themes, with an over-reliance on familiar topics like the family, as well as realistic toys limited to the use of children's ability to create substitutes.

One of the authors of this chapter watched children eagerly open new resources for the role play area (a well-known fast food chain), observed the children use it in exactly the same way as when they had eaten at the fast food restaurant, and after the initial flurry of excitement, the children were then observed leaving the area. Clearly the children had no long-term goals in mind, there was no planning as such which encourages individuals to develop self-regulation over their own short-term goals. There was only a brief interlude where children assigned themselves different roles, suggesting the development of other people's perspectives but little evidence of negotiating or problem solving, and importantly, no sustained interest as the play collapsed quickly.

Reflection 2.3: Immature and mature play

Reflect on the practice you have seen in this area, taking into account how play develops from simple repetitive actions to emerging and complex pretend scenarios as stated by Bodrova and Leong (2007) and explained in Figure 2.1.

Think about really absorbing play scenarios you might have seen –what made them so enriching?

What was missing in those you considered to be less effective?

Vygotsky suggests that children need to experience imaginative play that is rich in context as it stimulates the development of mental representations which leads to abstract thinking. For example, children's play matures from using replicas like a spoon to pretend to feed the baby to objects that are different in appearance but can perform the same function (a stickle brick becomes the spoon) to later using speech or gestures; feeding oneself without any sign of a tool (the gesture says it all). Children will also be able to develop other high-order thinking which requires active control

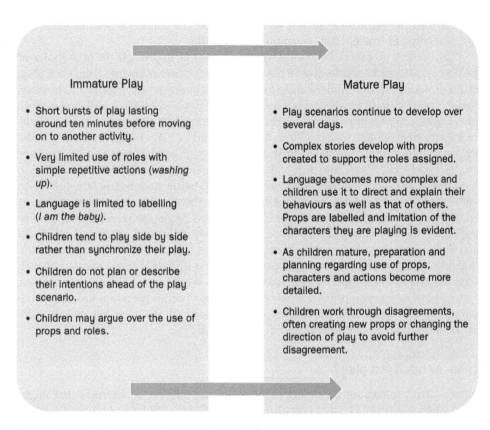

Figure 2.1 The development of pretend play.

Immature Play

- Short bursts of play lasting around ten minutes before moving on to another activity.

- Very limited use of roles with simple repetitive actions (*washing up*).

- Language is limited to labelling (*I am the baby*).

- Children tend to play side by side rather than synchronize their play.

- Children do not plan or describe their intentions ahead of the play scenario.

- Children may argue over the use of props and roles.

Mature Play

- Play scenarios continue to develop over several days.

- Complex stories develop with props created to support the roles assigned.

- Language becomes more complex and children use it to direct and explain their behaviours as well as that of others. Props are labelled and imitation of the characters they are playing is evident.

- As children mature, preparation and planning regarding use of props, characters and actions become more detailed.

- Children work through disagreements, often creating new props or changing the direction of play to avoid further disagreement.

over such cognitive processes as planning, self-regulation and remaining engaged (metacognition). Thus, children need time to develop mature forms of play in relation to social roles and relationships between people, with rules that have been experienced first-hand, and as Wood (2013) argues, Vygotsky's work related to children up to 7 years of age; therefore, phasing out opportunities for play during the Reception year means that the full potential benefits of play will not be realized.

Therefore, this is an area where Early Years Teachers really need to inspire and encourage settings to provide quality free-flow experiences that enable practitioners to gain insight into children's ways of being, where they are working just beyond their current ability (ZPD). As Bruce (2004) explains, in free-flow play, children take control, they make sense of what is happening, experience others' behaviours, face challenges and experience being both followers and leaders. These experiences provide the vital preparation for later life, when working as part of a team or being assertive in their role as leaders. Bruce also highlights the importance of free-flow play as a way of opening up the brain, and while it does not create new learning as such, it does consolidate learning in varied and interesting ways; for example Joe played indoors at being in the animal hospital yesterday and he is playing it again today but with different children and outdoors. So while it is the same theme, the context is not the same, and this, according to Bruce (2004), encourages flexibility.

Therefore, it is essential that all staff within a setting appreciate the importance of the flow of play and are attentive to the unfolding stories that emerge from such play, as this provides valuable understanding of children's interests and dispositions towards learning both as individuals and in groups. Observing how children collaborate with others opens up new possibilities for children's learning and offers practitioner opportunities for pedagogical framing. Broadhead and Burt's (2012) fascinating study in the 'whatever you want it to be place' identified that though play themes and interests are culturally personal, they often provoke cooperative engagements, which, according to them, revealed commonalities in children's quest to better understand how the world works and how individuals interact in that world. There are many themes that most children are fascinated by: mini-beasts, dinosaurs, changing seasons; similarly there are times when one child's visit to the seaside or a setting visit to a farm has sparked a shared excitement with the whole group. While this will be interpreted by each individual in a unique way, according to Broadhead and Burt (2012), the sharing of such experiences provides opportunities for children to see it from different perspectives. Such opportunities may provide teachers with opportunities for adult-directed activities which once again raise the challenges associated with the balance between child- and adult-initiated activities and your pedagogic role.

Child- or adult-led play?

Rogers (2011) makes an important point about the conflict of interests that might occur when one views children's play as separate from the adult's pedagogical requirements which may be a result of external pressures. However, Rogers also provides a useful perspective in that if the adults view the physical and social space as providing the potential for negotiation and enhancing relationships, then opportunities to really explore identities, individual needs and group interests may remove some of the constraints associated with play-based learning and assessment. But it is also worth remembering that regardless of whether the play is free-flow or adult-led, it is, as Moyles (1989) reminds us, still structured by the resources and materials offered. The resources and materials as previously highlighted really do influence the quality of play and, as an Early Years Teacher, you need to focus on the importance of the adults having a clear understanding about what they are hoping the children might gain from the play resources and materials on offer. This is why the children need to be involved in their play spaces with adults who value the importance of reciprocal relationships, because it is through such relationships that meaningful learning opportunities emerge.

As Fleer (2010) states, the importance of how much should be directed by the adult or how much space children should be given to become people in their own right is always incredibly challenging and can be related to a dance, and if you get it wrong, you tread on somebody's toes. But children need cultural as well as real tools if they are to develop deep and meaningful understanding that encourages them to make connections and transfer these skills to other activities. Therefore, Moyles's (1989) play spiral becomes a useful tool for the adult to consider. First, children need to freely experience novel resources or materials during free play episodes. This provides the opportunities where, according to Hutt (1979), epistemic play can be observed; children will often appear deeply intent on becoming familiar with the object; and according to Moyles (1989), the child, with the help of other children's ways of viewing the object, may develop some mastery. But it should be recognized that if left to their own devices the children may never know the full potential of the object. Hence the importance of some adult-directed play, as this opens up the full potential of the resource. Moyles then goes on to explain how the exploratory stage experienced by the children coupled with the learning from the adult-directed session, further enhances later free play, or as Hutt (1979) states, becomes ludic play where the children proceed to apply the knowledge gained through exploration and direct teaching. This model encourages us to recognize the fluidity of learning without over-emphasizing the instructive elements of play-based learning. While fluidity is vital to the quality of play experiences, one final consideration related to theoretical perspectives is necessary regarding free play and the adults' pedagogic role; when do you play alongside or observe from a distance? This is vital in relation to the complexities associated with tuning into children's emerging stories during free-flow play.

Fleer's (2010) valuable work on concept development through play is complex and for the purposes of this chapter only a snapshot is provided to whet your appetite for further reading. As previously stated, everyday imaginary play situations require rules that relate to the topic and these can often be stimulated by the resources available. These resources may spark in the child a connection to a real item at home, for example, a frying pan and eggs. However, in reality what you see is a plastic bucket and some small plastic balls. Tuning into the child's imagined world is therefore challenging and needs some careful observation for fear of not understanding the child's story at that moment in time and interrupting their flow to answer unrelated questions. Equally you may have set out play resources with particular learning for the children in mind; however, as Fleer states, you cannot just leave it to the resources to meet your intended learning because the children may have made an entirely different connection with the resources. Fleer (2010: 8) uses a wonderful example of a teacher who wanted children to explore the concept of changing materials by mixing different fluids together (potion play). However, the bottles with pump action, tubes and coloured water were near a few soft toys which included Humpty Dumpty and this prompted an entirely different play scenario. Instead, according to Fleer (2010), the children's play script was about caring for Humpty Dumpty who had fallen off the wall and this was combined with their everyday experiences of medicines. Hence if you have a specific learning intention in mind, it is essential that you frame the play right from the beginning. This clarifies the importance of the role of the Early Years Teacher in inspiring and leading a new generation of professionals who truly understand the importance of play to children's learning and development and your role as a pedagogic leader.

Leading a new generation of professionals

The concept of a visionary leader in the Early Years has been transformed into a reality with the government's drive in creating 'high quality early education and childcare, delivered with love and care' (DfE 2013e: 13). Consequently government policy intentions have raised determination and aspirations for the sector to substantially increase the quality and status of the workforce. In order to raise the status of the profession further, a continuum to build upon the strengths of the Early Years Professional has seen the introduction of Early Years Teachers, high-quality pedagogical leaders who will be specialists in early childhood development, trained to work with babies and children, leading the Early Years Foundation Stage curriculum. Being a successful Early Years Teacher will involve, as Doyle and Smith (1999) suggest, people who are able to think and act creatively in routine and non-routine situations and who set out to influence the actions, beliefs and feelings of others.

Reflection 2.4: Graduate leaders

In your view, how will you as a graduate leader improve outcomes for children?

What, in your view, makes a good leader in the context of an early years environment and the theoretical perspectives above?

Can leaders be trained or are they born leaders?

Consider the questions above and reflect on your own experiences of being led and leading others to help you to answer the questions.

The role of an Early Years Teacher is viewed as critical to the successful implementation of the EYFS curriculum (DfE 2012) despite a change of government in 2010. Without doubt, the pedagogical leadership role of an Early Years Teacher is primarily concerned with leading and implementing EYFS, however, as Whalley (2011: 68) reminds us, it also sets out to support others to make effective personalized provision for the children within the setting.

Reflection 2.5: Leading practice

As a trainee or established Early Years Teacher, why is leading practice particularly important in early years?

You may have reflected that leading and supporting responsibilities are required at all levels among practitioners, however, an influential leader in the Early Years cannot only articulate a vision for quality practice within the setting, but they will also introduce their role to the wider sector, promoting professionalism of the sector with awareness of their role in leading a new generation of professionals. This is supported by Smith and Langston (1999: 20), who suggest that leaders should have the vision, yet show sensitivity to others in the way they lead and innovate.

Historically, the early years sector had little recognition as a profession until political influence from the Rumbold Report (DES 1990) urged new attention to quality in all early childhood provision. Amazingly, considering the level of responsibility and skills required by early years practitioners, training was never a statutory requirement for employment in, or provision of, childcare services. Today, with the emerging role of the Early Years Professional (EYP) and the developing role of the Early Years Teacher, there is a drive and expectation to 'take responsibility for leading practice through appropriate professional development for self and colleagues' (NCTL 2013b: S8.5) and 'reflect on and evaluate the effectiveness of provision, and shape and support good practice' (NCTL 2013b: S8.6).

Today, the political influence in professionalizing the workforce has created excellent practice and a graduate-led workforce to improve outcomes for children (Miller and Cable, 2011). A recent qualitative study exploring early years employers' views of staff studying on a work-based foundation degree programme revealed that staff have more confidence in their role and demonstrate better knowledge and understanding which is shared with others, resulting in immediate impact on practice.

Plan high-quality provision that inspires babies and children

As a pedagogical leader, your role is to implement the EYFS (DfE 2012) in the setting by establishing and developing effective playful pedagogical practices with your staff team. More importantly, Whalley highlights that 'as a graduate leader, you are expected to model an informed and reflective approach to practice, which will include a high level of knowledge and understanding of theoretical views of children's learning and development' (2011: 66). It is also important to remember that there has been a shift towards understanding the individual needs of each child by creating a framework that supports effective partnership working between the wider context of the community, the family and the provision of children's services.

A core aspect of your role as an Early Years Teacher is that you are required to lead and support the team to establish and plan effective personalized provision and learning opportunities for children as well as groups. Note that a key requisite is to strengthen team knowledge and participation in planning the education and care of children. Therefore, your allocation of time and willingness to support individual practitioners to observe and plan quality care and learning opportunities is paramount to embedding a broad, balanced play-based EYFS curriculum. Following on from this step is to provide feedback on practice at regular intervals to engage staff to adopt a reflective practitioner culture.

Activity 2.1: Personal reflective practitioner model

1   Write the word 'Reflection' on a large piece of paper or a mirror; look in the mirror.
2   Write down key influential moments that have impacted on your journey towards being a leader in Early Years.

3   Identify a goal that you would like to achieve as an Early Years Teacher
     relating to your personal and professional role.
4   Write a plan of how you will achieve this goal.
5   Share with another trainee, mentor or colleague.

Enhancing specialist knowledge

The specialist knowledge of child development and planning playful pedagogical
experiences for children is important in a leadership role and must be in accordance
with EYFS (DfE 2012) as a baseline. Additionally, the ability to communicate is a key
aspect of the role of an Early Years Teacher, therefore, the transfer of theoretical
knowledge is essential to support quality provision and engage staff to update their
understanding of the field, through your intervention.

How to inspire a culture of effective planning

It is imperative that you work towards a culture of coaching staff on a regular basis,
talking and modelling planning meetings about how to plan and lead activities that
promote children's interests and intellectual curiosity with discussion that promotes
reflecting on the effectiveness of provision within the setting as a whole. For example,
discussion points at a planning meeting: What is the experience for babies and children
under 3 in the setting? What is the planning cycle and how can it be developed in the
setting?

Reflection 2.6: Nursery education and childcare

New Labour, from 1997, emphasized the importance of nursery education.
Refer to the current Coalition government DfE documents *More Great Childcare*
(DfE 2013e) and *More Affordable Childcare* (DfE 2013d).

What is your view now of the importance of nursery education as a leader in
the field?

Case study 2.1: Early Years Professional in private day-care setting

Sarah is an Early Years Professional (EYP) in a private day-care setting. Compare and
contrast her story below with your experience to date:

As an EYP in the setting, I have observed the practice in all the different areas of
the setting. I am pleased to be given this responsibility and have confidence in

looking at the care and the learning opportunities that are being planned by the staff. I see my role as an experienced staff member who can help the others to understand the importance of child development and use their experience to plan for each child's individual needs. I give feedback to staff and have been asked by management to observe fortnightly. When I am in the different areas, I encourage staff to talk more openly and reflect on elements of their work that they are finding challenging. I do feedback to management with my observations and pick up areas where I know I can immediately support staff to improve their practice or address a concern they have about a child or their work. I encourage staff to observe their designated key children in order to track their learning and development and then use their observations to plan for each child. Although I work in one area of the setting, I have so much experience from my past roles and remedial work in this country and abroad that I share and model to staff. The key areas where some of the staff need a better understanding, are managing behaviour, feeding and mealtimes, planning appropriate activities for children and focusing on better quality interactions.

Planning education and care

A core area of practice that you will be required to lead, support and be involved in is the regular daily and weekly planning for individual and groups of children. If you have other responsibilities such as managing the setting or leading one specific area, then now may be a good opportunity to review your role to ensure your involvement in leading and supporting planning (NCTL 2013b: S4.1, S4.4) with 'all staff' within your setting is effective and transparent. This would need a flexible approach and being available to support 'all' staff to meet the needs of children according to their interests, individual needs, age range, stage of development, circumstances and ability.

Activity 2.2: Planning

1 As a newly appointed Early Years Teacher in full day care, based in the pre-school room, you are asked to observe planning practice within the four main areas of the setting.
2 You observe that practice varies and there is a lack of understanding and confidence in using observations, photographs and other evidence to plan for the individual needs of children.
3 Supporting the knowledge and professional development of staff is your responsibility, so what are the key actions you would take to support the staff within each area of the setting?

Historically, you may recall the debates for and against bringing care and education together. Teachers' Standards (Early Years) (DfE 2013f) affirm that children learn from all their experiences, not just those seen as educational, therefore, highlighting the separation of education and care as a false division.

Reflection upon your practice here will enable you to demonstrate leadership responsibilities for planning both the education and care of children (NCTL 2013b: S4, S5) and the understanding of staff when planning and using the setting's planning policy.

Remember that staff and students often appreciate support in planning so you can identify and lead training or co-ordinate learning to embed the process, evaluating the effectiveness of planning procedures in your setting and propose an alternative approach. This involves a flexible approach and supporting staff to meet the needs of children according to their interests, individual needs, age range, stage of development, circumstances and ability.

Activity 2.3: Planning for education and care

1   Make a list of five activities you have planned, and ask yourself, does this include both the education and care of children or not? Before you begin, think about practitioners singing rhymes to a child when changing their nappy or at feeding time, do you call this education or care?

2   Is there a clear distinction or do both overlap in almost all aspects of your provision? Teachers' Standards specifically ask you to evidence both education and care, so you need to make reference and demonstrate both aspects.

In an era of care and education children need to be nurtured from birth to become curious learners. Curiosity needs to flow through any curriculum, and as Mindham (2005) reaffirms, practitioners and pedagogues should view children not solely as in need of an education but also should provide opportunities that support the children's imagination and creativity, including music, dance, storytelling, role play and arts.

Supporting the knowledge and professional development of staff is your responsibility. For example, an Early Years Teacher in a day-care setting observed practice in the toddler room and noted that one staff member lacked experience of behaviour management with this particular age group. To support the staff member's development she informed her of the setting policy and they worked on a strategy to manage the behaviour.

Conclusion

As an Early Years Teacher you are required to show competency in setting high expectations which inspire, motivate and challenge all children (NCTL 2013b: S1). The Introduction to the Standards claims 'Early Years Teachers make the education and care of children their first concern' (NCTL 2013b). As Palaiologou (2013: 231) states, 'When babies are born, they have a long way to go before becoming independent. If they are to survive, consistent care must be provided over an extended period of time.' It is therefore important to be aware that the role of the Early Years Teacher is to support practitioners to set high expectations by first establishing a thorough understanding of playful pedagogy and the principles of the EYFS framework from birth to age 5 years. This principled approach emphasizes the holistic nature of children's learning and development, with observation as a central monitoring and recording tool. This invaluable activity, expanded in Chapter 6, helps practitioners inform planning and share findings with children, parents, carers and other professionals.

So, draw on the theoretical perspectives of play and playful pedagogy shared in this chapter as you enjoy your role in leading and supporting staff to plan a range of flexible activities and individual care and education programmes. Be inspired through your reflective evidence on how children experience activities throughout the day. What are the children saying – verbally and non-verbally – about the experience? Are they experiencing a balance of activities suitable for their learning and development, indoors and outdoors? Are there physically challenging and quiet activities, adult-framed and free-flow, group and one-to-one opportunities with their key person?

Understanding how young children learn and develop remains fundamental to the role of the practitioner. As Neaum (2013:120) states, 'Early years pedagogical practice involves supporting children's learning through play in ways that are responsive to children's interests and motivations.' Furthermore, the timing of effective communication from responsive adults supports the richness of each experience and interaction which aligns with the Researching Effective Pedagogy in the Early Years (REPEY) study (Siraj-Blatchford et al. 2002), highlighting that the best learning takes place when children are motivated and involved.

3

Building and sustaining relationships
Early Years teaching with babies, young children and parents

Kelly Cooper and Vicky Mummery

> The most powerful influence on our capacity to manage life's hurdles is the quality of care we receive in childhood, especially the earliest years.
>
> (Kraemer 1999: 1)

Chapter objectives

By the end of this chapter you should be able to:

- understand the importance of attachment for children's well-being, learning and development;
- appreciate the role of the Key Person in supporting children's emotional development and formation of relationships;
- articulate why valuing parents'/carers' knowledge of their children is vital to building relationships;
- recognize the different perspectives of home and setting learning;
- discuss 'hard-to-reach' services in early years settings for parents and carers.

Link with Teachers' Standards (Early Years) 2013

S2, S6

Introduction

The first section of this chapter focuses on the importance of attachment (see the Appendix: Standard 2.3). It will give an overview of the suggestion by neuroscientists that children are born social and that the part of the brain that governs social development is dependent on relationships with others. There will be an exploration of how these relationships with others support children's personal, social and emotional development which in turn fosters their well-being, learning and development (Appendix: Standard 2.2). There will be discussion of the importance of being 'tuned in' to children's feeling states in order to support the formation of close relationships and enhance children's emotional development (Appendix: Standard 2.5).

The second section of this chapter will highlight how children's experience of day care needs to be carefully supported and will argue that the Key Person approach is not only a vital way to help 'contain' the intense feelings young children experience when they are separated from their parent/carer but helps children feel special, supported, cared for and thought about while they are away from home (Appendix: Standard 2.3). It will go on to explore the importance of practitioners valuing parents'/ carers' knowledge of their own child (Appendix: Standard 2.7), exploring how the 'secure base' and 'triangle of trust' are integral to building a supportive relationship with parents (Appendix: Standard 2.3). The importance of the home learning environ-ment will be discussed and how communication is key to parents/carers sharing infor-mation (Appendix: Standard 6.3). A debate on the services we provide, and whether they meet the needs of the communities of families we work with, will be considered. The chapter will conclude with a consideration of some of the barriers/obstacles that can impact on the formation of close relationships with children and their parents/ carers.

The importance of attachment for children's well-being, learning and development

Recent research in neuroscience suggests that babies are born social and are predis-posed with the knowledge and ability to build relationships and have their needs met (Dunn 1988; Gopnik et al. 2001). Farroni discusses research on babies making eye contact and face processing, and concludes that babies are born prepared to detect socially relevant information and use it as an early form of communication (Farroni et al. 2002). It is the opinion of neuroscientists that from birth, babies are orientated towards human faces and sounds and that they are able to imitate facial movements and can co-ordinate expression, gesture and voices to those of others (Gopnik et al. 2001; Gerhardt 2004).

Coupled with the suggestion that babies are born social, Gopnik et al. (2001) suggest that adults are designed to be powerful support systems that are devoted to helping babies. This is vitally important as young babies are deeply dependent on adults not only to have their fundamental physical needs and their need for affection, warmth and tenderness met, but also for their survival. The part of the brain that governs social development is called the orbitofrontal cortex. This part of the brain does not start to develop until after birth and does not begin to mature until toddlerhood. The orbitofrontal cortex is experience-dependent and Gerhardt (2004) argues that this is so the baby can be moulded to the environmental niche he/she finds themselves in and thus become part of that culture. The socio-constructivist Vygotsky emphasizes a similar view, arguing that the social environment enables the cultural transmission of knowledge. He argues that social activity shapes thinking, emphasizing that the child's mind is social and that cultural processes shape thought (Vygotsky 1962).

For the orbitofrontal cortex to develop well, a baby needs appropriate social experiences and is dependent on the available relationships with others. Crucial to the development of relationships with others and brain development is touch. Neuroscience research suggests that touch shows the child that they are loved and sends signals to the brain telling it to grow (Porter and Porter 2004). You can find support for this claim in Gerhardt (2004) who says that being lovingly held is the greatest spur to brain development. Smiling and making eye contact have also been shown to have a positive effect on brain development. Schore, as cited in Gerhardt (2004), suggests that it stimulates the growth of the social, emotionally intelligent brain and also makes the baby feel good as dopamine is released – dopamine being a natural chemical associated with feeling good and released during pleasurable times. Physical contact therefore not only helps build attachments but also stimulates the brain to develop.

These bonds or attachments to caregivers are therefore vital to children's development. Eliot (1999: 304) states that, 'Attachment is regarded by many psychologists as the seminal event in a person's development – the primacy of a child's security, self-esteem, self-control and social skills.' Eliot goes on to suggest that having secure attachments with caregivers enables children to learn how to identify their own feelings, read the feelings of others, adequately express their emotions, develop high self-esteem, become more resilient and develop relationships throughout life. Manning-Morton further highlights the importance of secure attachments, stating:

> Although having different perspectives and approaches, it seems that psycho-analytic theory, neuroscience and developmental psychology all emphasise the centrality of positive relationships between significant adults and young children in their earliest years in supporting healthy emotional, cognitive and physical development.
>
> (2006: 47)

Secure attachments, therefore, provide a base for children so they can build their personal, social and emotional development. Personal, social and emotional development in turn forms a base for learning and is the driving force upon which a child builds their cognitive development. Eliot (1999) supports this view, arguing that children's emotional abilities are the most important aspect of development because they establish the crucial foundations on which every other mental skill can flourish. Eliot (1999: 290) goes on to suggest that, 'Well before they can master language, babies communicate through these interactions that they develop the security, confidence, and motivation to master their more obvious motor, verbal and cognitive achievements.' Children need secure attachments in order to develop into emotionally, physically and intellectually healthy children (Berger 1999; Kraemer 1999; Penn 1999).

When children receive love with supportive and responsive interactions, they feel secure and know that they will have their needs and feelings met. This in turn helps children to develop self-confidence, a high self-esteem and a sense of worth. Knowing that they can rely on adults, what to expect, what will happen next and what the boundaries are, all help children develop a sense of consistency and continuity and in turn feel safe and secure. The knowledge that children are loved, safe and cared for enables them to focus their attention on exploring the world.

Bowlby (1998) argues that secure attachments provide a secure base from which the child can explore the outside world and return with the knowledge that they will be welcomed, nourished, comforted and reassured both physically and emotionally. This springboard for curiosity and exploration (Lieberman 1995) not only provides children with the opportunity to encounter new experiences but encourages children to develop a sense of self. By moving away from their attachments figure, children can 'try' being separate and exercise some freedom, power and control over aspects of their daily experiences (Stonehouse 1988).

It is extremely important that children are able to explore the world around them. Isaacs (1929: 73) highlights that, 'Children learn by their fingers – without active touch their vision as yet tells them little; and without their actual sensory experience of things, what other people tell them means hardly anything at all.' Piaget, an episte-mologist, expressed a similar view; arguing that children learn through acting on the environment and that by doing this they construct a knowledge and understanding about the world that are meaningful and personal to them (Bruner 1986; Miller 2002). Lieberman (1995) suggests that in every autonomous action, the toddler comes face to face with the paradox of being free to explore yet held hostage to internal limitations as well as external constraints.

Being sensitive to this 'struggle' means that we can support both children's learning and their emotional well-being. As well as providing a secure base for young children to explore, it is also vitally important that caregivers are 'tuned in' to children's feeling states. Stern (1998) argues that being psycho-biologically attuned to children and responding empathically not only demonstrates the quality of the relationship between infant and caregiver but also supports children's emotional development. Holmes (1993: 73) also supports this view arguing that, 'maternal responsiveness is a key determinant of the quality of attachment'. By being able to 'read' a baby's feeling state from their overt behaviour and, in turn, reflect back on this by performing a behaviour that corresponds, we encourage the baby's development of their sense of self and their recognition that internal feeling states are forms of human experience that can be shared with others (Stern 1998). Stern calls the above process *affect* and argues that not only does it act as a form of communication but is an organizing process that regulates relationships.

When caregivers are not attuned to an infant's feeling states, these will be experienced alone and isolated from the interpersonal context of shareable experiences (Stern 1998). Not only can this impact on children's emotional develop-ment but can also influence the formation of secure attachments. If babies' needs are not responded to, they learn that the world is a dangerous place in which other people are to be treated with great caution (Lieberman 1995). Not only does this teach them to expect little from close relationships, it also threatens their sense of well-being as they receive negative messages about their worth as a person (Manning-Morton and Thorp 2003).

When a child does not have a secure attachment where their needs and feelings are responded to in a predictable, positive way, they focus all their attention on having their needs met. Research indicates that in that situation, the brain shuts out the stimulation needed to develop healthy cognitive and social skills and produces more of the stress hormone, cortisol (Eliot 1999; Porter and Porter 2004). Having secure attachments with sensitive, responsive caregivers can block the elevation in cortisol levels and thus protect brain development (Vermeer and Van Ijzendoorn 2006). A securely attached child will store an internal working model of a responsive, loving, reliable care-giver, and of a self who is worthy of love and attention and will bring these assumptions to bear on all other relationships' (Holmes 1999: 78).

The role of the Key Person: Key Working vs the Key Person approach

In view of the above discussion on the importance of secure attachments, it is vitally important that when children attend a day-care setting practitioners actively encourage and support the development of close relationships between them and their key children, particularly for children under 3 years old. Through the Key Person approach, practitioners can aim to develop close relationships with a small group of children in order to foster and support their well-being and holistic development.

Many settings claim to operate the Key Person Approach but what is often seen in practice is Key Working. Key Working has a focus on systems and organization and includes tasks such as keeping records, observing and analysing information, planning for individual children, writing reports, communicating with parents on a daily basis, communicating with colleagues and other professionals and planning key group times. Although the above tasks do form part of the role as a Key Person, the main tenet of the Key Person approach is to develop secure trusting relationships with key children and parents. This is done through being available (both physically and emotionally), tuned in, responsive, consistent and able to contain children's feelings. Too often in practice the paperwork side of being a Key Person is valued above the importance of the quality of the relationships that Key People have with their Key Children. Opportunities for building and sustaining close relationships with young children are often missed.

Authors such as Greenman and Stonehouse (1996) and Manning-Morton and Thorp (2003) highlight the significance of using routine times as a means for deepening key relationships. Intimate moments in a child's day such as nappy changing, feeding and sleep are opportunities for Key People to spend sustained time with their Key Children. All too often these moments/events are seen as a 'chore' or just part of the daily routine which can result in children receiving 'collective care' rather than individualized personal care. One practitioner changes all of the children's nappies as if on a conveyor belt or hovers around the lunch table spooning food on to plates when in fact these are prime times for the Key Person relationship to be strengthened.

Too often practitioners claim that the conveyor belt approach ensures that 'work' is shared equally or stops children becoming too close – (an adult concept we will explore later in the chapter) – but this approach means that practitioners can often become too focused on practical tasks rather than children's emotional well-being. Imagine that you (as an adult) had an injury that meant you were unable to go to the toilet alone – who would you want to help you? Most likely it would be someone that you trusted and felt safe with and surely not a different person each time. Use the following activity to evaluate how much emphasis is placed on enhancing key relationships.

Activity 3.1: Evaluating the daily routine

1   Choose a child to 'follow' for the day. Observe and take notes on how often the child is 'handled' by an adult and how often they spend time with their Key Person/Key Group.
2   How often does the child's Key Person interact with the child?
3   Does the Key Person use key/prime times such as nappy changing, meals and sleep to enhance the relationship with their Key Child?
4   Does the Key Person provide times for their Key Group to come together?
5   Are there any changes that could be made to the daily routine to enable more focused Key Person time?
6   Who is benefitting from the way the routine is planned? Is it designed to meet the needs of the children or the adults?

Secondary Key Person

A 'secondary Key Person' is an approach whereby a second practitioner, based in the same room, aims to build a close relationship with another practitioner's Key Groups so that when a child's Key Person is unavailable, the children still have someone consciously respond to them in the way their Key Person would. Although other practitioners within the same room inevitably build close relationships with children (other than their Key Group), having a named secondary Key Person helps to ensure that the support children need while their Key Person is unavailable is more focused and planned for.

Degotardi and Pearson (2009) examined the impact of wider socio-cultural influences on relationship building in early childhood and argue that an infant will form multiple and different relationships within a group-care context. Although it is important to take into account that children build relationships beyond their Key Person – including with their peers – the secondary Key Person approach allows practitioners not only to support each other's Key Children during times of absence, but can provide additional support when new children are settling in, or when a particular child needs additional emotional support. This approach, however, is distinct from a collective care approach in that, in order for the child to build additional relationships, they first need to develop a secure Key Person relationship.

If we consider the concept of the secure base discussed earlier, once a child has developed their initial Key Person attachment, they can use this as a 'springboard' to explore not only the physical world around them but also the 'emotional world' in the context of other adult relationships. In order to have a successful secondary Key Person approach practitioners need to ensure that there is a named person who acts as the secondary Key Person and that regular information sharing takes place so that practitioners can deepen their relationships with their secondary Key Group.

The importance of being 'tuned in'

Manning-Morton and Thorp (2003: 89) remind us that, 'For a child, separation and loss is inherent of the process of entering day care.' Bowlby, as cited in Holmes (1993), further describes the experience of being separated as no less than that of a bereaved adult, in that they may experience intense feelings of mental pain and anguish, yearning, angry protests, despair, apathy and withdrawal. Goldschmied and Jackson (2005) highlight that, as practitioners, we can never remind ourselves enough that a very young and almost totally dependent child is the only person in the nursery who cannot understand why they are there.

In light of the intense feelings young children may experience when they are separated from their parent/s, practitioners need to be open, sensitive and tuned in to their Key Children. Winnicott (1960) uses the phrase the 'holding environment' to denote not just the physical holding of a baby but also the psycho-physiological system of protection, support, caring and containing. Shuttleworth (1989) describes this type of 'holding' as containment, i.e. the ability of adults to help a child manage feelings that may frighten, worry, overwhelm or threaten a child by acting as a 'container' for those feelings. By being able to get into contact with a baby's state of mind and supportively responding, a caregiver's mind can act as a container for the baby and enable the child to grow psychologically (Shuttleworth 1989).

In practice, practitioners need to be mindful of this so that through both their physical interactions (cuddles and holding, etc.) and emotional responsiveness they can help children cope with feelings that could overwhelm them. Manning-Morton (2006) further supports this approach by suggesting that children's physical and emotional needs are closely intertwined and that through meeting or having those needs met, the seeds of relationships are planted and grow. Therefore 'holding' or 'containing' children's emotions not only supports their well-being but in turn can further foster the development of secure attachments.

To be able to operate the Key Person approach, practitioners need to have an intellectual application of attachment theory and develop the skills necessary to form secure relationships with children. These include being attuned and responsive to children's cues, needs and feelings, making eye contact, and allowing physical contact such as being held closely.

The importance of parental influence

Having considered the importance of key relationships, we now need to explore the importance of parental influence in shaping relationships with children and practitioners. When working with young children, we need to appreciate the fact that we cannot do this in a vacuum, as children are part of a family unit. The type of family units children come from are often complex in the evolving society we live in today, which we will explore fully later on. Valuing how parents/carers impact on their child's learning and development is crucial to building a relationship with parents that can in turn become an effective and influential partnership (Wheeler and Connor 2009). There has been an abundance of research in this area, such as by Desforges and Abouchaar (2003) and the Effective Provision of Pre-school Education (EPPE) (Sylva et al. 2004), to name just a few, that support the notion that practitioners must work with parents'/ carers' knowledge of their children, as this is the most effective way to support young children in their development.

The National Children's Bureau (NCB 2012), in their guidance on the Progress Check at Age Two, stress to practitioners that parents/carers are the ones with the in-depth knowledge of their children. A question you need to consider is, how can I encourage parents to share this depth of knowledge? Clarke and French (2007: 160) state: 'In a truly collaborative relationship, parents are just as likely to be able to support professionals in their work.' As practitioners, the important thing you need to remember when working with parents is that sharing knowledge is beneficial to all those involved in the partnership.

One of the challenges of working with families is finding meaningful ways in which to keep them informed and abreast of their child's development and for them to have the opportunity to share moments with you. The Early Years Foundation Stage (DfE 2012) has made it a requirement that settings must keep parents informed of their child's progress and that each child must have an assigned Key Worker. However, as already highlighted, the Key Worker should be a Key Person and the main point to consider here is that a successful Key Person approach needs to be in place. The Key Person relationship is integral and starts from the minute a parent/carer walks into a setting. Attachment has been discussed in relation to children and how it supports their learning and development, however, this concept and that of the Key Person are impor- tant to the family unit as a whole. The Key Person should become the child's and parent's 'secure base' in a setting, a term used by Bowlby (1998). 'To create a secure base is to create an ambience that supports a child in their task of integrating their need to feel safe, in the protected sphere of intimate relationships, with their need for carefree unrestricted exploration' (Manning-Morton and Thorp, 2003: 23).

The secure base is important for parents/carers as well as the children; the secure base supports a parent/carer to feel safe and makes them want to share the valuable information they have of their child with you, which supports your relationship with the child and the parents/carer. This secure base will lead to a partnership that over time will be built on trust, time to have discussions with parents regarding the child's progress and give small intricate details of the child which should support the parents in feeling secure in the knowledge you hold. Taking time to get to know their child and having a meaningful Key Person relationship mean these points need to be firmly embedded in your practice and considered when developing a settling-in period.

The settling-in period is integral to building a Key Person relationship with the child and their parents/carers, as this is the time when a secure base is built and you should become a trusted adult by the family. Manning-Morton and Thorp (2003) refer to the importance of getting the balance right and this is something that should be considered from the very beginning, as this supports establishing a Key Person relationship based on trust. As practitioners, you need to consider what is really manageable in terms of supporting and managing parents' anxieties; it is unlikely to be realistic for you to be taking 20 phone calls in one day as well as looking after the other children in your care. You need to consider your approach and be as open as possible but also realistic in terms of manageability. This once again supports the building of foundations in a partnership based on real and manageable expectations. You need to ensure that if you agree to something with a parent that this commitment is followed through, as failure to do so can cause a very rapid breakdown in the relationship and the sense of trust is likely to be lost.

Another concept that is referred to when working with parents/carers is the 'triangle of trust' (Goldschmied and Selleck 1996). This concept has been of importance to many writers, for example, Elfer et al. (2012) advocate the 'triangle of trust' which needs to have the right ingredients, one of which is sharing information. There needs to be a triangle of care among the practitioners, parent/carers and the curriculum (Forbes 2004). For this triangle to remain balanced in its support, all contributions need to be valued. Whalley and the Pen Green Team (Pen Green Centre 2007: 157) suggest that, 'For this sharing of knowledge to be effective, each person involved has to understand the value of the contribution that they themselves make and appreciate the contributions of others.' This, in summary, encapsulates how the 'triangle of trust' should be in practice. The 'secure base' and the 'triangle of trust' are key factors in building a relationship with families, and these can only be developed if we value and empower parents with their own knowledge (Arnold and Rutter 2011; Blandford and Knowles 2009).

Importance of home/setting learning

Building a relationship with parents is not just about valuing the parents'/carers' knowledge; it is also about developing an understanding with parents/carers, and an integral part of this work is developing the links between the home/setting environments. The influential Effective Provision of Pre-school Education (EPPE) Report (Desforges and Abouchaar 2003; Sylva et al. 2004) refers to the importance of working with parents, and the term 'Home Learning Environment' features frequently, relating to the activities that happen in the home with parents/carers and children, such as playing with or reading to children. The Department of Health and the Department of Education have co-produced a report, *Supporting Families in the Foundation Years* (DfE/DoH 2011), containing the current Coalition government's views about the importance of working with families in the Early Years sector, and this provides instrumental information for practitioners to consider. This report discusses some key concepts, including the Home Learning Environment (HLE): 'The HLE has a greater influence on a child's intellectual and social development than parental occupation, education or income' (DfE/DoH 2011).

The HLE is referred to on many occasions in other writing related to working with parents, as Field discusses in his report, *The Foundation Years: Preventing Poor Children Becoming Poor Adults* (2010). In the summary of his independent report, many of the key recommendations refer to parenting and the Home Learning Environment (HLE) and the importance of this in improving a child's future life chances. Allen (2011) also highlights the importance of parenting, in a report based on the concept of early intervention, drawing on developments in neuroscience to highlight differences between the brain development of children who are stimulated and those who receive 'normal' opportunities to develop.

One of Allen's (2011) recommendations particularly focuses on the concept of a parenting programme, one which Patterson endorsed in his report *Parenting Matters* (2011) Patterson strongly argues in his report that the government needs a campaign to support parents/carers in their role if they are serious about improving social mobility. Patterson (2011: 27) directly compares children's experiences according to socio-economic status. He uses a study that compares 'Cumulative vocabulary experiences of children from differing backgrounds,' clearly highlighting the difference between children's experiences of vocabulary. Patterson exposes the difference in experiences for children according to their family background, the examples he uses place families into three categories: Welfare, Working Class and Professional. The study highlights that children from Professional families are more likely to be exposed to a wider vocabulary of words in the first four years of their life.

From reading this, one could argue the HLE is affected by the social status of parents. However, Wheeler and Connor (2009) and DfE/DoH (2011) argue that it is actually what parents do with children in the home environment that is key, not the parents' or carers' background. When working with families and considering how to support the HLE, it is important not to make assumptions about the kind of experience children have at home; the only way you can find out about a family is through developing a relationship of trust and this brings us back to the importance of the Key Person relationship. Once this is established then, in turn, you will have a sense of how you can better support families.

Arnold and Rutter (2011) advocate that practitioners need to make home learning relevant to the child and family for it to be truly effective. This point again links into the discussion on knowing your families, respecting that families come from different backgrounds and this can impact on how they view the relationship between home and setting, and how they wish to involve themselves (Nutbrown and Clough 2006). The tension for practitioners is respecting parents' and carers' views, along with managing their expectations as professionals. However, if you know your families well enough, both the home and setting learning environment should become as one, with each supporting the other and valuing each other's input.

In some ways, the home/setting approach has been formalized with the introduction of the Progress Check at Age Two in September 2012, which places a huge emphasis on parental involvement in the process of the check: 'Practitioners must discuss with parents and/or carers how the summary of development can be used to support learning at home' (DfE 2012: 11). The concept of working with parents/carers has developed over the years with a changing emphasis on the way we should work with them, according to the government in power at the time.

As practitioners, you need to develop and reflect on your approach to engaging parents. Communicating with parents is the key to engaging parents. Blandford and Knowles (2009) propose the idea that we should not confine communication arrangements. Clarke and French (2007) go further than this and suggest that communication needs to be considered from different perspectives, and is about which methods work best for the setting and parents/carers. In the current climate, communication takes place in various forms – email, text, phone and verbal just to name a few – and part of your role is to identify which method or methods individual families prefer to use. Communication with parents/carers is often highlighted when discussing how you should build relationships and partnerships and the Pen Green Centre (2007: 52) summarize the rationale for this as follows: 'If parents are listened to, their children receive the powerful message that their family, its culture and values are worth something in the wider world.' In essence, communicating with parents/carers is key in all elements of your practice as this supports the children in your care as valued, and contributes to building on home/setting learning.

Reflection 3.1: Practice with parents

When working with parents/carers, do you provide opportunities for parents to share with you their view of how their child is developing before you offer your view? When and how?

Do you have a 'triangle of trust' and 'secure base' for parents/carers, are your parents/carers sharing with you the practices they are happy with and not so happy with? A meaningful partnership needs to have both elements of feedback.

Do you work with parents/carers because you have a legal or moral obligation to do so?

'Hard-to-reach' services

The term 'hard-to-reach' services has been used deliberately here, instead of 'hard-to-reach' parents/carers, as this is a rather 'loaded phrase' as alluded to by the Early Learning Partnerships Engagement Group (ELPPEG 2010). Often the term 'hard-to-reach' is used to describe parents/carers who do not engage in services provided for them. The reason they may not wish to engage can be varied, for example, parents/carers may choose not to participate in services that do not meet their needs (Nutbrown and Clough 2006). Historically, services have been set up to support parents/carers where there seemed to be a lack of skills or knowledge (Fitzgerald 2004). Basing services on a perceived lack of knowledge or skill has been referred to as the 'deficit approach' to working with parents/carers. This had led to writers such as Clarke and French (2007), Arnold and Rutter (2011) and Wheeler and Connor (2009) suggesting that effective collaboration involves parents and carers sharing the decision-making process in order to engage them. The point being argued here is that it may not be the parents and carers who are 'hard-to-reach' but in fact the services. If communication is key, as already discussed, then we should be communicating with parents and carers about the services they feel they need, or empowering them in the decision-making process, so that they may well wish to engage.

The other factor we need to consider is that a 'one-size-fits-all' approach is not always appropriate. We are working within settings with diverse families, with diverse needs and differences. If we are going to approach families and ask about the services they would like and maybe identify some services we think appropriate after evaluation of parents'/carers' input, one main thing is that you need to know your community of parents well. Families cannot be all considered in the same way.

Robinson and Diaz (2006) argue that the definition of family should be fluid so as not to exclude different family structures. They put forward the idea that families should be viewed as social spaces and that our concept of what a family is will be influenced by our personal experiences. The idea of families being viewed as social spaces is an interesting concept, as it encourages practitioners to understand the complexities of different families. The ideology of the family structure is complex and a much bigger debate than the one being put forward here; however, the point being highlighted is, when we consider providing services for families, this needs to be considered within the context of the community where you work and with the understanding that all families are different and therefore will need different services. Blandford and Knowles (2009) make a very pertinent point that 'no presumptions' should be made when working with families as to what they may or may not wish to be involved in.

As practitioners, we need to consider that we work with various families and we need to be aware of the differing needs of families as, when these are not considered, this can lead to problems, and can impact on the relationship between the home and setting if a family does not feel valued and understood. ELPPEG (2010: 18) put forward the view that 'Practitioners need to find ways to actively engage parents, particularly those who have not accessed services in the past.' This involves reflecting on services and finding out what is working for parents/carers and what is not. ELPPEG (2010: 19) provides, in relation to practitioners, the following key points to engage parents/carers who do not traditionally access services:

- time – time to develop relationships with families;
- support – for themselves;
- flexibility – being responsive and flexible to families' needs.

In relation to the services themselves:

- fine-tuning – to support specific needs of particular families;
- outreach – taking the service to the parent/carer is just as important as in-house services;
- to be complementary and networked – a raft of services to meet the differing needs of families at different times.

The point about services is that they should create a community learning environment, an environment that children, parents and carers want to be part of. In essence, however, the key is providing a service that meets the needs of everyone accessing it.

Activity 3.2: Who initiates parent activities?

1   Examine the events you have offered for parents in the past six months, such as parents evenings, story sessions or cooking sessions.
2   Evaluate how many of them have been initiated by what you think parents want or need, how many have been initiated by parents?

3   Reflect on this aspect of your work:
    (a) Why have you set up such events?
    (b) Are they well attended?
    (c) Do they work and, if yes, how do you know that?
    (d) How can you improve these learning opportunities for all?

Barriers and obstacles to forming Key Relationships

We now turn to some of the barriers and obstacles practitioners sometimes experience when developing key relationships with children and their parents/carers. Although having a close attachment with practitioners is crucial for young children, some practitioners can resist (consciously and unconsciously) developing close relationships with young children. Manning-Morton (2006: 42) argues that, 'Psychological defences against demands of the job, often prevent practitioners from meeting the needs of very young children.'

Elfer (1996) suggests that one reason for this is that we respond in our relationships according to patterns from our past relationships and experiences. He describes this as a process of transference and argues that we transfer feelings and attitudes developed or 'left over' from our earlier experiences to new/present relationships. For practitioners, developing new close relationships with children may bring back painful memories of those they had been close to moving on, or trigger feelings from their own childhood and thus impact on an ability to develop close relationships with children in their care. This resistance to developing close, responsive and respectful relationships with children can act as a defence against the emotional impact young children's feelings can have on them. Manning-Morton and Thorp (2003: 32) further highlight this, stating:

> Children's expression of pain, distress and anger is particularly uncomfortable for adults, who often respond by frantic jiggling up and down of a baby or distraction of a toddler and then reassuring themselves with the false notion that the child will soon forget their distress.

Manning-Morton and Thorp (2003: 33) go on to suggest that in order to develop close relationships with children, practitioners need to develop self-awareness and a strong and flexible sense of their own identity. They state:

> By retaining their own adultness, practitioners can remember that they are in benevolent charge of managing their relationships with the child so will not expect babies or toddlers to understand and consider the practitioners' need or follow the adult's play agenda.

The provision can support the development of close practitioner relationships with their Key Children by providing regular opportunities for practitioners to talk about the feelings being a Key Person can evoke. By doing this, practitioners not only can develop an understanding of how their role as a Key Person positively impacts on the children in their care but also can identify any barriers they may have to developing these relationships.

Bain and Barnet (1980) discuss the past experiences of children attending day care and found that not only were the children handled by many different practitioners but they received little close individual attention. They highlighted that one reason practitioners resisted developing close relationships with children was that they were concerned that this would weaken or undermine parents' relationships. Hopkins (1988: 102) describes this concern as:

> Proponents of the old ideal argued that if a child became closely attached to a nurse, he would suffer a great deal when she left or went off duty, and that it would both weaken his relationship with his mother and make him more difficult to manage by his nurse.

In contrast, rather than close relationships with a Key Person being potentially damaging for children, Bowlby highlights that:

> When a child has more than one attachment figure it might well be supposed that his attachment to his principal figure would be weak, and conversely, that when he has only one figure his attachment to that one would be specially intense. This, however, is not so: indeed precisely the opposite is reported.
>
> (cited in Bain and Barnet 1980: 73)

It is therefore important that the provision helps practitioners understand that becoming 'too attached' is an adult concept that practitioners use when they are worried about parental reactions or mistakenly think that keeping an emotional distance shows greater professionalism (Lindon 2006). Having a strong and clear ethos on working closely with parents can encourage practitioners to discuss any concerns parents may have about their child developing close relationships with a practitioner (Goldschmied, cited in Lindon 2006) As highlighted earlier, it is the practitioner's role to manage the implications of the essential triangular relationship between practitioner, child and parents and which may include the parent needing to feel that they will not be 'cut out', and the child's need to witness positive interactions between the practitioner and their parent/s.

The settling-in period is one way in which the provision can support this triangular relationship. By sensitively planning the settling-in process so that there is only one child settling in at one time and not during a time where staff are on leave or training, practitioners will be able to devote more time to supporting the child and parents during this difficult time. The settling-in period provides an opportunity for parents and practitioners to work through any mixed feelings and it is important that practitioners are able to openly discuss with parents how their child starting nursery can evoke a mixture of emotions. The settling-in period can quite often be a 'rollercoaster' of emotions for parents; in that they may desperately want their child to develop close relationships with their Key Person so that they are happy and settled but they may also feel apprehensive that they will become too close and not 'need' them any longer. By voicing these concerns, parents are not only provided with the opportunity to talk through their feelings but practitioners can demonstrate that they genuinely empathize with their feelings and want to develop a close relationship with them as well as their child.

For a Key Person to be able to devote this time to parent and child during the settling-in period, they need the support and understanding of the rest of the team. This includes other practitioners in the room understanding that a lot of the Key Person's time will be spent with the new family and helping to facilitate this. The provision will also need to support this very unique and vital time by giving staff autonomy to adapt to the children and alter the routine as necessary. Elfer highlights the benefits of developing a close relationship with parents stating:

> Every parent is a specialist, in relation to his or her child. And every worker in early childhood education and care is also a specialist, in child development. The best possible start that babies and young children can have is when these two specialists come together to share their knowledge and experience and understanding with each other.
>
> (2002: 2)

Bain and Barnet (1980) also highlight that practitioners sometimes resist developing close relationships with children because of concerns over professionalism; which include treating all children the same by spending equal amounts of time with each child. If, however, practitioners have a deeper understanding of the importance of developing close relationships with the children in their care, they can discover that this in fact provides the opportunity for practitioners to build individual, meaningful relationships with their Key Children rather than just spending time with all of the children. Further exploration of this aspect of the Key Person approach can be found in Manning-Morton (2006) and Page (2011), where the concepts of professionalism within the context of close loving relationships are explored. Both authors advocate the need for appropriate professional intimacy in order to ensure that the emotional needs of our youngest children are met. Given that, 'The most powerful influence on our capacity to manage life's hurdles is the quality of care we receive in childhood, especially the earliest years' (Kraemer 1999: 1), appropriate professional intimacy should be the core of what we as Early Years Teachers implement and advocate in practice.

Case study 3.1: An 11-month-old and his Key Person

Read through the following example from early years practice, compare and contrast with your own experience to date.

Shane (11 months) had been in the baby room for about three months and seemed to spend much of the day crying and upset. His Key Person was finding working with him difficult so I came in to observe. From my observations and discussions with the practitioners in the room we felt that Shane had not built an attachment with any of the staff in the room – his Key Person seemed unresponsive to Shane's distress and labelled him a 'whiny child'. Observations found that she did not spend any significant time with Shane and, though he was safe and 'cared for', he was not supported emotionally. When I shared my findings, we decided to move Shane to another Key Person who empathized with how he was experiencing being away from his mother. She agreed to try to build a closer relationship with Shane and discussed our concerns with his parent who agreed to do some 'settling visits' as she had when Shane first started nursery. Over the following few weeks his new Key Person worked hard at building a close relationship with Shane and found that he responded. Once Shane had formed this close attachment with his Key Person, he became calmer and began to explore the environment with confidence. The practitioners reported that Shane seemed to be making more progress in his development and, most importantly, he seemed happy and content.

Reflection 3.2: Leading and supporting the Key Person approach

Now, reflect on your own practice in relation to the example above.

What opportunities do you provide for practitioners to meaningfully talk about the emotional aspects of the Key Person approach and settling-in?

Are there any changes you might make to your practice to encourage a culture of trust and collaboration?

Conclusion

This chapter has focused on the importance of relationships between families, children and practitioners with an emphasis on the Key Person approach. It has drawn attention to the impact of attachment for babies and young children, and argued that positive, consistent and attuned adults have a positive influence on children's well-being, learning and development. In the chapter there has been a consideration of the importance of valuing parents' knowledge of their child and the contribution they make to both their child's learning and development and the practitioner's knowledge. Valuing the home learning environment has been explored, and the significance of practitioners not making assumptions in relation to the families' social status and home experiences has been highlighted. The concept of 'hard-to-reach' services has been examined in order to challenge the concept that some parents are 'hard-to-reach'. Finally, an overview of some of the barriers and obstacles that inhibit the formation of close relationships with children and their parents/carers was reflected upon. The chapter argues that in order to be able to develop close relationships with children and their families, practitioners need to have an intellectual application of attachment theory and the importance of parental influence in order to develop the skills necessary to form secure relationships.

4

Curious engagement
Creating learning opportunities within the Early Years Foundation Stage
Jessica Johnson

> Development is not an automatic process ... It depends on each unique child having opportunities to interact in positive relationships and enabling environments.
>
> (EE 2012: 2)

Chapter objectives

By the end of this chapter you should be able to:

- use knowledge and understanding from the previous chapters to create ongoing developmentally appropriate learning opportunities with babies, young children, families and colleagues;
- recognize learning and development within a continuum from birth through to 18 years, encompassing Foundation Stage and National Curriculum requirements within lifelong learning;
- promote an ethos of relational, playful, purposeful pedagogy across early years to encourage lifelong learning dispositions.

Link with Teachers' Standards (Early Years) 2013

S1 S2 S3

Introduction

The aim of this chapter is to ensure you have a secure knowledge of the uniqueness of early childhood development and are able to demonstrate a clear understanding of how to widen children's experience, raising expectations (Appendix: Standard 3). Current research will be introduced to stimulate critical thinking about your role in relation to the EYFS areas of learning and development (EE 2012). These will include the use of systematic synthetic phonics as one strand within early literacy and a range of appropriate strategies for engagement with early mathematics (Appendix: Standard 3). As you provide opportunities for young children to develop positive learning dispositions, you will be able to identify how these lead to successful learning and development at school and throughout life (Appendix: Standard 3).

Early learning and the Early Years Foundation Stage

Key aspects of early childhood development have been encountered in the previous two chapters. Now is an exciting time to be actively, and hopefully curiously, learning about yourself within the Early Years Foundation Stage (DfE 2012). As an Early Years Teacher you are, or will most likely be, working in a private, voluntary, home-based or independent setting, with some in maintained Nursery and Reception classes. As you explore learning with birth-to-5-year-olds, their families and colleagues, consider the skills and expertise required by specialists delivering a child-led play-based curriculum across these different forms of provision (Roberts-Holmes 2012: 36). Important underlying tensions – such as those between 'child-led' and the 'tested curriculum' – will be apparent along the way, as acknowledged with the ongoing 'Too much too soon' campaign (House 2011) so, as graduates, it is imperative that you use critical thinking skills within your own reflections to do your best for children and families.

Make the most of placement opportunities in full day care provision, pre-schools, children's centres, nursery and reception classes to look for ways to extend your own personal practice, as well as leading and supporting practitioners. You will also observe Key Stage 1 (KS1) learning and teaching, again with a chance to look for connections that enrich your own provision and can aid vertical transitions for children and families from early years to KS1 (Dunlop and Fabian 2007; Brooker 2008; Bayley and Featherstone 2009; Allingham 2011). You are in a unique position, through these opportunities, to develop and share your own knowledge and expertise of stimulating practice that can 'widen children's experience and raise their expectations' (Appendix: Standard 3.2).

Current research from different perspectives highlights how babies really are 'born ready, able and eager to learn. They actively reach out to interact with other people and in the world around them' (EE 2012: 2). As an Early Years Teacher, with your specialism from birth to age 5, you need to be equally ready to respond to this ability and eagerness to learn. As you explore ways to nurture these early learning dispositions, you will be able to engage with 'the educational continuum of expectations, curricula and teaching of Key Stage 1 and 2' (NCTL 2013b).

Activity 4.1: Educational continuum of expectations

1 Read sections from the Introduction to EYFS (DfE 2012) and the Aims of the National Curriculum.

2 List what is *expected* in England for all children, within this educational continuum.

EYFS Introduction

I Every child deserves the best possible start in life and the support that enables them to fulfil their potential. Children develop quickly in the early years and a child's experiences between birth and age five have a major impact on their future life chances. A secure, safe and happy childhood is important in its own right. Good parenting and high quality early learning together provide the foundation children need to make the most of their abilities and talents as they grow up.

II The Early Years Foundation Stage (EYFS) sets the standards that all early years providers must meet to ensure that children learn and develop well and are kept healthy and safe. It promotes teaching and learning to ensure children's 'school readiness' and gives children the broad range of knowledge and skills that provide the right foundation for good future progress through school and life.

National Curriculum aims

3.1 The National Curriculum provides pupils with an introduction to the essential knowledge that they need to be educated citizens. It introduces pupils to the best that has been thought and said; and helps engender an appreciation of human creativity and achievement.

3.2 The National Curriculum is just one element in the education of every child. There is time and space in the school day and in each week, term and year to range beyond the National Curriculum specifications. The National Curriculum provides an outline of core knowledge around which teachers can develop exciting and stimulating lessons to promote the development of pupils' knowledge, understanding and skills as part of the wider school curriculum.

Reflection 4.1: Providing learning opportunities

How can you provide learning opportunities with babies and young children that are 'mindful of the moment' – going with the spontaneous needs/ interests – while also creating a 'right foundation for good progress'?

What works well?

What can be developed?

As you engaged in this activity, you may also have become aware of some changes in terminology between EYFS and the National Curriculum (NC). When do 'children' become 'pupils', defined as 'a person, especially a child at school, who is being taught' (Cambridge University Press 2013)? Does this have implications for variations in the meaning of 'teacher' within the EYFS, to that in the National Curriculum? Your knowledge and understanding of early childhood development will influence your professionalism as an Early Years Teacher, with the recognition that 'good parenting and high quality learning together provide the right foundation' (DfE 2012: 3). 'Cultivation of child-responsive "childcare" and "education" are both important for the well-being and development of a young mind and neither should be promoted at the expense of the other' (Trevarthen 2011b: 187).

Trevarthen (2011b: 173–93), as a neuroscientist, alert to the rapid growth in brain development through quality interaction in early years, argues for an understanding of what babies and young children bring to a setting's learning community and culture, impacting on the dynamics of the teaching process for all. So, as an Early Years Teacher, rather than being a fount of all knowledge with the child as recipient of your wisdom and power, you acquire specific skills of 'relational pedagogy' as you learn together with babies, young children, families and colleagues (Moyles and Papatheodorou 2009; Johnson, 2010: 74–80). Learning and care opportunities combine throughout the day, requiring professional expertise during meal-times, nappy changing and toileting, rest and sleep times, as well as activities. Physical development is rapid in these early months and years, so you are continually on the alert for the latest attempts to increase mobility. Celebrate with babies, toddlers and their families those initial achievements of rolling, crawling, standing, walking, running and climbing as you are often the provider of opportunities to perfect these individual skills. Trust is built up through these shared moments that intermingle and need to be valued. But, are they valued? What are the values and principles that underpin EYFS, and are they the same as your own personal and professional values and beliefs about early learning?

Activity 4.2: Educational continuum of teaching and learning – underlying principles and values

Look at what is seen to be important or valued by EYFS and the National Curriculum principle statements below.

Rank the principle and value statements accordingly:

1   those you fully agree with and are able to meet consistently;
2   those you agree with, but have difficulty always meeting within your professional role;
3   those you are asked to meet within your professional role but find difficult to agree with;
4   those you do not agree with and would not do.

Principles of EYFS: Overarching principles (DfE 2012: 3)

Four guiding principles should shape practice in early years settings. These are:

1   Every child is a *unique child*, who is constantly learning and can be resilient, capable, confident and self-assured.
2   Children learn to be strong and independent through *positive relationships*.
3   Children learn and develop well in *enabling environments*, in which their experiences respond to their individual needs and there is a strong partnership between practitioners and parents and/or carers.
4   Children develop and learn *in different ways and at different rates*.

The framework covers the education and care of all children in early years provision, including children with special educational needs and disabilities.

Principles of the National Curriculum (DfE 2013g: 5)

Every state-funded school must offer a curriculum which is balanced and broadly based and which:

*   promotes the spiritual, moral, cultural, mental and physical development of pupils at the school and of society;
*   prepares pupils at the school for the opportunities, responsibilities and experiences of later life.

The school curriculum comprises all learning and other experiences that each school plans for its pupils. The National Curriculum forms one part of the school curriculum.

All state schools are also required to make provision for a daily act of collective worship and must teach religious education to pupils at every Key Stage, and sex and relationship education to pupils in secondary education.

Maintained schools in England are legally required to follow the statutory National Curriculum which sets out in programmes of study, on the basis of Key Stages, subject content for those subjects that should be taught to all pupils. All schools must publish their school curriculum by subject and academic year online.[1]

All schools should make provision for personal, social, health and economic education (PSHE), drawing on good practice. Schools are also free to include other subjects or topics of their choice in planning and designing their own programme of education.

Reflection 4.2: Impact of personal and professional values on widening children's experiences and raising their expectations

Can you identify any differences between your personal and professional values?

How may these influence your current role or expected role within early years?

How can this impact on your own learning and your ability to widen children's experiences and raise their expectations?

Awareness of the impact of your personal and professional values and beliefs on practice is important within relational pedagogy. Learning together implies a degree of vulnerability on your part as an Early Years Teacher, creating a level of empathy with a young child as well as parents and colleagues. How does this relate to the theories and theorists encountered in the previous chapters? Those that you remember most are likely to support your practice, but have you found new information that challenges you to change? If so, how does it fit in with 'learning together'?

Curious engagement

What makes these quality relationships that enable learning? How will this show itself? Consider the key aspects of effective learning characteristics as stated in the EYFS Profile (STA 2013):

- Playing and exploring – innate curiosity, representation through imaginary play.
- Active learning.
- Creating and thinking critically.

Bandura's social learning theory recognizes how young children imitate those around them, learning and developing skills in the process. One of the joys of visiting a range of early years settings is that each is likely to have its own 'projects' under way as a result of the play and exploration relevant to the interests of those particular individuals/groups. The level of curious engagement depends on how adults and children are interacting with each other and how 'rich' the learning environment is, enabling adventurous play (Trevarthen 2011b: 175). Your environment can support or hinder any attempt to build constructive relationships, so this needs to be considered in relation to learning opportunities.

Curious engagement is evident as young children develop learning dispositions through activities that enable them to experiment, take risks, learn through mistakes and practise new skills (Carr 2008; Katz 2011). Observe children who are willing to have a go, keen to practise even though they may find something hard. Linking to Vygotsky theories in Chapter 2, you are able to scaffold learning, enabling the children to build resilience as they work through problems. Do identify how you value the effort of children and adults alike, providing feedback about this essential skill.

Activity 4.3: Interactive observation identifying Space, Voice, Audience and Influence

1   When in your setting, complete the observation template in Figure 4.1, noting what happens during a shared learning opportunity – whether between peers or with adults.
2   What does this tell you about relationships and learning opportunities?
3   Who is learning, and what are the outcomes?

Interaction observation
Date: _____ Time started: _____ Time ended: _____ Adults present, e.g. staff, parents: _____ Children present: _____
SPACE: *for views to be formed and expressed* Note below examples of the environment that enable infants/toddlers/young children to express views. Consider the physical features, e.g. the room layout, the materials, and the emotional environment, e.g. the human contact
VOICE: *expression of views* Identify below examples of verbal and non-verbal signs and symbols that the infants/toddlers/young children use to express views. What are these views?
AUDIENCE: *who is watching the performance?* Indicate who the audience is . . . the peer group, staff, parents, others . . . and how they demonstrate this. What happens to any infant/toddler/child view expressed?
INFLUENCE: *influencing change in practice* Identify examples of infants/toddlers/children influencing change in setting practice. What have they changed?

Figure 4.1 Interaction observation: Space, Voice, Audience, Influence.

Source: Adapted from Lundy (2007: 927).

As you set up your environment each day, consider where the spaces are that will allow children to remain involved and concentrate on their chosen ways of doing things ... whether with others or alone. How will the new ideas they bring with them each day be developed? How ready are you for surprises? Curious engagement encompasses all these and should enable adults as well as children to enjoy achieving what they set out to do (STA 2013: 10). Often assessment and monitoring outcomes focus on individuals, yet within early years provision these achievements develop in participation with others, including peers, through learning opportunities. They give rise to collaborative skills that allow learning through 'mistakes' for all and help to manage conflict. Aim to identify, and value specific communication skills as they occur, such as asking for help as needed. Remember that active listening requires hearing as well as 'the ability to notice that someone is speaking to you, attending to what the speaker is saying, processing what is heard and responding' (Jones 2013: 27). All these aspects deserve recognition as children relate to each other and to adults.

Case study 4.1: The volcano

As you read through the excerpt below, evidence from Ulla's EYPS summative assessment, compare and contrast the specific skills of the Early Years Teacher with your own experiences.

The volcano project came out of the observation of a child's activity. The child was making a picture, and when I asked what he was doing, he said: 'I am making a picture of a volcano. Then the volcano erupts and lava is coming out and after that floods, earthquakes and hurricanes can happen.'

The child demonstrated great interest in volcanoes, hurricanes and earthquakes. He showed understanding of a cause and effect relationship – 'lava comes out after the volcano eruption, then floods and earthquakes can happen'. The child used the language of science which reflected the breadth of his interest. I recorded the observation of child's activity and shared my observations with his parents.

The child's mother confirmed that he was really interested in volcanoes and spent hours at home looking at books about the volcanoes. The next day he brought the book, *Volcano*, by F. Branley to nursery, which he had borrowed from the library. He showed the book to the children. The children observed the pictures, talked about the volcanoes, hurricanes, floods and earthquakes. The child also brought a volcano model which he had made together with his Dad at home. The children were very interested and excited about the volcanoes and we started to discuss what resources we could use to make a volcano in a nursery. The children offered to make a playdough volcano and decorate it and to build a volcano out of bricks in the construction area.

To extend the children's knowledge, I introduced the papier mâché technique to children and suggested they make a papier mâché volcano model as well. We planned the activity and first prepared the resources – a bottle, cardboard, newspapers, ingredients for papier mâché paste. Then the children learnt how to make the paste. They measured the amount of glue and flour, using mathematical language – full, empty, more, less. They counted the number of cups of flour and water. The children were developing their sensory skills – touching the papier mâché paste, discussing what it looks like, how it smells and how it can be used and why. The children were very interested in the activity and spent lots of time creating a volcano model. I involved the children in the creative thinking process by asking questions: 'What shape does a volcano usually have?', 'Where is it narrow and where is it wide?', 'What should we do to make it look like a real volcano?', 'What colours will you use to decorate the volcano?', 'Why?'

To make our 'Volcano' project enjoyable fun, and to extend the children's knowledge about volcano eruptions, we tried an awesome experiment of a volcano eruption. Mixing baking powder and vinegar is the equivalent of a volcano eruption, which brings the exciting world of science to life. I prepared the resources and the children measured the amount they needed. The baking soda experiment is a non-toxic one, but nevertheless before doing an experiment we talked about the risks children should avoid. They should be careful and try not to get the substance into the mouth, or eyes or on the skin. When one of the children added vinegar inside the volcano, and the children saw how the volcano was fizzing and spurting red lava they were amazed. It was great fun for the children but also a great learning experience.

To make more fun out of the learning project, I suggested baking a chocolate 'Volcano' cake. When the children were making a cake, a lot of mathematical learning was involved: counting spoonfuls, estimating 'how many more', as well as science: weighing, noticing the changes in textures created by heat. The children used their skills of mixing ingredients, mixing colours for the decoration of the cake, making the shape of a proper volcano.

We made a display of the children's volcano pictures and models. In our report it was noted that the staff 'carefully preserve the models children make so that they can return to them and continue their designs. In this way, the volcano that the children made is still available to play.' When displayed, the pictures and volcano models were annotated, so the children could see that their curiosity, creativity and exploratory skills were well rewarded.

Reflection 4.3: Curious engagement

Consider times when you have been 'curiously engaged' with:

- babies
- toddlers
- young children
- colleagues
- parents.

Do you have a preferred group . . . and if so, why? What have you learnt together with this group?

Is there a group that you have not yet engaged with? How can you set up opportunities to do so?

.Can you, as an Early Years Teacher, create 'multiple zones of proximal development, respecting, simultaneously, children's psychological, social and cultural differences' (Oliveira-Formosinho and Barros Araujo 2011: 223–35)? Bear this in mind as we continue to look in turn at how you can provide learning opportunities that address key and specific areas of EYFS. These areas also provide an opportunity to compare and contrast with National Curriculum requirements.

Activity 4.4: Compare the curriculum content of EYFS, KS1 and KS2

Identify similarities and differences in the key curriculum content areas shown in Table 4.1.

Table 4.1 Comparison of the curriculum content of EYFS, KS1 and KS2.

EYFS	National Curriculum KS1 and KS2
Prime areas	*Core subjects*
Communication and language development	English
Physical development	Mathematics
Personal, social and emotional development	Science
Specific areas	*Foundation subjects*
Literacy development	Foreign languages
Mathematics development	Computing
Understanding of the world	Geography
	History
Expressive arts and design	Art and design
	Music
	Physical development
	+
	Religious education
	Personal, social, health and economic education (PSHE)

1   How may the principles of EYFS, explored previously, underpin both?
2   What tensions may arise?
3   How can you alleviate these for children, families and staff?
4   What prime and specific areas of learning are acknowledged in the Volcano case study above?
5   How do you acknowledge daily learning opportunities for physical development, as a Key Area? How may this differ in KS1 and KS2?

Learning opportunities

As an Early Years Teacher, you have scope to provide opportunities for all the above, making connections across areas and, as Gerver states:

> Perhaps the answer to the future is already staring us in the face. The most powerful learning environments in our schools currently are to be found in the schooling of our youngest children, known as the Foundation Stage ... the children are given broad learning opportunities, often role-play based, that encompass the skills required throughout the learning journey.
>
> (2010: 60)

So how can 'broad learning opportunities' develop these life skills? Although holistic planning within early years provision – whatever your setting – is crucial, each EYFS area of learning and development can be explored individually. A supportive resource – not a statutory checklist – is Early Education's *Development Matters in the Early Years Foundation Stage* (2012) document, enabling you to consider each area in relation to the key principles of the Unique Child – as you observe what a child is learning, Positive Relationships – as you see what adults could do to support learning, and Enabling Environments – what you could provide. Chapter 6 acknowledges the observation, assessment, planning cycle that supports early learning (DfE 2012). The focus here is on how you critically use your knowledge and skills to develop strategies that enable children in your specific context to engage with stimulating learning opportunities.

Personal, social and emotional development (PSED)

From the start of this chapter, it has been emphasized that relationships are seen as central to the learning process for all. Looking back, and to previous chapters, it will be clearly evident that PSED development is integral to all the learning opportunities. So what can widen PSED experiences further? The next activity looks specifically at your role in relation to being a learning companion with babies and young children.

Activity 4.5: Four companionable As

1   Consider each of Rosemary Roberts's 'Four companionable As' in relation
     to the examples of how they are demonstrated in practice (2011: 202).

Anchored attention	Sense of belonging with another
Authoritative companionship	Reliable, regular, consistent establishing routines and rules belonging-and-boundaries
Apprenticeship	'Helping' their companion/s in daily tasks
Allowing time and space	Time and space to play, a place for 'down time' and for reflection

2   Identify, for each, one example of being a 'learning companion' from your
     own practice/experience.
3   What are the strengths?
4   What may be the challenges?
5   How can you increase the quality of these relationships?

Reflection 4.4: 'Well-being play'

When specifically thinking about well-being, Roberts identifies three rich
learning opportunities for 'well-being play – child-initiated, open-ended,
un-rushed, adaptable, available, intense, intentional, leisurely, creative,
free . . . and profoundly satisfying' (2011: 203):

- Food: growing it, shopping together, cooking, eating, clearing up, picnics, parties.
- Familiarity: people (companions), books, pets, songs and rhymes, places.
- Going out: everyday expeditions, getting around – walking, bus, train.

Thinking back to your own examples of companionable learning:

- Were any the same as Roberts's three, and if so how?
- Were any different from Roberts, and if so how?
- What key and/or specific areas of development were acknowledged within each 'rich, learning opportunity'?
- How may you expand your provision of rich learning opportunities to encompass well-being?

Prime area: communication and language opportunities

Communication and language development involve giving children opportunities to speak and listen in a range of situations and to develop their confidence and skills in expressing themselves (STA 2013: 24). Early Learning Goals (EE 2012: 15–21), note the order, are grouped under:

- Listening and Attention
- Understanding
- Speaking.

Knowledge of how babies communicate is important, even if your first interactions with them are from 3 months or later, as you need to continue with the rhythms and patterns they are familiar with. 'An alert newborn can draw a sympathetic adult into synchronised negotiations of arbitrary action which can develop in coming weeks and months into a mastery of the rituals and symbols of a germinal culture, long before any words are learned' (Trevarthen 2011a: 121). Engaging with these rhythmic proto-conversations, mirroring facial language and body movement, requires the skill of responsiveness that really does 'tune in and out' to individuals and groups. Consider how you demonstrate this yourself, as well as support other practitioners to develop these skills. This is especially important in relation to the Key Person role and how transitions occur within the setting when staff change shifts or duties. These skills continue even as vocabulary develops, as children will gravitate towards peers and adults who respond to their needs and interests. A listening culture (Williams 2009) values the interactions between children and adults throughout the day wherever and whenever they occur. Within such a listening environment, the extent of children's verbal and non-verbal communication develops and their individual and group perspectives become clear. So how much influence do they have on setting procedures? As a growing area for research there is scope, as an Early Years Teacher, to identify what is happening in your context.

From an Australian early years education background, Jones (2013) shares a range of suggestions for specific communication skills to engage all staff and children across the age range that help to develop a 'consciousness of others':

- naming strategies, use of a child's name in different contexts blending throughout the day;
- group sessions that talk about the need to listen, why we listen, what would happen if we didn't . . . and when we listen (Jones 2013: 27);
- self-control opportunities: yoga, music, breathing and relaxation exercises, transition games that give specific directions to children to practise listening and responding to another person (Jones 2013: 28);
- thinking and problem-solving opportunities can be set by children as well as adults, using small group or circle opportunities;
- use of conflict management frameworks, such as mediation or restorative justice, to manage disagreement.

During these processes, children are becoming increasingly able to de-code what others say within the nursery context, and try out a range of strategies to own a valuable life skill. For bilingual learners, be alert to ways to 'recognize and build upon their linguistic and cultural "funds of knowledge" in the early years' (Drury 2013: 391). While they may seem to have a period of silence, as they absorb communication around them, this is also a learning opportunity for adults and children, seeking ways to involve bilingual staff as mediators between the home and setting environment.

Case study 4.2: Literacy with parents and children

Compare and contrast the example below with your own experience to date.

Parents at Blenheim Playgroup, Dewsbury, have created their own book to encourage literacy (Blenheim Playgroup Parents 2012). Composed in question-and-answer format, with photographic illustrations, it covers concerns, with responses, such as:

Question: What language should I use?

Answer: This is up to you and your child!

Question: Which language(s) do you feel comfortable in?

Answer: I read to my son in English and Arabic.

Answer: I use mainly Urdu and some English.

Answer: We read in English but sometimes explain in Urdu. My children like the English cartoons! If we read an Islamic story, we read it in English and Urdu.

Answer: I use English a bit but occasionally have to use Punjabi to explain or to translate . . . or sometimes to ask a question. I also use the pictures to help understanding.

Answer: English, Urdu.

(Blenheim Playgroup Parents 2012: 4)

Creation of this book is an example arising from Sheffield's Raising Early Achievement in Literacy Project (Nutbrown and Bishop 2013).

Reflection 4.5: Encouraging a parent initiative relating to an early learning opportunity

The earlier example shows one creative way parents shared their knowledge and understanding of early reading, supported by staff.

Consider one way you can encourage and support a parent initiative relating to an early learning opportunity.

How will you achieve your 'next step' to move this forward?

Case study 4.3: Sustained shared thinking

Read through the two conversations below during free-flow play outdoors in day care, and identify the skills of the Early Years Teacher (EYT).

Conversation 1 with Connor

C: This is a field; this is the sheep, he's the only one left in the field because all the others have escaped.

EYT: How did they escape?

C: There was a hole in the fence.

EYT: How did the hole get there?

C: The big sheep ate it and made a hole and they ran away.

EYT: How can we get the sheep back?

C: We can't, they're gone now. But I need to fix the fence.

EYT: What will you use to fix the fence?

C: The wooden blocks, but they have to be straight so there's no gaps.

Conversation 2 with Jake

J: This is the rubbish bin, we're not going to shut the lid tight so that Mr Fox can eat the food.

EYT: Why does Mr Fox want to eat the food?

J: Because he's hungry and he likes to eat the left-overs.

EYT: What do foxes like to eat?

J: Rubbish.

EYT: How do you know that?

J: Because mummy always puts the lid down at night so Foxy Loxy doesn't eat the rubbish.

EYT: Where do you think foxes live?

J: In the woods.

EYT: The fox that comes to your garden, how does he get there?

J: In his car.

EYT: What colour is his car?

J: Grey, . . ., no, black, so that the grown-ups can't see him.

Consider developing your own collection of 'conversations', possibly supported by photos as these were – of the 'fence' and the 'rubbish bin' – that can be displayed around your setting and used to extend discussions and promote sustained shared thinking.

Communication, language . . . and literacy

Language has a discourse of its own within communication. Create your own glossary of specific terminology as new words emerge, expanding your own lexicon (words you understand and use verbally and/or in writing).

In Early Years you are continually increasing verbal content for babies and young children as they come across sounds for the first time. As new vocabulary is heard and seen, word meanings are sought, and connections identified that relate words to one another. Basic concepts – letters and sounds – surround the young child so they become immersed in language construction.

As an Early Years Teacher, you can fine-tune what is happening. Formation of words arises through a combination of sounds (phonology). There are rules that govern how words are formed (morphology), and rules that determine how words can be combined to create sentence structures (syntax). Three words for your glossary! These words and sentences are then adjusted for use in various forms of communication – verbal, written, text, symbols, rhymes, poetry, song and stories.

As you talk with children about language, as well as increasing their vocabulary, you are involving them in metalinguistics – 'the ability to think about language' (Wandschneider and Crosbie 2013: 25). However, there are lots of fun ways to become immersed in vocabulary – 'receptive' vocabulary being the words the child understands and 'expressive' vocabulary the words the child uses. General vocabulary knowledge is the single best predictor of reading comprehension (White and Kim 2009, cited in Wandschneider and Crosbie 2013: 25). During a national press interview, psychologist Dr Jo Van Herwegen reminds us: 'Pre-schoolers need the basic building blocks, as their working memory and language isn't complete before they reach five or six, so developmentally they're simply not ready for formal learning before that' (Paton 2013).

Playing with synonyms – two or more words with the same meaning – and antonyms – words with opposite meaning – can occur through games, activities and stories looking at matching similarities/pairs or contrasts, e.g. light and dark, high and low, big and small. When children have met a word several times, they 'map' it, storing limited information about it. As they gain multiple exposures to a word over time, it becomes established in a child's store of words (lexicon).

Activity 4.6: Opportunities for vocabulary development

Be creative, and think of a way you can provide a specific opportunity for each of the suggestions below, showing involvement across the birth-to-5 age range:

- Create a sense of curiosity around specific words and meanings.
- Provide clear explanations of new words, with illustrations, using different mediums/multi-sensory contexts (try 'transparent').
- Play with synonyms and antonyms around a word.
- Link a word to experience.
- Talk about the sound structure . . . clap rhythm/number of syllables.
- Provide meaningful opportunities to use a new word.
- Tell stories, making them up together.

As Taylor et al. recognize:

> Children are born into a world of storytelling . . . over time and through repeated conversations about and telling of their stories, they move from this focus on hearing themselves talk to an awareness that their stories can have an impact on others. As this occurs, they begin to understand that what can happen to them and their world could happen to others.
>
> (2011: 54)

Reflection 4.6: Who's a story-teller?

When did you last hear a 'story'?

What was your response?

How can you create opportunities for 'story-telling' and 'story-listening'?

As understanding and use of vocabulary increase, links can be directly made to reading. The importance of developing speaking and listening skills has to take priority before specific reading and writing approaches. In 2006, an independent review of the teaching of early reading, in its Final Report, emphasized:

> the importance of fostering speaking and listening skills from birth onwards in the home environment, in early years settings and in schools, making full use of the great variety of rich opportunities for developing children's language that all these provide through use of a multi-sensory approach.
>
> (Rose 2006: 1)

The prime recommendation was then for 'systematic high quality phonic work as the prime means for teaching beginners to learn to read' (DfES 2007: 4). Phonics consists of knowledge of the skills of segmenting and blending, knowledge of the alphabetic code and an understanding of the way the code is used in reading and spelling (DfES 2007: 18). The 'simple view of reading', shown in the Review, acknowledged two dimensions of reading – 'word recognition' and 'language comprehension' – as discussed above (DfES 2007: 9). When children are becoming proficient in decoding words, they are *learning to read*, systematic phonics aims to help this process. When they are competent with doing this, they become more able *to read to learn and enjoy*.

The government at the time responded with the production of a toolkit for practitioners presented within the Primary National Strategy, the 'Letters and Sounds: Principles and Practice of High Quality Phonics' pack (DfES 2007). Some providers also draw on Ruth Miskin's online sources for teaching systematic phonics, available via ReadWriteInc. You may like to compare the sources. With awareness of EYFS and the National Curriculum expectations for learning systemic phonics, Letters and Sounds highlights seven aspects in Phase One that can help provide learning opportunities for children:

- General sound discrimination – environmental sounds, e.g. a silent walk.
- General sound discrimination – instrumental sounds, e.g. making and using a variety of instruments.
- General sound discrimination – body percussion, e.g. variation in sound using the body.
- Rhythm and rhyme – timing, beat, patterns.
- Alliteration – similarities in sound across different words, tongue twisters.
- Voice sounds – pitch, tone.
- Oral blending (sounds that make up a word) and segmenting (how words are broken down into different sounds).
- Discriminate phonemes – the smallest unit of sound in a word that can change its meaning, e.g. b/ed, l/ed. There are 44 phonemes in the English language. When writing, in alphabetical code, phonemes are symbolized by graphemes – a letter or group of letters representing a sound, e.g. b, l, ed. There is always the same number

of graphemes in a word as phonemes. Reproduce audibly the phonemes they hear, in order, through the word. Use sound-talk to segment words into phonemes.

'The ways in which practitioners and teachers interact and talk with children are critical to developing children's speaking and listening' (DfES 2007: 4).

The above acknowledge three strands:

- tuning into sounds (auditory discrimination);
- listening and remembering sounds (auditory memory and sequencing);
- talking about sounds (developing vocabulary and language comprehension).

Only later, in Phase Two does systematic phonics support the skills of oral blending and segmenting, exploring phonemes, starting a process with the simple aspects and moving in sequence to the more complex ones. As an Early Years Teacher, if not delivering a systematic phonics programme yourself, try to observe a trained colleague . . . and find an opportunity to see a Phase Two session and one further along, reaching Phase Six. For the first time in 2013, children at the end of Year 1 have been assessed on their phonological awareness, with the understanding that they did not all start at the same level.

So consider, within EYFS, to what extent does current practice extend children's language comprehension and word recognition processes? How are staff competencies increased, if needed, to enhance developmentally-appropriate practices for individual children? National Curriculum KS1 English has a clear expectation of previous learning:

> Teachers [in KS1] should build on work from the Early Years Foundation Stage . . . accurately using the phonic knowledge and skills they have already learnt [p. 9]. Writing is seen as a specific fine motor skill to be taught in KS1 [p. 14], using lower case, capitals and digits 0–9.
>
> (DfE 2013c: 9, 14)

This is a subtle reminder that children need to have good short-term memory as well as working memory (the ability to do two things at the same time) in order to read and write. These may be useful points to share with parents and colleagues when planning how best to develop early literacy skills.

Early mathematics

As an Early Years Teacher you will be able to demonstrate a clear understanding of appropriate strategies in learning early mathematics (NCTL 2013b: S3.5). So what is recognized within EYFS by early mathematics? According to the EYFS Profile (DfE 2012), mathematics development involves providing children with opportunities to practise and improve their skills in counting numbers, calculating simple addition and subtraction problems, and to describe shapes, spaces and measures.

Early Learning Goals (ELG) 11 and 12 focus on:

- Numbers
- Shape, space and measures.

Practical examples are again provided against each ELG, and also in *Development Matters*, in relation to observing the Unique Child, how positive relationships with adults can support learning and how an enabling environment can provide stimulating resources.

But what do we know about how babies and young children learn mathematics? From birth, we are aware that babies identify shape – especially the human face – so this could be seen as an innate recognition. They become aware of patterns, regularity and numbers through subitization (recognizing small quantities like two) (Montague-Smith and Price 2012: 8). However, Piaget's work on constructivism has a clear mathematical focus, showing how children build on concepts. Then Vygotsky and Bruner's socio-constructivism identifies the role/s of the scaffolders, whether peer or adult, in extending knowledge and understanding of concepts (Chapter 2). Where children learn through 'social practice' theories to follow adults and learn the 'tools of the trade', they have been found at a young age to be cooks or stall holders, involving mathematical decisions (Montague-Smith and Price 2012: 8). So what are the implications for curious engagement relating to early maths in early years provision?

Activity 4.7: Curious engagement and social practice involving mathematical concepts

We know young children are eager to problem solve. Opportunities with block play, junk modelling and imaginary play can identify these experiences, with the adult as astute companion, making connections relevant to mathematical concepts.

- Identify daily social practices within your local community where babies and young children are engaging with:
  - the number concept itself (e.g. quantity of 5);
  - the spoken word, the oral concept of number (e.g. five);
  - the written numeral, the number concept in written form using symbols (e.g. 5) (McGregor 2013: 18).
- Then, identify specific play strategies that can be added to support understanding, including experiences with written numerals as well as spoken word. Include opportunities for subitizing – 'establishing quantity by recognising a stylised number pattern' (McGregor 2013: 22).

The above activity valued routine, spontaneous and structured learning opportunities that occur throughout the day. Structured play is created to suit individual and group developmental levels, including feedback that enables each child to learn something new.

Case study 4.4: Structured play using approximate number systems

Dr Jo Van Herwegen, an educational psychologist, and her research team at Kingston University have been trialling eight games as a flexible training programme (PLUS) for early years staff with children aged 2½–5 in full day care sessions. As she shared:

Maths is more than just counting. To be good at maths you also need to know 'where is more or less' very quickly. Approximate Number Systems (ANS) is very important for mathematical abilities later on in life . . . The games are designed to improve ANS and to give children confidence in maths (it's OK to guess). For example, in one game two children each take a handful of pasta shapes and they then look at how much each of them has and we ask them to quickly guess who has the most.

(pers. comm.)

For more information, see www.jovanherwegen.co.uk.
Compare and contrast the above with your own experiences, considering:

- When you are involved in a learning opportunity how do you balance providing the child with opportunities to consolidate the knowledge they have while also challenging appropriately to learn new things as well?
- How can you provide feedback, enabling the child first to guess for themselves and form theories by making comparisons with similar problems to be solved?
- How can you share these learning opportunities above with parents?

Conclusion

By looking at both EYFS and the National Curriculum, above, can you now identify the specific nature of your role as an Early Years Teacher? There may be 'pedagogic tension noted in reception classes between the child-led play based on EYFS and the knowledge led National Curriculum' (Roberts-Holmes 2012: 39), that is also evident across different forms of early years provision. There is some evidence that 'by informally extending the EYFS principles and practices through to the end of KS1, head teachers are engaging with the concept of "making the school ready for the child"' (Roberts-Holmes 2012: 40). You will have a key role to play in this ongoing discussion.

So the 'curious engagement' of children and adults in creating learning opportunities together, within the Early Years Foundation Stage, deserves to be valued in its own right as well as providing a secure foundation for the future. Scaffolding now, within positive relationships, the flow of each baby, toddler and young child's physical development is essential to release freedom to explore, experiment and create. The knowledge, skills and understanding encompassed here can provide a basis for consideration of specific requirements relating to inclusive practice, observation and assessment, safeguarding and leadership in the following chapters.

Recommended reading

Moyles, J. and Papatheodorou, T. (eds) (2009) *Learning Together in the Early Years: Exploring Relational Pedagogy.* London: Routledge.

Note

1 From September 2012, all schools are required to publish information in relation to each academic year, relating to the content of the school's curriculum for each subject and details about how additional information relating to the curriculum may be obtained from http://www.legislation.gov.uk/uksi/2012/1124/made.

5

Adapting education and care to respond to the strengths and needs of all children

Reflections on practice by senior professionals in early years

Lalitha Sivalingam and Fiona Dearman

> Never ever do nothing.
>
> Area SENCO

Chapter objectives

By the end of this chapter you should be able to:

- identify a range of parameters for effective differentiation to address diverse needs of babies and young children;
- reflect on the value of sharing expertise with a range of professionals;
- confidently create an enabling learning environment for children, families and colleagues.

Link with Teachers' Standards (Early Years) 2013

S1 S4 S5 S6 S8

Introduction

This chapter will help you explore a number of parameters for effective differentiation, as five professionals reflect on their practice. Babies and children have diverse needs, different learning characteristics and unequal patterns of progress. Efficient planning seeks to build access to education and care for all children. The phrase 'one size fits all' does not apply when providing for children, as the Early Years Foundation Stage is an inclusive curriculum based on the individual needs of each child (DfE 2012). You can build your confidence, as Early Years Teacher trainees and Early Years Educators, to set up and adapt an environment that meets the needs of all children based on sound knowledge of the Early Years Foundation Stage (DfE 2012).

In this chapter, the authors have engaged in informal meetings or discussions with five professionals in senior positions in the early years field to invite them to share their experiences and expertise. This method of informal discussion has been chosen as it creates a relaxed atmosphere where professionals can reflect on their practice and engage in conversation, perhaps providing a model you can use to collect your own evidence. The authors are aware that the professionals chosen for this discussion are mainly from one authority and that it is not representative of the whole population. However, the reflection and points raised by the professionals could be the starting point for further reading and exploring the subject. Care has been taken to keep the names of the participants anonymous and to explain to them the purpose of sharing some of their daily experiences in their professional roles.

1 Area Special Educational Needs Co-ordinator (SENCO)

Question: What would you advise settings to look out for in order to know when a child is in need of additional support? How do you think settings can assess these needs?

Answer: Settings have a number of tools that they can use to assess the child's learning and development such as Early Years Foundation Stage, *Development Matters* (EE 2012). They need to look and assess a child over a period of time and look at specifics of each area of learning and development to find out where their concern lies. For example, if you are considering whether the child is able to follow instructions, in a contextual situation, you need to consider whether the child really understands what is being asked before using tools to check against the average development level.

They also need to look at observations systematically to collect data that will help them to assess the needs more accurately.

A tool such as ECAT (*Every Child a Talker*), a language development list, will be useful if the concerns are about speech and language development (National Strategies 2008).

You also need to cross-reference, using information from parents, carers and other professionals.

Another example, for instance, is, when observing a child who has chosen to do a 12-piece insert puzzle, you could be assessing fine motor skills, problem-solving skills to match shape; ability to manipulate; ability to persevere; whether they scanned information in front of them, whether they had referenced eye contact or used any language to communicate at the same time. You should be clear what exactly you are looking to assess. However, this could lead to you becoming aware of the need to support the child in other areas such as the inability to divert their attention to what you are saying.

No specialist toys are needed to test cognitive skills. Simple practical toys that the child is familiar with, such as pegs, can be used to check for problem solving. If a child is unable to fit a piece, you may intervene saying, 'What about———?' If the child is still only focused on one thing, it could be that either he/she did not understand or may lack social communication skills.

Points to note in practice

- Observe and assess systematically over a period of time.
- Use a development tool to check the child's development stage.
- Cross-reference against other given records and areas of learning.
- Use simple practical toys the child is familiar with when making assessments.

Question: What are the main difficulties settings encounter when approaching parents to discuss a child's learning and development needs, and how is this best addressed?

Answer: Practitioners need to deal more with their own feelings of anxiety about how the parent will react; how to break the news; feelings about how and when to do this. If parents have been given regular feedback on observations of the child and about the child's progress in the areas of learning, this should not come as a shock to parents. Hence, there will be a negative response from parents mainly when the news is unexpected, such as unexpected findings in the end-of-year report or when given in front of others instead of confidentially. It is all about building trusting relationships and respecting parents. Give regular feedback, that is, there must be formative assessment and feedback to parents before any discussion on summative assessments.

Parents should also be given concrete examples of what you have observed and encouraged to share their own observations of the child in the home environment. If concrete examples are not given, it may sound like you made up a value judgement. A well-informed parent is usually grateful and happy to work with practitioners to meet the identified needs of their child.

It is also important that the practitioner is backed up by the senior management team. The child's needs should have been talked through so that everybody in the team understands the parent's view or concern and how the child can best be supported. Ways of talking to parents and other matters can be talked through during staff supervision sessions. It is also important that more experienced staff give feedback and support to parents to avoid any mixed messages.

Points to note in practice

- Parents should be given regular feedback based on formative assessments.
- Check against what the parent has observed in the home environment.
- Staff will benefit from supervision sessions on how best to work with parents.

Question: Which professional services are currently most sought after and why?

Answer: Speech and language seems to be the most sought-after service. This is because it is a physical need and in some cases fairly obvious to the parent and staff if the child's speech is not at the developmental level.

Some authorities have a tracking tool within a key STEM area and settings in the authority know how to use it. Before a speech therapist in the authority will accept a referral, they expect practitioners to have completed one of these (further information is given in *Every Child a Talker*, National Strategies 2008). Practitioners need to use more than the *Development Matters* as this is a general overview of the developmental stages of a child. They need more concrete and better information to get early support.

Points to note in practice

- A tracking tool should be used to assess the child's need.
- *Development Matters* is a general guide so practitioners need to look for a book or document that gives more detail on child development.

Question: How are education and care adapted to support parents and families while they wait for this service?

Answer: Never ever do nothing. As soon as you find out, action should be taken. You should not wait for an appointment for the speech therapist as the expectation is that you can do something positive before the appointment. For example, the practitioner needs to think about what she gathers from her observation and how she can plan the next steps for the child. It could be as basic as learning to listen to simple instructions in order to be in the environment, e.g. 'Stop, listen.' The practitioner should use their knowledge of what the child is good at and build on the strengths instead of trying to sort out the difficulty or do nothing. For example, if child Z zooms around the room, swiping toys off the table, the practitioner's first reaction might be to stop the child. Instead, observe and reflect further, paying attention to all the information shared by the parents and staff. Check the development level of the child and they might come to the conclusion that the child does not know what to do with the toys on the table. Therefore, the practitioner needs to show the child how to play with one or two toys on offer. The practitioner should eliminate negative preconceptions. Instead, they should try to find out the reasons for the child's actions and plan positive actions.

During the support process, the practitioner should carry on supporting the child, bearing in mind that you are a social setting, providing experience; you don't want to turn into a therapy group. You don't have to specialize your group, instead, you need to adapt the group so the child is included, not excluded, in a social situation. Some children need more one-to-one attention for specific work, while the majority can do with the practitioner adapting the environment to meet their needs. We need to remember that each child is an individual. Some children need more support than others.

Points to note in practice

- Look closely at how you can meet the individual needs of the children in your setting.
- Do not wait for specialist advice, instead take immediate positive actions to support the child, based on your observations.

Activity 5.1: Observations and tracking to support planning for individuals

1 Look at different types of observation, their purposes and how they can best be used to support your planning for the child.
2 Look at the ECAT language tracking tool (National Strategies 2008). How can you modify this to use in your setting?
3 Check what system is in place in your Local Authority that is used as a tracking tool before seeking help from a speech therapist.
4 Reflect on how parents and children are supported during transition.

2 Local Authority Early Years Adviser

Question: What does your main role involve?

Answer: I advise childcare providers including nurseries in the private, voluntary and independent sector, children centres, crèches and childminders. Support and advice are focused on meeting the Early Years Foundation Stage to provide high quality, inclusive early years care and education.

I make pre-inspection visits and also visit to address actions or recommendations given in an Ofsted inspection, to put together a development plan with SMART targets. I deliver training on different aspects of the EYFS and prepare settings for an Ofsted inspection.

I have been involved in Local Authority childcare settings colour categorization, rating settings red, green or amber, which determines how much support a setting needs. Red signifies that the setting is providing inadequate service, so will need more advice and support. Amber rating could be for a setting having a new manager who would benefit by support but there are no major concerns. Finally, a green rating signifies that the setting needs minimal support.

Points to note in practice

- Local Authority Childcare Advisers advise all childcare settings registered on Ofsted's Early Years Register.
- Local Authority Childcare Advisers offer training on meeting the requirements of the EYFS to provide high quality inclusive early years care and education.

Question: How are childminders supported in understanding and adhering to the Early Years Foundation Stage?

Answer: In my role as a Local Authority Adviser, I do a pre-registration visit to those intending to register to be childminders to check their understanding of the requirements. They are encouraged to put together a portfolio of policies, registration documents, insurance certificates, regulation certificates, and planning formats for documenting the learning and development of children in their care. They are signposted to training on the Statutory and Safeguarding requirements and the Learning and Development requirements of the EYFS framework.

I make annual and pre-Ofsted visits to childminders as well as post Ofsted visits to support childminders in addressing action and recommendations from Ofsted inspections. During visits I carry out audits to assess the quality of the provision and identify areas in need of improvement.

I also support prospective childminders through the pre-registration process. Prospective childminders are offered a training programme and visits to support them in preparing for the Ofsted registration visit.

Points to note in practice

- Childminders are given training on EYFS.
- They need to be able to demonstrate a thorough understanding of the EYFS.
- Portfolios are a useful tool to store all their necessary documentation.

Question: How do you support a childminder to adapt her home to meet the needs of babies and children in her care?

Answer: I refer the childminder to the EYFS statutory and safeguarding requirements (DfE 2012) and the learning and development requirements (EE 2012). I advise that they should adapt the home environment to provide the child with a safe and stimulating environment, hence they need to look around the home and assess it for safety and age-appropriate resources. For example, I would advise that they avoid using a tablecloth, especially when looking after very young children, particularly those learning to walk. It is important that there are appropriate resources for children in the developmental stages to provide interesting and challenging activities. The resources should be easily accessible to promote children's independence. Children should be able to take and return resources confidently without fear. The childminder needs to ensure the environment is safe from hazardous material by placing these in locked cupboards. If they are unable to offer a variety of activities, childminders should try to take the child to 'drop-in' sessions in the local area. The environment needs to be child-friendly with appropriate age-related equipment such as carry cots, high chairs and play mats for the very young. In the garden, childminders could consider a small area for children to dig or grow plants and vegetables. They should take children outdoors daily and offer opportunities for playing or using larger equipment. There should be an area for the child's personal belongings, for example, for coats and bags. If the child has any particular needs, consideration should be given to adapt the environment to meet the needs of the child. If the need is very specific, the childminder could get advice from specialists who can demonstrate and give details of what to do in certain situations related to the condition. For example community nurses can help with training on using epi pens; draw up care plans; organize review dates for support and link to other professionals. There is advice and support to signpost what needs to be done to meet the child's needs. If a childminder is not confident, they might not agree to look after the child. Hence it is important to reassure them that there is support for them to help children with specialist needs.

Points to note in practice

Childminders are supported in the following areas:

- in implementation of the EYFS;
- to provide a safe and stimulating environment;
- to provide children with a sense of belonging;
- to work with parents and other professionals;
- to use facilities in the local community.

Activity 5.2: Childminder provision

1   Draw up a 'do' and 'don'ts' list for the childminder on ways of making their home a safe and stimulating place for children in their care.
2   Look at the services that are available for childminders to access in the local community.
3   Think of ways the childminder can work with schools and nurseries to support the child in their learning and development.

3 Nursery manager

Question: How do you plan for the children in the setting on a daily basis to ensure you meet the needs of all the children in the setting?

Answer: We ensure children feel they are part of the group, if they do not feel comfortable, they will not feel they belong. Children need to have their space and their basic needs met, hence the importance of the Key Person system. The Key Person's role is to liaise with the child's parents to exchange information to ensure the child's needs are being met so they can learn and develop to achieve their full potential.

When children start at the nursery, Key Persons complete an 'entry profile' with the parents to gain information about each child. We discuss their likes and dislikes, interests and their daily routine. We also gather this information by talking to the children, listening to them, and observing them. The entry profile is also used to assess children's stage of development on entry to the nursery and is used to start their 'Learning Journey' which is recorded by staff via on-going observation and liaising with parents throughout the child's time in the nursery.

As a team, we discuss how each child learns and provide appropriate resources for their learning, to reinforce what they have learnt and to extend their learning. We give opportunities for children to develop their creativity. We recognize that children learn through sensory experiences and by doing things themselves, so we provide an environment which allows children to explore and discover using knowledge of the individual child to provide appropriate resources that meets their developmental stages. We recognize the need to differentiate activities to ensure all children can participate. We also use opportunities in our daily routines to further develop children's learning.

We are conscious of avoiding negative messages to children such as 'don't do', 'don't touch' and 'can't'. Instead we encourage children to believe they 'can' achieve by use of encouragement and praise.

Points to note in practice

- Ensure children are made to feel valued so they experience a sense of belonging within the group.
- Key Persons work with parents to ensure child's needs are met and that learning and development are extended to the home environment through shared communication.
- Plan to meet the child's needs and extend their learning through daily routines and planned activities.

Question: How do you support children through transition?

Answer: For most of the children in our setting, it is their first transition from home into nursery. We have developed a transition policy and we reflect to improve on it.

During the settling-in period, parents are encouraged to stay with the child until the child is more familiar with us, the surrounding and the routines. The parent is introduced to the Key Person who works closely with the parent and child. They spend time talking about the child's interests and routines and share information on a daily basis. The Key Person gets to find out the child's likes and dislikes, the home language and the level of understanding and communication. We do not have home visits prior to starting but are aware of the value of home visits. However, as the Key Person, parent and child are not rushed, a good relationship is established, which helps the child to settle. We continue to work closely with the parent by sharing information on our noticeboards and newsletters. There are lots of photos on the wall which show how and what children do when they are at the setting. There is a communication book that is sent home which is completed by both the setting and the parent. This keeps parents and Key Person updated with information to support the child.

Key Persons also work closely when children transfer between rooms to support them in a similar way. The Key Person will spend time with the child in the new room until they are familiar with their new Key Person and environment. Usually they make friends quickly and are happy in the new environment. If they are not, we give them time to get more used to the new Key Person and children in the room by joining in more activities with them for example, during outdoor activities, etc. We recognize the value of transition objects, such as a cuddly toy or muslin. New environments, both indoor and outdoor, can be daunting for some children. We are very aware of this and create cosy areas where some children might be more comfortable.

We work closely with schools in the local area. Our pre-school children use facilities at our local school throughout the year. In the summer term we take children to visit the reception class in school. The reception class teacher from the school also comes to visit the children in our nursery. We share books about moving to the 'big school'. We also take photographs of the new classrooms and teacher and talk to the children to get them ready for the new environment. We listen to them, give them time to ask questions and reassure them. If the school has pets, we talk to the children about the pets and have a pet week in the setting so that they look forward to looking after the pets in the new school. These summer holidays we looked after the guinea pigs from the reception class. It made our children look forward to seeing the guinea pigs in school in September. Throughout, we work closely with parents to let them know what we do and to share any information.

Points to note in practice

- Adhere to a well-reflected transition policy and procedure.
- Establish links between the Key Person, parent and child.
- Keep parents informed by talking to them, sharing information and lots of photos on the wall for them to see their child in the new surroundings.
- The child can be supported by the use of transition objects.
- Help the child build links by giving them time and reassuring them.

Activity 5.3: Setting support

1   Think of introducing supervision for new staff to help them develop confidence in settling children and supporting parents through transition.
2   Use an audit tool (Figure 5.1) to reflect upon the effectiveness of supporting parent involvement. Give any suggestions for improving the service.

How do you support parent Involvement?	What do we do?	What could we do better?
How do you make staff aware of the importance of involving parents/carers in their children's learning?		
How do you ensure parents/carers feel welcomed in the setting?		
How do you show that staff respect and value parents/carers?		
How do you share information with parents/carers at the beginning and end of a session?		
How do you engage parents/carers in their child's learning and development?		
How do you build parents'/carers' trust?		
How do you communicate (for example, newsletters) with parents/carers in your setting?		
How do you support families with differing needs, for example, languages, literacy and culture?		
How do you support the transition from home and ensure that parents/carers are involved?		

Figure 5.1 Setting audit: reflect on how you support parent involvement.

4 Portage worker

Question: What would you consider to be your main roles and responsibilities?

Answer: As a portage worker I provide a home visiting educational service for pre-school children with additional support needs and their families, and support the development of play, communication, relationships, and the learning of young children within the family.

I use a broad range of materials, including observational records and developmental profiles or checklists, to provide a framework for parents and carers to discuss their children's individual strengths and needs. I set goals with the parent or carer, ensuring the child's participation and inclusion within the daily life of the family.

One of my main roles is to teach children through play particularly through the small steps approach. There might be one big goal to achieve, but I break it down into tiny steps as the child will have a disability, so the learning or development does not come naturally to them. For example, the child might have a physical or cognitive disability.

I identify the child's areas of strength and use this as a base to work with the child. I work closely with the parent throughout the programme. If the child is about to learn a skill, I work closely with the child and parent to support the child through each stage of the development. I always take the lead from the parent as they know their child best. I keep notes of what is done during each visit. If the child has developed any new skill or if there is a need for a joint visit with another professional, I try to organize this meeting. In my role, I work closely with other professionals and services such as speech therapist, physiotherapist, hearing and visual impairment service. I follow the advice given by the other professionals and work with the parent to help put in place any recommendations. I am also involved in writing six-monthly reports about the progress of the children I work with.

Points to note in practice

- Work with parents supporting their understanding of how children learn and develop.
- Identify small steps towards children's learning.
- Work with other professionals to support the child and parent.

Question: How do parents come to know about the portage service?

Answer: Some parents know about us from other parents. However, on the whole, they are referred to us by other professionals. When a child is six months or younger, they may be identified as needing extra support by their local general practitioner or professionals from the neo-natal clinic, the health visitor, the community nursery nurse, the children's centre or staff from nurseries. It is then decided at a meeting where other professionals from all agencies are present, which services can best support the child.

Points to note in practice

- Parents share their knowledge with others about the role of the portage system.
- Portage workers are aware of the importance of working with other professionals to support the child and family.

Question: What makes them decide that portage service is needed?

Answer: The child might have:

- an identified syndrome;
- birth injury resulting in, for example, cerebral palsy;
- developmental delay, showing that the child is not meeting milestones;
- different development patterns from their other siblings, thus causing the parents to be concerned.

To receive portage, a child needs to have a delay in two or more areas of development. Some portage services see children between the ages of 0–5 years even though they get 15 hours of funding.

In cases where the child is at nursery, the portage services may be able to offer the nursery advice on the best methods of adapting the environment to suit the child, including methods of communicating such as the use of Makaton or visual timetables. They will work with the staff in the setting to help draw up an Individual Education Plan (IEP) for the child. This is based on the child's strengths, likes and interest. Emphasis might be on encouraging any form of communication. The portage worker might demonstrate how they work with the child, such as modelling what they do when talking to the child. This may include some or all of the following:

- get down to the child's level;
- call them by name;
- use simple language;
- use repetitive phrases or words;
- use visual cards or materials such as pictures, symbols or photographs.

The above are what any good setting do, to adhere to the Early Years Foundation Stage curriculum (DfE 2012).

The portage worker will also share the portage goals with the setting. Throughout the process, the parent is fully involved and any goals set are shared with the parent so that they might be followed in the home too.

If a child is not at a setting, for instance, not of nursery age, and the parent has been referred to portage services, a portage worker will write to them giving the date of an initial visit. At the visit, the portage worker will give information about portage services, clarifying that it is not a therapy or medical service. The weekly or fortnightly visits are to see the child and parent/carer.

During the visit, the portage worker

- will observe the child with their own toys;
- will get the history from the parent and any information from other professionals;
- might use check lists, to get baseline assessment which should give an idea of gaps in development, or an idea of goals to set;

- will go through the check list and set goals with the parents based on the child's strengths and interests;
- will develop a programme to enhance the child's skills;
- will build bonds with the family to support the child.

Often strong bonds are formed between the parent, the child and the portage worker. Hence, the portage worker may need to prepare the parent to cope with the end of the support system. One way this is done is by directing them to coffee mornings where they can meet and share their experiences with other parents. All portage workers are trained as EarlyBird (EB) presenters to support the families of children in pre-school, and as EarlyBird Plus for those in school. EarlyBird is a programme of support for parents whose child has been newly diagnosed with autism (EarlyBird 2013).

Points to note in practice

- Adhere to the principles of the EYFS.
- Follow the steps to meet the needs of the unique child.
- Follow the rule of: observe, assess and monitor.
- Give parents ideas for activities to support the child.
- Support parents whose children have been newly diagnosed with autism.

Reflection 5.1: The step-by-step approach to learning a skill

Reflect on a step-by-step approach on how you support children to develop a particular skill such as a manipulative skill.

Reflect on ways you give feedback to parents on children's learning and development.

---

5 Head teacher of a Local Authority-maintained children's centre

Question: How do you plan for the needs of each child?

Answer: First, it is very important to get to know the child and family. This is a 'partnership of learning with parents.' You find out more from parents when you talk to them in an informal way than when you only use forms. We use the information from parents and carers to plan for children to help make them feel safe and secure in their new setting. We visit every child in their home before they join us. We take photos of the children in their homes and, with the parental permission, use them in the classrooms. This helps make the child feel very special on their first day. A photo is placed on their coat pegs so that children can recognize where to put their coat and they feel a sense of belonging. Photographs of all of the children are placed outside the classrooms, supporting the opportunity for a discussion with the children and parents about their new friends.

We aim to visit all children in their homes. A teacher and a nursery nurse make the planned visit and either the teacher or nursery nurse will be the Key Person for the child. The Key Person is responsible for building a relationship with the child and family. They are responsible for compiling a Book of Learning Experiences for the child during the time they are with us. If the family is already attending the centre, we aim to make the Key Person a member of staff that they are familiar with and with whom they have formed a good relationship. Generally, we are all responsible for working with the child and family. I feel, most children will respond to the kindness and enthusiasm of a caring adult. If a child has any special or additional needs, we need to find out as much information in order to help the child access the curriculum with the support of other professionals.

Points to note in practice

- Build up a partnership with parents and carers.
- Use information to support the child through transition.

Question: How do you know what the child's learning needs are?

Answer: We observe the children in our setting and use the Early Years Foundation Stage curriculum (DfE 2012) to plan appropriately for each individual child. We use our knowledge of child development to track every child's learning and development from the time they start. Through observation and assessment we are able to assess, 'where the child is in terms of their developmental stage, and ensure they should be making progress.'

We offer group activities in which we address the needs of individual children. We listen to them, talk to them and give them lots of opportunities to develop and practise skills. We plan using the child's interests to engage them in their learning. We attempt to expand their interests in a creative way. For example, we would try to encourage a child who only likes to play with the space toys and never uses the paints, to paint a planet for the rockets to zoom around.

We have regular team meetings after school. It is the responsibility of the Key Person to discuss some of their children in depth, sharing evidence of progress and concerns. The team set some targets for the children and these are worked through the week and shared at the following meeting. An example could be that staff have observed a child playing alone, so a plan would be made for the Key Person to engage in an activity with a group of children encouraging that child to begin building relationships with others. Children who choose not to play outside can be encouraged to do so by their Key Person providing the activity outdoors and working alongside them.

Points to note in practice

- The importance of observation, assessment and planning for the individual needs of each child.
- Sharing information and planning the next steps of learning for each child on a regular basis.

Question: How do you work in partnership with parents whose child may need extra support?

Answer: Initially we will observe the child and talk with the team, gathering as much information about the child as we can. We use photographic and video evidence to share with parents. We have an informal meeting with the parents and this is an opportunity to talk about their child's development in school and at home. It is at this meeting we introduce the idea of involving other professionals in our work with the child. Our SENCO is always at these meetings and it is her role to make any necessary referrals with the parents' permission. This is a very anxious time for parents and it is important that staff are trained to work in partnership with parents. Newly qualified teachers (NQTs) will benefit from someone who will support them in the initial parent consultations to gain experience. We offer mentoring sessions to our newly qualified staff and this would include how best to talk in a non-threatening way; how to overcome a communication barrier, and the importance of being honest and open to parents. The NQT is further supported by training provided on our Inset days, working closely with other schools and training by the Local Authority. In our LA, we have leading Foundation Stage Teachers located in various schools across the authority who offer additional training to NQTs and other staff. My belief is that as a teacher you never stop learning and personally you are always looking to improve your practice. We should always look at a variety of ways and strategies to support children.

Points to note in practice

- Remember that parents are the child's first educators.
- Staff need to be well trained to be able to work with parents to gain their trust and confidence.
- We need to be aware of working with other professionals.

Question: How do you support children for whom English is an additional language?

Answer: This is a priority as many more children speaking a variety of languages join our school. Last year, for example, English was an additional language for 33 per cent of the children attending the school, with a total of 19 different languages spoken there.

We make home visits to all of the children and work with parents by showing them photographs of the nursery and a visual timetable to help them familiarize themselves with the child's daily routines at school. When they visit us, we show them around and they can see what their child is involved in and how children are engaged in learning through play. We explain that we use lots of visual aids and Makaton signs to help children understand what is happening and this helps them to feel more confident. Visual timetables are displayed so that children can see or point to what they are doing or going to do next.

We do lots of small group work, depending on the child's ability to speak or understand English. We encourage other fluent English speakers to join the play so that language is modelled indirectly. We also plan around themes that make sense to the children. We have several opportunities for children to learn the language in small informal groups such as in the role play areas, or the small world play, both inside and outside. We have resources that reflect the diversity of the families attending our school. We have dual language books alongside our books in English and parents can borrow these. We encourage all parents to come and help in the school. We acknowledge where the families and children come from by learning about their culture and displaying some of their family photos and resources. We learn to say 'hello' in their language to greet them and they recognize that we are not saying that English is the only spoken language in school. I am passionate about children speaking their home language at home. The children need to learn their home language really well and English will come, as it is role-modelled in the setting. We are continuing to work in our school improving and acknowledging the importance of building the child's self-esteem. We are aware that the environment needs to reflect the child's background and culture. Parents are encouraged to come in to celebrate Diwali, the Chinese New Year, Eid and other special events.

Parents are invited to attend workshops. Through the use of photos and video we can show how children are developing in the seven areas of learning through play opportunities. We video children in school and talk to parents about what the children are doing. We role-model how we use lots of praise and positive language to support a child through their learning and development.

Points to note in practice

- Develop positive relationships with parents and understand the differing needs of families.
- The resources in the setting need to reflect the diversity of the community.

Question: What will you include in your planning if you have a high level of children who arrive hungry and are inadequately clothed?

Answer: It is important to have a trusting relationship with the parents. It is never our intention to make any moral judgements about how parents bring up their children but we are in a position of authority to ensure that the children are well cared for and kept safe. If we see children arriving in school hungry, we are able to offer breakfast in our extended day provision. There is a charge for using our extended day provision but we waive any fee if we know the parent is unable to pay. It is in the child's best interest to ensure they have a good breakfast to start their busy day. We know research has shown that hungry children do not learn well.

In our children's centre we have professionals who are able to discuss with parents how to organize their day, encouraging routines to take place in the home. Professionals work with parents helping them budget money and provide training to cook nutritious meals on a low budget such as the Cook and Eat Project. We monitor the families and seek to help out wherever we can. However, if we believe that a child is not being fed properly or is seen to be unkempt, we would have no hesitation in referring the family to children's services. We communicate well across the services and it is usually the health visitor whom we contact to see how the child and family can be supported. Working in a multi-agency team has the best outcomes for children and families.

Points to note in practice

- The child comes first – always work in the child's best interests.
- Engage with parents in a supportive role.
- Be aware of the expertise and support from other professionals.

Question: Could you give some suggestions to support children with additional needs in the setting?

Answer: The environment should be supportive of all children. It is a good idea to look at your classroom/setting with a critical eye to ensure that the needs of all children are met.

- Visual timetables should be displayed and individual schedules made to help the children know what will happen next in their day. These should be used all of the time and Makaton signing could be used too. Children unable to communicate verbally can use the picture symbols and signing to make their needs known.

- Some children find it difficult to sit still for a short period of time and the use of a 'wriggle cushion' can help them to sit on the spot which then helps them focus.

- If a child finds it difficult to keep their hands to themselves while sitting, it could be a good idea to give them something to hold such as soft, stretchy and squidgy resources. A piece of 'theraputty' works well but is not a good idea if they are likely to put it in their mouth.

- Children who like to suck their fingers and hands might benefit from a 'chewy tube' this is a soft rubber tube that they can use to suck and bite and not hurt themselves.

- Ensuring that all resources are clearly labelled using photos helps all children become independent learners and tidying up at the end of the session becomes more manageable. The use of music at tidy-up time alerts the children to something different happening. Each time they hear the music, it reminds them that they have to help tidy up.
- Furniture should be of the right height for children using a walking frame or in a wheelchair. Activities should be planned to be accessed by all. Sometimes it is necessary to use the floor, if a child is unable to stand up at a table or walk in the room.
- When you look around your environment, imagine you are the child and think about the difficulties he or she may have in accessing the learning.
- Talk with your team and be confident to make changes in the setting for the benefit of all children.

Points to note in practice

- Look carefully at your setting to see how you can make resources accessible.
- Use Makaton and visual timetables to help children understand the routines and to communicate.

Activity 5.4: The setting audit

1 Carry out an audit of the indoor and outdoor environment to reflect on your provision.
2 Make several visual timetables which can be left for children and staff to use.
3 Involve children in making a few picture books to develop their language.

Conclusion

The discussion with the senior professionals in this chapter has highlighted the importance of adhering to the EYFS principles of Unique Child, Positive Relationships, Enabling Environment and Learning and Development (DfE 2012). Throughout, there has been reference to working closely with parents, key workers and other professionals. The child has been, in all cases, considered as the main focus of discussion and the environment is set up to cater for the needs of individual children based on knowledge shared between parents and other professionals. According to the EYFS, to plan for a child's learning and development we need to follow the cycle in Figure 5.2 of observe, assess and plan, introduced in detail in Chapter 6. It is crucial that we

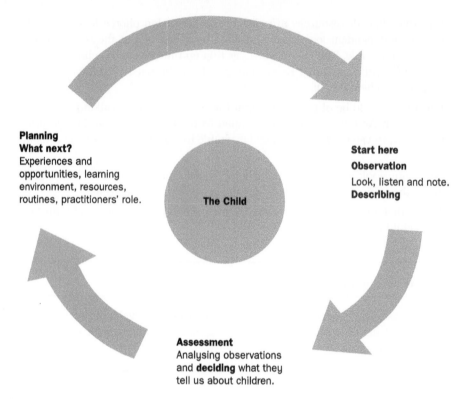

Planning
What next?
Experiences and
opportunities, learning
environment, resources,
routines, practitioners' role.

The Child

Start here
Observation
Look, listen and note.
Describing

Assessment
Analysing observations
and **deciding** what they
tell us about children.

Figure 5.2 The observe, assess, plan cycle.
Source: Early Education (2012: 3).

reflect on what knowledge we have of the child before we plan for their learning and development.

In order to plan to support a child, we should know what the child is able to do, their likes and dislikes, and any background information relating to their current development. Next, we observe the child to gain information from what we see for ourselves. We then assess and plan for the child which activities and experiences will aid their development, based on their age and stage of development.

This cycle is followed and the information gained is shared with the parent. The Pen Green Centre for Under Fives and Families recognize that: 'We need to begin with the firm belief that all parents are interested in the development and progress of their own children,' reinforcing the important role of parents and knowledgeable adults: 'Warm, trusting relationships with knowledgeable adults support children's learning more effectively than any amount of resources' (DCSF 2008a: PiP card 2.3).

Recommended reading

Clark, A. and Moss, P. (2011) *Listening to Young Children: The Mosaic Approach*, 2nd edn. London: National Children's Bureau Enterprises.

Fabian, H. and Mould, C. (eds) (2009) *Development and Learning for Very Young Children.* London: Sage.

May, P. (2010) *Child Development in Practice: Responsive Teaching and Learning from Birth to Five.* London: Routledge.

Meggitt, C. and Sunderland, G. (2012) *Child Development. An Illustrated Guide*, 3rd edn. London: Heinemann.

Nutbrown, C. (2011) *Threads of Thinking*, 4th edn. London: Sage.

Palaiologou, I. (ed.) (2013) *The Early Years Foundation Stage: Theory and Practice*, 2nd edn. London: Sage.

6

More than just a Post-it!

Making accurate and productive use of assessment

Helen Sutherland and Angie Maxey

Chapter objectives

By the end of this chapter you should be able to:

- see how the Teachers' Standards (Early Years) (NCTL 2013b) can be used to make accurate and productive use of assessment by examining the importance of observing and assessing children;
- know how the on-going cycle for observation and assessment can be used to promote a holistic view of the process. To enable reflection and improvement of practice within a well-established learning environment, as well as enabling the development of children's learning needs;
- value the underlying principles of observation and assessment by exploring different techniques and tools and the challenges raised when observing and assessing young children;
- reflect upon how observation and assessment and the Early Years Foundation Stage impact and underpin the Early Years Foundation Stage Profile and the two-year progress check;
- explore different ways of recording and collecting evidence alongside children, parents and other professionals and giving feedback to all stakeholders.

Link with Teachers' Standards (Early Years) 2013

S1 S2 S3 S4 S6 S8

Introduction

This chapter will support early years teachers in exploring how observation and assessment can be used to understand children's learning, and can inform planning and next steps for possible lines of development. Observing children is all about watching them carrying out different tasks; recording observations can be achieved in lots of ways, so that we can refer to what has been observed. This can be completed in a variety of different forms, from a Post-it note to the formal structured planned observation. Observations are used as an assessment tool and analysis of these observations tells us about the whole child or area observed, demonstrating their learning strengths and needs, interests and areas for development. This allows gaps in learning to be identified, reflecting on the need to change the environment and/or specific teacher/practitioner input. This also feeds into the process of planning and next steps.

It is important when recording an observation that it is objective and it should be positive and focus on the children's achievements as opposed to what they cannot do. By providing new challenges or continuing to support transferable skills with adult input, future observations will reflect progress in the children's learning. Remember to consider the language being used so as not to label inadvertently or make comparisons. '*Development Matters* can help practitioners to support children's learning and development, by closely matching what they provide to a child's current needs' (Early Education 2012: 3).

Observation and assessment have undergone radical changes in the past few decades especially due to the influence of the Assessment Reform Group, supported by the Nuffield Foundation. This has had a huge impact on the assessment being used in Key Stages 1 and 2 with the publication of *Inside the Black Box* (Wiliam and Black 1998), *Assessment for Learning Beyond the Black Box* (Assessment Reform Group 1999), *Working Inside the Black Box* (Black et al. 2002) and *Assessment for Learning 10 Principles* (Association for Achievement and Improvement through Assessment (AAIA) 2013). This, in turn, has impacted upon the development of assessment practices as it has 'advance[d the] understanding of the roles, purposes and impact of assessment' (AAIA 2013), driving forward meaningful informative assessment approaches. Currently, the Early Years Foundation Stage Profile (EYFSP) (STA 2013), with the inclusion of the two-year progress check (NCB 2012), is the process adopted in early years settings to record the achievements and recognize the learning development of young children. The EYFSP is a culmination of observations and assessments carried out using formative assessment to create a summative assessment. Discussion of formative and summative assessment will be covered in the assessment section of this chapter, to feed into Key Stage 1 (STA 2013). The most recent development is that of the non-statutory guidance *Early Years Outcomes* (DfE 2013b).

The on-going cycle for observation and assessment (Figure 6.1) provides an overview of the whole process, highlighting approaches for supporting the use of observation and assessment in meeting children's needs. The cycle demonstrates the process of observation, assessment, next steps and planning, including the principles, concepts, approaches and strategies that are involved in each of these aspects.

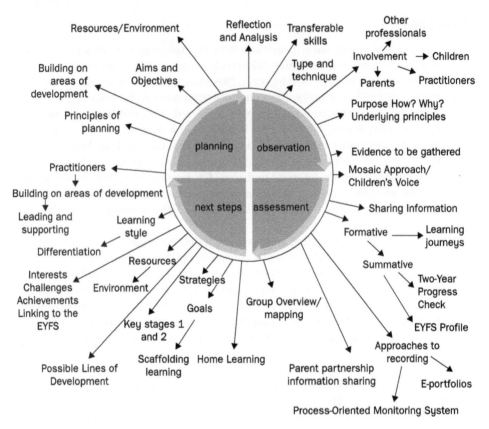

Figure 6.1 Ongoing cycle for the process of observation and assessment.

Source: Adapted from Royal Borough of Kingston. Early Years Advisory Team (2012).

The on-going cycle for observation and assessment will be referred to throughout the chapter to show how each of the spokes of the cycle is interlinked and informs the observation and assessment process. It is so much more than just a Post-it note!

Observation types and techniques

There are many different types and techniques of observing that can be used to gather evidence on a child. Here are just a few of the better-known ones:

- *Written records* are the most popular way of gathering observational evidence as they are a straightforward representation of what has been observed. This written narrative can cover any area or aspect of development and learning.

- *The tracking observation* follows a child over a period of time to discover what they are doing. This diagrammatic format of a room layout tracks where the child has been and how long they have spent there. To add more substance to this type of observation, it is beneficial to include a short commentary of their engagement in each area. This type of observation has limited usage but can be invaluable in identifying a child's movement, use of resources and particular interests.

- *Time samples and event samples* are observations that again record a child over a period of time. They enable the observer to detect any recurring or specific behaviour. They provide precise focused data on a child that is easy to access. However, it is not always easy in a busy setting to remember to make a record of what the child is doing.

- *The target child* observation provides the observer with a more focused observation on a particular area, such as language and social interaction. It can identify any barriers to learning or recurrent events which an observer can use to inform the next steps for the child's learning and planning.

- *Activity records* are a good way of recording what a child might be engaged in independently. This provides the opportunity of observing without having to try and describe everything that the child is doing, as it enables the observer to record the child's activity using diagrams or a sequence of photographs alongside a written narrative. This is a good technique if you are using iPads or tablets in your setting.

- *Socio-grams* provide the observer with an opportunity to observe the social dynamics of the group of children being observed. Use them to observe the interaction of the group through tracking their communication and engagement with each other or by asking the children who their friends are to see what their friendship groups are in the setting.

- *Check lists* are a quick and easy way to record the presence or absence of particular predetermined behaviours such as skills, competences, traits, reactions, achievements or stages of development. There are many different kinds of check lists and it is a good way of observing a group of children. It is important to record the child's achievements so that they are valued and celebrated.

- *The Mosaic approach* will be covered in the assessment section of this chapter. This approach supports the involvement of children, parents, other practitioners and professionals in the observational process.

What is the purpose of observation?

It is important for Early Years Teachers to lead practitioners in their understanding of the observation process, so that they recognize the value and importance of observations in contributing to the assessment process. It is through observation that children's progress, skills and development can be identified and recorded. Early Years Teachers should recognize that practitioners are not able to record everything they observe, but should in time gain an understanding of how to use both planned and spontaneous observations to support the identification of all aspects of children's learning and development to ensure that the whole assessment process has been fully engaged with and achieved.

When carrying out planned observations, an Early Years Teacher should support practitioners to record in the appropriate ways, for example, using templates, signing and dating observations and ensuring that the information gathered is suitable, informative, legible and professional, and describes what is seen in a non-judgemental way. Practitioners should consider what is going to be observed, where and how this will take place, and why, so as to acknowledge the aims and objectives for the particular observation. Some observations will need some preparation in relation to how they are going to be carried out and what is required to fulfil the desired outcome. Early Years Teachers can support practitioners to consider their role in completing the observation. As an Early Years Teacher, consider whether the practitioners are going to be involved with the activity while observing or be unobtrusive by not engaging in the activity.

It is important to be objective in the recording of observations so that they fully describe what is happening and are not just a practitioner's interpretation. People all have different perceptions of what they see and hear and this will affect how they interpret the meaning of what they observe. It is therefore important that observations are recorded as objectively as possible, not letting one's own values and beliefs affect what is recorded in relation to the observations on the child.

Activity 6.1: Objective statements

1   Look at the statements in Figure 6.2 and identify which are objective or not and say why.
2   Share this with your colleagues to support their knowledge and understanding.

Are the statements below objective or not?	✓ or X
1. Kwan smiled a lot and bounced up and down on the seat.	
2. Kwan is happy and energetic.	
3. Alice fetched the ball from under the chair.	
4. Alice rolled the ball under the chair, she reached to get it and crawled under the chair and picked up the ball.	
5. Tomas sat at the table and banged the pens with both hands to make marks on the paper.	
6. Tomas enjoys mark-making.	

Figure 6.2 Objective statements.

Observation plays a key role in formative assessment and clearly underpins this within the Early Years Foundation Stage (DfE 2012) and the Early Years Foundation Stage Profile (STA 2013). Use Activity 6.2 to support your own knowledge and understanding and those of your colleagues when using different observational techniques.

Activity 6.2: Comparing the value of using different observational techniques

1   Using the three Post-its shown in Figure 6.3, identify how Tom is developing and progressing in each of the three prime areas using *Early Years Outcomes* (DfE 2013b) to support in the identification of his age and stage of development and learning. Tom is 2 years and 1 month old; he has been attending the day nursery for 1 year and 7 months. His home language is Polish.

Post-it 1	Post-it 2	Post-it 3
Tom says 'give it to her' telling the adult to give another child playdough.	*Tom listens to the adult when he is asked to move back from the bubbles.*	*Tom explores different ways of using the slide.*

Figure 6.3 Three observations of Tom

2   Using the three different observational techniques shown in Figures 6.4, 6.5 and 6.6, identify how Tom is developing and progressing in each of the three prime areas.

Tom climbs up the slide, steps forwards one step at a time, using alternate feet. When he gets to the top, he turns his body round and sits on the slide. He pushes off with his hands and slides down backwards. When he gets to the bottom, he rolls over and pushes himself up to a standing position. He then lies on the slide and pulls himself up to the top. He hangs upside down for a few moments before pushing himself back down again.

Figure 6.4 Narrative/written record

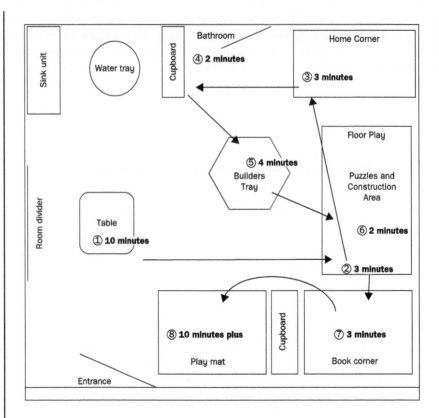

① 8:00am – Tom arrives first and sits at the breakfast table, he points to the trolley and an adult serves him breakfast, he sits and eats his Shreddies with a spoon.

② 8:10am – Tom moves to the construction area and pulls out the tray of animals. He uses two hands to rummage through the box and looks at the different animals until he finds a horse and a cow.

③ 8:13am – Tom moves around the room tapping the animals on different surfaces. He starts off in the home corner banging the table, the food boxes and the pots.

④ 8:16am – Tom stands at the low cupboard and moves the animals along from one end of the cupboard to the other. A child on the other side laughs and Tom joins in.

⑤ 8:18am – Tom sits with adult, 2 other children with more animals. 1 of the other children takes one of Tom's animals. Tom growls at the child and the adult intervenes, stopping both children's inappropriate behaviour.

⑥ 8:22am – Tom moves off to sit alone with a box of animals ⊗.

⑦ 8:25am – Tom lies on a cushion in the book corner with an animal in each hand.

⑧ 8:28am – Tom is encouraged by an adult to come and join her on the play mat. He bangs the animals as he goes over to her and sits with her putting the animals in and out of the blocks.

Figure 6.5 Tracking.

Time	Setting/Activity	Language	Social group
10:00	Story corner – the adult reads the story of *Dear Zoo*	Listening to adult and making animal noises	Adult Small group
10:10	Tom and Charlie stay in the story corner looking at the book together	Charlie lifts the flaps and Tom repeats the animal names – frog, camel, monkey and pup.	Tom and Charlie playing cooperatively together.
10:17	Charlie leaves and gives Tom the book	Tom lifts the flaps saying, 'elephant, giraffe roar'	Solitary play
10:20–10:30	Tom puts the book in the book rack and walks over to the construction area and takes a basket of animals out. Adult joins Tom as he lines up the animals	Tom names some of the animals as he lines them up making the noises of each animal. Adult asks Tom to name the animals that he has not named and names them with him	Adult and Tom

Figure 6.6 Time sample.

Reflection 6.1: Observational techniques

Compare and contrast the difference in the evidence gathered when using the Post-it note format and other more formal observational techniques.

Reflect upon how valuable the information gathered from using the different observational techniques in comparison to the Post-its has been in identifying the child's age and stage of development, linking to the Early Years Foundation Stage (DfE 2012) and *Early Years Outcomes* (DfE 2013b).

Reflect upon how you as an Early Years Teacher lead and support other practitioners by auditing observations to develop a richness and depth to the observations. Use Activity 6.2 to support with this.

Activity 6.3: Practitioner observations

This task can be used to support colleagues in understanding the value of using a range of observational techniques to inform practice.

1   Ask two practitioners to observe the same child using different observational techniques at the same time.
2   How much information is available from the observations?
3   Following the observation, discuss together the outcomes and interpretation of what they have each observed.
4   Did either of the practitioners face any challenges or issues? How could these be resolved? What strategies could be developed to support them in completing observations effectively?

Challenges, issues and strategies

Use the information in the grid in Figure 6.7 to support in the identification of any further challenges or issues that the practitioners recognize during Activity 6.3. What strategies can be identified to support the practitioner further? Some suggestions have already been inserted to support discussion.

Challenges	Issues	Strategies
Time constraints when completing formal observations	Practitioner carrying out an observation is not readily available to other children and may be distracted from the observation being carried out	Other practitioners to be aware that observations are taking place and support. Build time into the daily routine and have templates easily accessible to record formal observations as you observe them, rather than having to write them up later, which could lead to a different perspective being recorded
Understanding formal observational techniques	Lack of knowledge which in turn leads to a lack of quality within the observations carried out	Regular training, guidance and support in using different observational techniques and as an Early Years Teacher auditing Key Person files to ensure consistency across the setting

Figure 6.7 Challenges, issues and strategies.

Reflection 6.2: Leading and supporting others with observational techniques

In relation to achieving the Teachers' Standards (Early Years), identify:

- how Early Years Teachers can lead and support other practitioners in the development of different observational techniques;
- what value there is in using different techniques to inform practice;
- how the children can be part of the observation and assessment process;
- how the viewpoints of other stakeholders vary in regards to observational techniques and how their understanding has developed.

This section of the chapter has addressed the importance of carrying out informed observations, highlighting the value of using different types and techniques of observation. The purpose of carrying out observations with activities and tasks that can be used to lead and support other practitioners in developing their knowledge, skills and understanding of observing children has been addressed. This knowledge is used in the next section of this chapter to demonstrate how observation feeds into the assessment process.

What is assessment?

Assessment is a form of measuring the learning that has been achieved. It is through the development and implementation of assessment criteria that particular levels of skill, knowledge and competences prior, during and after learning can be determined. Assessment and its recording and reporting must also be meaningful, useful and have a purpose. Sometimes practitioners feel that they are just assessing because it is part of their role but it is essential that they realize the importance and potential usefulness of the assessment process and why it must be completed properly.

There are two main types of assessment found in practice within early years:

- *Formative assessment* is about gathering information about the child during their learning experiences, and can happen at the beginning to measure what the child's starting point is. Home visits and 'All about me' information will form part of this formative assessment. This feeds into the summative assessment process and is an essential part of the learning process. It has been identified as Assessment *for* Learning by the Assessment Reform Group (AAIA 2013).

- *Summative* assessment happens at the end of a learning experience, the end of a term or end of a year, to see what the child has learned and achieved in relation to the Early Learning Goals within the Foundation Stage. The formative assessment process will support and inform this assessment. This ascertains what a child has learnt and is carried out at regular intervals to summarize what has been achieved. The Assessment Reform Group has identified this as Assessment *of* Learning (AAIA 2013).

Both of these approaches to assessment feed into completion of children's records and reports. According to (DCSF 2008d: 5), for continuity of assessment, the assessment must therefore be:

- accurate
- fair
- reliable
- useful
- focused.

Types of assessment can include:

- observations
- questions
- self-assessment
- standardized tests such as SATS
- pre-produced tests such as portage check lists
- activities
- check lists to determine group achievements.

Some of these would probably be more evident in later stages of development or carried out by other professionals working outside of the setting.

What is the purpose of assessment?

The purpose of assessment is to clearly record a child's development and significant achievements. Assessment identifies learning needs and supports planning for individual children to be able to access activities which will enable them to progress. Assessment can be used to support children to recognize and celebrate their own achievements and to identify what they would like to learn next. It serves as a reporting mechanism when giving information to parents, and assessment profiles can be shared as part of the consultation process. By collecting whole-group assessments, Early Years Teachers can identify any gaps in learning which can then be rectified through planning appropriate learning opportunities. Whole-group assessment involves plotting children's development and learning as a whole group to show the patterns and to inform for differentiation within the planning process. This can be achieved by plotting individual children on a grid for the area of Personal, Social and Emotional Development (PSED) (Figure 6.8).

PSED – Aspects	0–11	8–20	16–26	22–36	30–50	40–60+
Self-confidence and self-awareness			Charlie Rav	Tomas Oliver Sarah Kwan	Lucy Sophia	
Making relationships			Tomas Oliver Rav	Charlie Sarah Lucy Sophia Kwan		

Figure 6.8 Personal, Social and Emotional Development (PSED).

All the children in the aforementioned group are two-year-old funded children, aged between 24 months and 35 months. As shown in Figure 6.8, there is a gap in the area for 'Making relationships', and this informs the practitioners that the children would benefit from further activities and experiences to develop this area.

How does this feed into government agendas and initiatives?

The Standards and Testing Agency is an 'executive agency' and is part of the Department for Education. They develop and deliver the statutory assessments for all statutory testing which includes the Early Years Foundation Stage Profile (STA 2013) and the statutory tasks and tests carried out in Year 2, Year 6 and Year 9 which is at the end of each Key Stage.

The Early Years Foundation Stage Profile is the statutory summative assessment at the end of the Foundation Stage (STA 2013). This supports transition into Key Stage 1 by providing the receiving teacher with information on each child's needs and abilities and their age- and stage-related achievements in the 17 Early Learning Goals. This information also informs both the Local Authority and the Standards and Testing Agency of the progress of every child in the Local Authority and across the country. This data is then analysed by the Standards and Testing Agency to identify the trends and patterns of development. This goes on to inform government agendas and initiatives, for example, the Williams Review (Williams 2008) has fed into the changes to the EYFS (2012), changing Problem Solving and Reasoning to Mathematical Development, giving a deeper focus on play-based learning relating to maths in the everyday environment. It also recommends that practitioners are mathematically confident and this can be seen with Early Years Teachers being required to be qualified at GCSE level in Maths, and this now forms part of the Teachers' Standards (Early Years) Standard 3.5 (NCTL 2013b).

When completing the Early Years Foundation Stage Profile (STA 2013), Early Years Teachers should consider drawing upon all the information available to form the summative assessment, including observations, learning journeys, previous assessment, the knowledge of the child supplied by parents, children, other professionals and the teacher. The Assessment and Reporting Arrangements (ARA) (STA 2013) provide example materials for the EYFSP on the Department for Education website: http://www.education.gov.uk/schools/teachingandlearning/assessment/eyfs/b00217443/eyfs-exemplification (accessed 30 October 2013).

Activity 6.4: Collating observations for the purpose of assessment

1   Referring back to Activity 6.2 and the information gathered from the observations, can you plot where Tom is on the *Early Years Outcomes* (DfE 2013b) point in the ages and stages of typical behaviour in Figure 6.9?

2   The current link to *Early Years Outcomes* (DfE 2013b) is available at: http://www.foundationyears.org.uk/wp-content/uploads/2012/03/Early_Years_Outcomes.pdf (accessed: 28 October 2013).

Prime Areas:	0–11	8–20	16–26	22–36	30–50	40–60
Personal, Social and Emotional Development						
Communication and Language						
Physical Development						

Figure 6.9 Observations for assessment.

3 *Development Matters* can be used as an alternative (Early Education 2012).

Reflection 6.3: Informed observations supporting assessment

Reflect upon how going through the process above has helped with the understanding of how informed observations support assessment.

What knowledge, skills, resources and support would practitioners need to be able to carry out the process effectively?

The two-year progress check

This is the first statutory summative assessment that is carried out within the EYFS and was introduced as part of the statutory guidance in 2012. This is carried out by practitioners in all early years settings on children between the ages of 24–36 months. This summative assessment informs the receiving Early Years Teacher when a child makes the transition into pre-school. If a child has not attended any setting prior to starting pre-school, there will not have been a two-year progress check completed and the EYFSP will then be the first statutory summative assessment completed on the child.

Activity 6.5: Viewpoints from an early years practitioner, a parent and a health visitor of their experiences of and perspective on the two-year progress check

1 Use the three viewpoints in Figures 6.10–6.12 to explore the experiences and perspectives of three of the stakeholders who have been involved in the two-year progress check for Tom (National Children's Bureau 2012).

Early years practitioner

I have completed six two-year progress checks and have actively involved the parents. I have also supported other practitioners in carrying out these checks. I have received training from the Local Authority and I have carried out independent reading and research to support in the completion of the checks. I have involved parents in the process by sharing information through the settings' newsletter and by providing the parents with a guide to the EYFS.

I use my knowledge of the child gained through observations and assessment to carry out the two-year progress check and then I meet with the parents to gain their input and feedback. This enables us to work together on the next steps and ways to support the child at home and in the setting. I have had experience of working with a health visitor when they came into the setting to observe a child whom I was concerned about. This was noted in the two-year progress check and action was taken by the health visitor. I have also used another two-year progress check to inform a health visitor who was carrying out a two and a half year check.

(Summary of answers from the questionnaire given to an early years practitioner)

Figure 6.10 Two-year progress check: early years practitioner.

Parent

My experience of the two-year progress check has been that I have been able to input into the check by talking with Carolyn [the Key Person]. She has completed her bit and I was able to add to this. I found that it was really helpful in providing information of Tom's learning and development as he is different at home to here – he eats differently here to at home. Carolyn has shared information and told us what she will do next with Tom. As a result, I now do different things with Tom at home. Carolyn has supported Tom's speech and development by encouraging him to use words to name the animals rather than growling or making the animal noises and I continue to support this at home. The nursery communicates with me on a daily basis and this along with the two-year progress check has helped me to support Tom.

(Summary of answers from the questionnaire given to a parent)

Figure 6.11 Two-year progress check: parent.

Health visitor

I have found the experience of carrying out the two-year progress checks alongside practitioners to be an extremely effective way of undertaking the review as you are able to look at all aspects of the child's development, especially their language and communication skills. I have received health visitor training and receive on-going CPD to support in the completing of the check. The parents are really happy to know that the setting and the health visitor work very closely together especially if there are any concerns. I have so far not found that I have faced any challenges in completing the two-year progress check. It has been excellent working with the Key Person and manager of the setting. I have found that the Key Person really knows the child well and that means that the assessment is not a snapshot view but a longer observation and monitoring. If actions are identified, the Key Person can put these into place and review the outcome.

(Summary of answers from the questionnaire given to a health visitor)

Figure 6.12 Two-year progress check: health visitor.

Challenges, issues and strategies

Use the information in Figure 6.13 to support in the identification of any further challenges or issues that may arise when working in partnership with parents and other professionals on the two-year progress check. What strategies can be identified to support practitioners? Some suggestions have already been inserted to support discussion.

Challenge	Issue	Strategies
Time constraints of gathering stakeholders together	Health visitor or other professional involvement not available	Completing several checks in one visit
	Parents may be working	Arranging appointments appropriate to their needs
Training for staff to be able to complete the check	Staff may not be confident even after training	Early Years Teacher to lead and support in the completion of the check
Parents not valuing the two-year progress check and providing minimal input	Confusion with the health visitor's $2\frac{1}{2}$-year health check only being carried out if there is a concern	Information to inform parents about what the purpose of the two-year progress check is and how it is carried out within the setting

Figure 6.13 Challenges, issues and strategies.

Using the sample two-year progress check for Tom in Figure 6.14, identify and highlight where the three observations on the prime areas of learning fed into this progress check.

Two-year Development Summary

Child: Tom

Age in months: 27

Completed on: 23 November 2012

Key Person: Carolyn

Health Visitor Check_Date_____

Personal, Social and Emotional Development

	0–11	8–20	16–26	22–36 W	30–50	40–60+
Self-confidence and self-awareness	0–11	8–20	16–26	**22–36** **W**	30–50	40–60+

Key Person's View:
Tom is very competent at expressing his own preferences and interests and displays this in his choice of play and activities, for example, using his current interest in animals to engage in play. He uses the animals to make marks in the sand and playdough. Tom will choose different songs and sings them confidently and independently or will lead his peers and adults in singing them. He will also choose books to read and will sit and go through them or will ask an adult to read them.

Parent's Comments:
Tom knows what he wants and won't change his mind. If he doesn't want to play with something or do something, he will clearly say no and continue what he is doing.

	0–11	8–20	16–26	22–36 W	30–50	40–60+
Making Relationships	0–11	8–20	16–26	**22–36** **W**	30–50	40–60+

Key Person's View:

Tom will join in other children's play and seeks out others to share play experiences with; for example, he will give adults books to read, join other children as they look in books and will offer children toys to join him in his play. Tom has formed friendships with other children in his group and will call them by name as he greets them in the morning and will play cooperatively with them during his time at nursery.

Parent's Comments:

Tom loves his friends from nursery as well as the staff. When asked who is in the nursery, he will say the names of his friends. When he comes close to the gate, he will call the practitioner's name ☺. Outside the nursery he has Polish friends and he loves to spend time with them. He makes friends with adults as well. He is even willing to try and talk to people on the bus or in the shop.

Communication and Language						
Listening and Attention	0–11	8–20	16–26	**22–36 W**	30–50	40–60+

Key Person's View:

Tom listens with interest to the noises adults make when reading stories and will sometimes imitate them, for example, when reading 'Walking through the Jungle'. He mimics and makes up his own sounds and enjoys singing nursery rhymes and songs. Some of his favourites are 'Hammer, hammer', 'Twinkle, twinkle little star', and 'I have a little turtle' and he will sing them along with adults or independently. Adults are able to get Tom's attention when he is engaged in other tasks, sometimes by calling his name, demonstrating his ability of single channelled attention.

Parent's Comments:

Tom loves music, we sing nursery rhymes while he is in the bath. When asked to bring something he will go and find it and is very happy with himself, 'Give to me'.

Understanding	0–11	8–20	16–26	**22–36 W**	30–50	40–60+

Key Person's View:

Tom identifies action words, for example, when playing with animals, he will move them along as if they were running, saying, 'Run, run, run', or 'Polar eating ice cream'. He responds to who, what, where in simple sentences, when reading the book, 'Walking through the Jungle', he will identify what he can see when asked by an adult. Likewise, if asked 'Where is the lion?,' he will point to it. He is able to correctly identify 'big' giraffe and 'little' giraffe showing his understanding of simple concepts of big and little.

Parent's Comments:

When watching TV, Tom will call me and say, 'Look at this, it's a truck'. When he drops his favourite horse, he will say, 'Oh dear', and kiss the animal. When going out in the rain, he will say, 'Look, it's raining and water' When asked to go to bed, he will say 'Night, night' and ask to read a book with him. .

Speaking	0–11	8–20	16–26	**22–36 W**	30–50	40–60+

Key Person's View:

Tom is bi-lingual, speaking both Polish and English. He is learning new words in English and uses them when communicating. He uses different types of everyday word, such as, banana, water, snack, ball, run, round, sleep, hot, wash, hands, and repeats words or phrases from familiar stories, for example, 'What can you see?'. Tom uses gestures sometimes with limited words to express himself, for example, he will hand the adult a book he wants to be read to him, saying 'book'. He sometimes uses simple sentences, such as, 'Mommy say morning', 'Oh look! It's horse', 'it's a horse', 'Oh, no thank you'. Tom uses language as a means of widening contacts and sharing thoughts, though this consists of his 'own words' but an adult is able to identify the words to use as context clues to ascertain what Tom is expressing verbally.

Parent's Comments:

When reading books, Tom will name objects and animals using both languages (Polish and English), saying English first.

Physical Development						
Moving and Handling	0–11	8–20	16–26	**22–36 W**	30–50	40–60+

Key Person's View:

Parent's Comments:

Next Steps to Support Learning and Development

Figure 6.14 Tom's two-year development summary.

> **Reflection 6.4: Two-year progress check**
>
> Reflect upon the layout and structure of the two-year progress check, consider how informed and varied observational techniques need to be part of the continual process to be able to be collated into a format for summative assessment.
>
> How does this form part of, and impact on, the educational continuum of the assessment process?
>
> How important was the parent's feedback when completing the progress check?
>
> By using this example format, how can you lead and support other early years practitioners through the process of the two-year progress check?

The use of information communication technology (ICT) in the observation and assessment process

With the growth and development of ICT, more settings are using different multimedia to support their recording of observations and assessments, giving instant observations. This forms part of Computer Mediated Communication (CMC) as observations and assessments are recorded and shared immediately they are uploaded. The types of media used are: digital cameras, digital recorders and iPads or tablets. These media can feed straight into an electronic portfolio forming the learning journey. Different companies, such as the Early Years Foundation Stage Forum (Tapestry and PRAMS – Progress Recording And Monitoring System) and Interactive Learning Diary have developed different applications, online resources and forms to support settings with electronic ways of observing and recording child observations and assessments.

The Mosaic approach

The Mosaic approach, while designed as a framework for listening to children and gaining their perspectives, provides researchers and practitioners with a range of different tools and approaches to listen to children but also enables them to be actively engaged and participating in the assessment process. This can also be used to actively engage children in the making of decisions as to what they would like to include in their assessment. This provides another dimension to the assessment process and clearly gives the children a voice in the process. There are three different stages to the Mosaic approach that complete the mosaic picture. A variety of different tools can be used to gather data and include the child's voice: observations, tours, interviews, questionnaires, children's photographs, children's drawings, structured activities, map making, audio recording, art activities, role play and persona dolls (Clark and Moss 2011).

The process-oriented monitoring system (POMS)

The Research Centre for Experiential Education, at Leuven University, Belgium (Laevers et al. 2005) have developed the Process-Oriented Monitoring System to record and evaluate young children's learning and development, particularly in relation to well-being and involvement. The Process-Oriented Monitoring System provides practitioners with another way of recording a child's learning journey and draws upon in-depth observations to record what the child has learnt and how they are developing. It provides a 'portrait' of the child, drawing upon the Key Person and parental information to complete the record. This includes information about the child, 'developmental domains', showing what the child has achieved, and the next steps 'The paradigm behind this instrument is "holistic" in this [*sic*] sense that the assessments are based on observation in real life situations' (OECD 2004: 7).

Reflection 6.5: Leading and supporting others with assessment, the two-year progress check and the EYFS Profile

In relation to achieving the Teachers' Standards (Early Years) (NCTL 2013b) identify:

- how Early Years Teachers can lead and support other practitioners in their knowledge, understanding and completion of the assessment, the two-year progress check and the Early Years Foundation Stage Profile;
- what value there is in using different assessment to inform practice;
- how the children can be part of the assessment process;
- how the viewpoints of other stakeholders vary in regards to their experiences and perspectives of the assessment process.

This section of the chapter has addressed what assessment is in relation to formative and summative assessment, the purpose of assessment procedures and how these feed into government agendas and initiatives. The activities provide opportunities to reflect upon how formative assessment, such as observations support the summative assessment process. The knowledge gained from this section will be used to support the development of next steps and planning for children's learning and development.

Next steps and planning

This part of the chapter shows how the observation and assessment material collected informs the next steps for learning and planning, using practical examples and reflection points to help lead and support planning. Next steps and planning play a vital role in the continuation of the assessment process and validate the play-based learning led and supported by Early Years Teachers.

When reflecting upon the child's assessment records, practitioners should build on areas that require development and differentiate activities according to individual children's needs and learning styles. Early Years Teachers need to lead and support practitioners by identifying areas for development within the environment and provide resources which support the next steps for learning. When planning learning experiences for children, practitioners need to ensure that the aim and objectives relate to the learning outcomes desired. Practitioners need to have clear assessment criteria for this, that link to the aim and objectives so that the activity/experience will provide children with clear learning opportunities. This forms the last part of the on-going cycle of the process of observation and assessment.

Activity 6.7: Two-year progress check: next steps

Using the two-year progress check for Tom in Figure 6.15, complete the next steps to support his learning and development.

Two-year Old Development Summary
Child: Tom Age in months: 27 Completed on: 23 November 2012 Key Person: Carolyn Health Visitor Check _Date_____
Next Steps to Support Learning and Development
Next steps:
How the setting will support:
How parents/carers could support learning at home:

Figure 6.15 Two-year check on Tom: next steps.

Reflection 6.6: Leading and supporting others to extend development

Looking at the two-year progress check, what aspect of development and learning has been identified and how would you lead and support practitioners to provide appropriate activities and experiences to extend and encourage Tom's continued development?

Reflect on how identifying the next steps for learning for individual children feeds into the planning process for the whole group.

How does this completed focused activity sheet (Figure 6.16) incorporate all aspects of the learning cycle from observation, to assessment, to next steps and planning?

This process of planning for the individual or group of children is beneficial in developing underpinning knowledge.

Focused activity: Reading *Percy the Park Keeper*

Duration: 15 minutes

Date: _____-

Children's previous experience related to this activity:

Tom has shown a real interest in different animals from the storybooks, Dear Zoo and Walking through the Jungle.

Aim of activity/experience

To provide the children with the opportunity to:

* Develop his language and communication skills through one-to-one interaction with an adult.

EYFS Areas of Learning and Development objectives

We are learning to:
* Name the different animals (Speaking, 22–36 months)
* Identify their habitats (The world, 22–36 months)
* Describe the weather (The world, 30–50 months)
* Count the animals in Percy's shed (Number, 30–50 months)
* Match the animal puppet to the animal in the story (shape, space and measure, 22–36 months)

Needs of individual children/Differentiation of activity to meet the children's needs:

Name and age of child:	Differentiation and needs of child:
Tom 27 months	Be specific in describing the words to identify the animals and their habitats to support language

Health and Safety aspects (Risk Assessment):

Follow guidelines for setting

Relevant legislation:

Statutory and non-statutory guidance

Activity/experience

Adult reads the story with Tom identifying what is happening in the story using the story and animal puppets

Teaching points

To ensure that the children have opportunities to identify what is happening in the story through open-ended questions:

- What animals are in the story? Match to the puppet.
- Where do they live?
- Why do they need a new home? Talk about the weather.
- Where are the animals going to live? Count how many are in his shed.

Resources

Story of *Percy the Park Keeper* and animal puppets

Assessment

What I'm looking for:

- Tom is able to name some of the animals in the story.
- Tom demonstrates an understanding of the story sequence.
- Tom can identify some of the habitats.
- Tom can count one up to five and beyond with support.
- Tom can recognize the change in weather in the story.

Evaluation:

To be completed following the activity

Next step planning:

To link into following planning informed through observation and assessment of the activity

Figure 6.16 Focused activity sheet.

Reflection 6.7: The EYFS planning cycle

In relation to achieving the Teachers' Standards (Early Years) identify:

- how Early Years Teachers can lead and support other practitioners through this planning cycle;
- how Early Years Teachers can support other practitioners in identifying the links between aims, objectives and the assessment part of the planning process;
- how Early Years Teachers can draw evidence from individual observations, evaluations of activities and assessment to develop next steps within the planning.

Conclusion

This chapter has explored the on-going cycle of observation and assessment to demonstrate how the Early Years Teacher can develop strategies to support good practice within a well-established learning environment. This has been achieved by demonstrating the value and importance of detailed observations which, when gathered, create a rich source of evidence for the summative assessment process. Within the summative assessment process, this chapter has shown how the two-year progress check is completed, drawing on experiences from a practitioner, a parent and a health visitor. The reflective process is evident throughout and demonstrates how the Early Years Foundation Stage impacts and underpins the Early Years Foundation Stage Profile and the Progress Check at Age Two.

Recommended reading

Featherstone, S. (2011) *Catching Them at It!* London: A & C Black Publishers.

Papatheodorou, T., Luff, P. and Gill, J. (2011) *Child Observation for Learning and Research.* Harlow: Pearson.

7

A safe environment
Safeguarding and promoting the welfare of children
Jo Elsey

Safeguarding children, the action we take to promote the welfare of children and protect them from harm, is everyone's responsibility.

(DfE 2013h)

Chapter objectives

By the end of this chapter you should be able to:

- know and act upon the legal requirements and guidance on health and safety, safeguarding and promoting the welfare of children;
- establish and sustain a safe environment and employing practices that promote children's health and safety;
- know and understand child protection policies and procedures, recognize when a child is in danger or at risk of abuse, and know how to act to protect them.

Link with Teachers' Standards (Early Years) 2013

S1 S7 S8

Introduction

Working Together to Safeguard Children (DfE 2013h) clearly states that 'safeguarding children, the action we take to promote the welfare of children and protect them from harm, is everyone's responsibility'. What does this really mean for an Early Years Teacher and how can you carry out this responsibility effectively day to day?

This chapter focuses on current legislation and the role of the Early Years Teacher in safeguarding children and how, as an Early Years Teacher, you can support and lead others to ensure they understand their role and associated responsibilities in protecting children from harm.

Parents have primary responsibility for looking after their children and for making sure they are safe and cared for. Agencies working with children and their families, irrespective of the capacity that they are working within, have a role in supporting parents to fulfil their responsibilities. It is, therefore, important to understand the context in which you are working.

Early Years provision should not work in isolation but should see themselves as an integral early intervention provider for children and their families. Multi-agency working, integrated working and children's services are all terms that we are familiar with, however, the level of partnership working between different sectors within children's services can vary from area to area. *Supporting Families in the Foundation Years* (Department for Education/Department of Health 2011) identifies that those working in the Foundation Years are best placed to identify children and families who would benefit from early intervention and support from professionals, and that Early Years Teachers, health visitors and GPs all have a role to play in ensuring families receive the support they need quickly and appropriately.

The importance of early intervention as detailed in *Supporting Families in the Foundation Years* (Department for Education/Department of Health 2011) came about as a result of several reviews, including those led by Graham Allen MP, Dame Clare Tickell, the Right Honourable Frank Field MP, and Professor Eileen Munro. They all identified that universal preventative services do have an impact on reducing the abuse and neglect of children. Early Years provision is a universal preventative service though it is not seen generally as this.

Legislation and associated statutory guidance

The legislation that now governs child protection practices has been informed in part by investigations and inquiries following several serious case reviews. The Department of Health (1991) carried out an inquiry report which focused on cases from 1980 to 1989. These included cases that had received media coverage such as Jasmine Beckford (London Borough of Brent 1985), Kimberley Carlile (London Borough of Greenwich 1987) and Tyra Henry (London Borough of Lambeth 1987). The associated media coverage raised the issue of child protection and allowed for increased public debate around improving practices and increased collaboration between agencies.

The Cleveland Inquiry (Butler-Sloss 1988) raised serious concerns in relation to the assessment processes undertaken by agencies when working with children and families following 121 cases of suspected child sexual abuse being diagnosed by paediatricians at Middlesex Hospital. This, and the Department of Health (1991) report, informed the revision of family law. The Children Act 1989 had a wider remit than just child protection, however, it clearly emphasized that the welfare of the child must be paramount and that professionals should work in partnership, both with parents and with each other to ensure that all children are protected from potential risks.

The Children Act 1989 identified two main areas of concern: children in need and significant harm.

Children in need

Under Section 17 of the Children Act 1989, children are defined as in need:

- if their health and development are unlikely to reach a satisfactory level or it is likely to be significantly or further impaired without the support of relevant services supporting the child;
- if they are disabled.

Significant harm

Under Section 47 of the Children Act 1989, significant harm identifies the threshold for compulsory intervention by services in the best interest of the child. Significant harm is defined as when a child is suffering or is likely to suffer ill treatment or impairment to their health and development.

The Children Act 1989 established the categories of abuse recognized in law. These categories of abuse are defined in the guidance, *What to Do If You Are Worried a Child Is Being Abused* (DfES 2006b) as:

- *Physical abuse* may involve hitting, shaking, throwing, poisoning, burning or scalding, drowning, suffocating, or otherwise causing physical harm to a child, including by fabricating the symptoms of, or deliberately causing, ill health to a child.
- *Emotional abuse* is the persistent emotional ill-treatment of a child such as to cause severe and persistent adverse effects on the child's emotional development. It may involve conveying to children that they are worthless or unloved, inadequate, or valued only insofar as they meet the needs of another person; age-inappropriate or developmentally inappropriate expectations being imposed on children, causing children frequently to feel frightened, or the exploitation or corruption of children.
- *Sexual abuse* involves forcing or enticing a child or young person to take part in sexual activities, whether or not the child is aware of what is happening. The activities may involve physical contact, including penetrative (e.g. rape or buggery) or non-penetrative acts. They may include involving children in looking at, or in the production of, pornographic material, or encouraging children to behave in sexually inappropriate ways.
- *Neglect* is the persistent failure to meet a child's basic physical and/or psychological needs, likely to result in the serious impairment of the child's health or development, such as failing to provide adequate food, shelter and clothing, or neglect of, or unresponsiveness to, a child's basic emotional needs.

These definitions are an important starting point for practitioners in assisting them in the identification of potential safeguarding and child protection risks for children. In addition to these definitions, the following possible signs of abuse and neglect assist practitioners further in their responsibilities in safeguarding and promoting the welfare of children.

Possible signs of abuse and neglect may include:

- significant changes in a child's behaviour;
- deterioration in a child's general well-being;
- unexplained bruising, marks or signs of possible abuse or neglect;
- a child's comments which give cause for concern;
- any reason to suspect neglect or abuse outside the setting, e.g. in the child's home;
- inappropriate behaviour displayed by other members of staff or any other person working with the child. For example, inappropriate sexual comments, excessive one-to-one attention beyond the requirements of their usual role and responsibilities or inappropriate sharing of images.

The publication of *Working Together to Safeguard Children* (Department of Health/ Department for Education and Employment 1999) offered clear guidance on the legal requirements on agencies to safeguard and promote the welfare of children and how agencies should work together in order to fully carry out their duties as set out in primary legislation and relevant associated guidance. This included an emphasis on training for all practitioners working with children and their families within these agencies.

The processes introduced through the Children Act 1989 (HM Government 1989) and *Working Together to Safeguard Children* (DH/DfEE 1999) did have an impact on how agencies carried out their duties individually and on multi-agency co-operation in relation to protecting children. However, insufficient communication and co-operation between agencies are still key factors in subsequent child death inquiries.

In February 2000, Victoria Climbié died following significant harm inflicted upon her by her great-aunt and her great-aunt's boyfriend. The subsequent inquiry into her death conducted by Lord Laming (2003) made 108 recommendations directed at agencies working with children and their families. The key message of Lord Laming's inquiry was that the lack of co-ordinated communication between the agencies involved with regard to the concerns that they had about Victoria resulted in insufficient appropriate intervention being made, resulting in her death.

Lord Laming reviewed the recommendations he had made in 2003, following the death of Peter Connelly in 2007. Peter was 17 months old when he died following severe physical abuse and neglect by his mother and her boyfriend. Peter was, at the time of his death, on Haringey Council's child protection register (now known as being under a child protection plan) and had been seen more than 60 times by a variety of different professionals in the months preceding his death, including being examined by a paediatrician 48 hours before he died. Again the key messages from this later review of those recommendations, made following Victoria Climbié's death, centred on improved training for professionals, including council leaders and senior managers and not just front-line staff.

In 2003, *Every Child Matters* was published by the UK Government. *Every Child Matters*, though now an archived document, underpins more recent statutory frameworks in supporting practitioners working with children and their families to use a holistic approach when considering a child's needs. The five outcomes that were identified support a child-centred approach, allowing children and young people to share their views and experiences of the services that directly and indirectly affected them. The *Every Child Matters* five outcomes are:

1   *Be Healthy*: This includes being physically healthy, mentally and emotionally healthy, sexually healthy, adopting healthy lifestyles and choosing not to take illegal drugs.

2   *Stay Safe*: This includes being safe from maltreatment, neglect, violence and sexual exploitation, safe from accidental injury and death and bullying and discrimination and safe from crime and anti-social behaviour in and out of school, therefore having security and stability.

3   *Enjoy and Achieve*: This includes being ready for formal education, and attend and enjoy school, achieving national standards at primary and secondary school and developing personally and socially while enjoying recreation.

4   *Make a Positive Contribution*: This includes engaging in decision-making and supporting the community and the environment, plus engaging in law-abiding and positive behaviour, in and out of school. Developing positive relationships includes choosing not to bully and discriminate. Develop self-confidence and successfully deal with significant life changes and challenges while developing enterprising behaviour.

5   *Achieve Economic Well-Being*: This includes engaging in further education, employment or training on leaving school and therefore being ready for employment, living in decent homes, in sustainable communities and in households free from low income and having access to transport and material goods.

The Children Act 2004 built upon the Children Act 1989 (HM Government 1989) and gave clearer accountability for children's services, in order for agencies to work together in a more efficient way, in particular, in relation to safeguarding and promoting the welfare of children. It also placed a duty on Local Authorities to establish Local Safeguarding Children Boards (LSCBs) which have the role of co-ordinating and quality assuring the safeguarding children activities of all the partner agencies as defined by the Children Act 2004 (HM Government 2004)

A key role within the LSCB brief is the co-ordination of training that is relevant and in line with core principles as set out in *Working Together to Safeguard Children* (DfES 2006c). The training that Early Years Practitioners have access to through their relevant Local Authority will be quality assured by the Local Safeguarding Children Board. Although each Local Authority will have a different delivery method, the core content of the training will be consistent.

Reflection 7.1: Leading and supporting staff in safeguarding responsibilities

Under the Children Act 2004 (HM Government 2004), each individual agency, which includes all early years and childcare providers, is responsible for ensuring that their staff are competent in carrying out their safeguarding responsibilities. This includes ensuring staff in regular contact with children attend child protection training relevant to their role within the organization. How does your setting/placement ensure that this responsibility is met?

Although not specifically related to the safeguarding of children, the Childcare Act 2006 was the first piece of legislation that focused on improving services for young children in England (HM Government 2006). The two areas of focus of the Act are:

- to improve the well-being of young children and reduce inequalities;
- to improve the quality of childcare provision in order to establish a minimum national standard that parents can be assured of.

Section 40 of the Childcare Act 2006 (HM Government 2006) places a duty on all early years providers to comply with Section 3 of the Statutory Framework for the Early Years Foundation Stage and to implement both parts of the Early Years Foundation Stage, the Learning and Development requirements and the Safeguarding and Welfare Requirements.

In 2012, the revised Early Years Foundation Stage was published and included several changes to the Statutory Framework in relation to child protection (DfE 2012: 13, 14). Safeguarding was given a higher profile within the Safeguarding and Welfare Requirements. Early Years providers, under the Safeguarding and Welfare requirements must:

- have a written policy and procedure that safeguard children, which includes the use of mobile phones and cameras. More importantly, they must implement this policy and procedure when necessary;
- identify a designated safeguarding lead within the setting who is trained in the identification of the signs and symptoms of possible abuse and neglect and how to respond effectively to these;
- ensure that all staff are aware of and understand the setting's policy and procedures and act appropriately within this;
- train staff in order for them to understand and identify the signs of possible abuse and neglect at the earliest opportunity;
- have regard to the *Working Together to Safeguard Children* statutory guidance.
- ensure that all staff who have regular contact with children are suitable for this role through safer recruitment procedures;

- inform Ofsted of any allegations of serious harm or abuse by any person at the premises.

As an Early Years Teacher, you will need to meet Standard 7 of the Teacher Standards (Early Years). This Standard relates to health and safety and safeguarding. Statutory and non-statutory guidance provide the framework that Early Years Teachers work within, however, it is the individual and collective practice of the staff employed that will effectively ensure that children are safe and their welfare is promoted within a setting. Before we look at the welfare and safeguarding requirements in relation to the Teacher Standards (Early Years), let us consider a wider practice context.

Child-centred practice

Effective safeguarding practices can only be achieved if an organization and the people working in it have a child-centred approach to the services that they offer. Having a clear understanding of the needs and views of the children is paramount when carrying out your responsibilities in safeguarding children.

As an Early Years Teacher, it is important to ensure that the views of the children attending your setting are actively sought.

Reflection 7.2: Are children's opinions heard and acted upon?

How often do you ask for children's opinions on the experiences that you offer them and then act upon their responses in a timely way?

Building a safe and open culture

If you have a safe and open culture within your setting, where children can express their views, wishes and wants and where these are heard, taken seriously and acted upon, you will be creating an environment that supports the safeguarding of children. Children benefit from feeling and knowing that they will be believed and that their voice and opinions are important. This safe and open culture supports and fosters attachment and positive relationships, both for the child and adults but also between children (see Chapter 3).

In order for a safe and open culture to be integral to a setting, you as an Early Years Teacher will need to model an open approach to communication with your colleagues and parents. Staff and parents also need to know that their voices will be heard, that you take their thoughts, opinions and ideas seriously and that you welcome feedback. In relation to safeguarding children, you will need to encourage and support colleagues to talk about their concerns, however small, that they may have about individual children. Early Years Teachers also need to sensitively challenge the values, beliefs and opinions of colleagues in relation to safeguarding children. Naturally we do not want to consider that children could be at risk of harm, however, early years practitioners need to reflect on situations and question appropriately and not always accept situations for what they are.

Case study 7.1: Mary and her mother

Mary is 42 months old and attends a pre-school setting in a small village in an area that is perceived locally as affluent. The majority of children attending the setting are white and have parents who are professionally qualified. Mary's mother takes and collects her from pre-school every morning. Mary has been attending the pre-school for a year and staff have a positive relationship with Mary and her mother.

On one morning Mary's mother does not arrive at 11.30a.m. to collect her. Staff follow the setting's policy for when children are not collected and try and contact Mary's mother. After 90 minutes of not being able to contact either of Mary's parents, staff are pleased to see Mary's mother arrive at the pre-school. She apologizes, explaining that she had fallen asleep and hadn't realized the time. Staff accepted the explanation and Mary left with her mother.

Reflection 7.3: Concern and response

What would you do in this situation?

Would you accept Mary's mother's explanation without further consideration?

Consider: is it normal for an adult to fall asleep at 11a.m. in the morning?

Could Mary's mother be:

- working nights as they are having financial difficulties?
- ill, physically, or does she have mental health problems?
- coping with alcohol or drug addiction?

Are things generally well for the family?

Such questions need to be considered and followed through to ensure a child like Mary is safe and the family can receive further support if they require it. How many times are questions not asked and situations accepted in your setting? In an open and safe culture questions can be raised between colleagues and parents in a sensitive and supportive way.

Before the specific responsibilities for early years providers (contained in the Early Years Foundation Stage Safeguarding and Welfare Requirements) are explored in depth, it is important to consider and clarify the meaning of safeguarding and child protection.

Working Together to Safeguard Children (DCSF 2010, Section 1.20) defines safeguarding and promoting the welfare of children as:

- protecting children from maltreatment;
- preventing impairment of children's health or development;
- ensuring that children grow up in circumstances consistent with the provision of safe and effective care;
- taking action to enable all children to have the best outcomes.

Safeguarding is essentially the overarching umbrella that encompasses the preventative approaches to promoting the welfare of children – child protection is an element of safeguarding and refers to the specific activity associated under Section 17 or Section 47 of the Children Act 2004 (HM Government 2004).

Meeting the Teachers' Standards (Early Years) and the Welfare and Safeguarding Requirements

All registered early years providers have to have a written policy and procedure that safeguard children, which includes the use of mobile phones and cameras. The policy should align with guidance in *What to Do If You Are Worried a Child Is Being Abused*. Any policy should be transparent and applicable for staff and parents and all other visitors to the setting. Primarily it should ensure that the child's needs are the priority. In order for the policy and associated procedures to be transparent, parents and staff should be asked to sign a declaration confirming that they have read and agree to the policy. It should be explained to parents that practitioners will act within the policy if they have any concerns that a child is at potential risk. This practice also supports practitioners when communicating with parents about any concerns that they have as they can relate back to the parents that they have agreed to the setting's safeguarding policy. This approach supports an open and safe culture within an organization where concerns can be discussed openly with staff and parents and where safeguarding and the needs of the child are central to the ethos of the setting.

Reflection 7.4: Policy review and amendment

How often is your setting's policy reviewed and amended if required?

Do you know who is responsible for this or do you complete this as a staff team taking a collective responsibility for safeguarding within your setting?

All registered early years providers must identify a designated safeguarding lead within the setting who is trained in the identification of the signs and symptoms of possible abuse and neglect and how to respond effectively to these:

The lead practitioner is responsible for liaison with local statutory children services agencies and with the Local Safeguarding Children's Board. They must provide support, advice and guidance to any other staff on an on-going basis and on any specific safeguarding issues as required. The lead practitioner must attend a child protection training course that enables them to identify, understand and respond appropriately to signs of possible abuse and neglect.

(DfE 2012: 13)

The designated safeguarding officer within a setting should be someone who has responsibility for the safeguarding policy and for ensuring that staff are supported in working within it and carrying this out. It is important that parents are aware of the policy and understand the role and responsibilities of the designated safeguarding officer. The designated safeguarding officer is not solely responsible for safeguarding children who are attending the setting. Every member of staff has a responsibility to identify when a child is potentially at risk and act upon this concern in accordance with the setting's policy. In line with the Children Act 2004 (HM Government 2004) and *Working Together to Safeguard Children and Promote the Welfare of Children* (DfES 2006c), there is safeguarding training that is specific to the role of designated safeguarding officer within an early years setting. This training explores the role and its associated responsibilities and details the process that needs to be followed if a practitioner has concerns about a child's welfare.

Guidance for all practitioners working with children and families, as detailed in *What to Do If You Are Worried a Child Is Being Abused*, states: 'If you are responsible for making referrals you should know who to contact in police, health, education, school and children's social care to express concerns about a child's welfare' (DfES 2006b: 11).

It is usual for the designated safeguarding officer to be the first person that is alerted to any concerns. They then have a responsibility to discuss these concerns with the child's parents and any other professionals relevant to the situation. As an Early Years Teacher, you may be the designated safeguarding officer within your setting. Even if you are not in this role, as an Early Years Teacher, you will be supporting colleagues to discuss concerns, however small, and ensuring that these concerns are acted upon appropriately.

Reflection 7.5: Differences of opinion

How would you approach a situation where the designated safeguarding officer has not, in your opinion, acted appropriately to a concern raised about a child and their family?

Who within your setting can you discuss this with?

Who outside of your setting can you discuss this with?

What responsibility do you have to safeguard children?

Leading practice: ensure all staff are aware of and understand the settings policy and procedures and act appropriately

This requirement can initially be met through a comprehensive induction course for new staff. New members of staff should not just be given a copy of the setting policies and procedures or just shown where they can be accessed. They should have the opportunity to discuss policies and procedures, allowing for explicit clarification of what they actually mean and recognition of the implications for their individual responsibilities. This process should ideally be completed by the new staff member's line manager and/or their mentor within the setting. Further meetings should be conducted to discuss again the policy and procedure to ensure that the practitioner has an understanding of the role they have in safeguarding children.

Reflection 7.6: Staff induction

How is induction of new staff undertaken in your setting?

Is it a 'first day' process or a supportive process over a set period of time?

How is support offered to new members of staff?

Do you identify a mentor who can support them through the initial six months at the setting?

Policies and procedures need to be reviewed on a regular basis and this process should include and involve all staff. Revision to safeguarding policies will be led by the designated safeguarding lead within the setting and should include any changes to legislation and LSCB recommendations. This is an opportunity to have a professional discussion about safeguarding and to re-confirm with staff the collective and individual responsibilities in relation to safeguarding children. When changes are made to the setting's safeguarding policy, staff and parents will need to be asked to read and sign a new declaration stating that they have read and agree to the policy.

Reflection 7.7: Reviewing policies and procedures

How often is your safeguarding policy reviewed?

Who is responsible for this?

Are all staff involved in this process?

How do you engage with parents?

It is important to remember that parents do need to be informed of any changes to policy and procedures and that they understand why the changes have been made.

Training staff in order for them to understand and identify the signs of possible abuse and neglect at the earliest opportunity

LSCBs have responsibility for the co-ordination and quality assurance of the safeguarding training that will be available through services and organizations represented on the LSCB. Staff in early years settings should be supported in attending training that is appropriate to their role and responsibilities. *Working Together to Safeguard Children* (Department for Children, Schools and Families 2010) guidance clearly states that all employers have the responsibility to identify adequate and reliable resources and support for multi-agency training and release staff to attend appropriate multi-agency training courses. The guidance also gives definitions of training and which groups of practitioners should have access to the different levels of training, depending on the level of contact they have with children and young people:

- *Universal (Groups 1 and 2)*: This training is mandatory for all staff who are in regular contact with children and young people, adults who are parents or carers and vulnerable adults.
- *Targeted (Groups 3 and 4)*: This training is mandatory for all staff who work predominantly with children, young people and families and who may be asked to contribute to assessments of children in need.
- *Specialist (Groups 5 and 6)*: Staff in this group should require a higher level of expertise: a fuller understanding of how to work together to identify and assess concerns and to plan, undertake and review interventions.

Using these definitions, all early years practitioners should attend multi-agency universal training. The designated safeguarding lead within the setting should also attend specialist designated person's training. Other specialist training may also be appropriate for the designated safeguarding lead to attend, such as an introduction to domestic abuse. Staff will need to undertake 'refresher' safeguarding training every three years or after significant changes to legislation or local policy.

Attending safeguarding training at any level can have an emotional effect on practitioners and as an Early Years Teacher you may need to support practitioners who have been affected by the course content. This should allow for open discussions that support the safe and open culture within the setting.

Reflection 7.8: Emotional support for staff

What opportunities are available for staff to talk about the feelings and emotions that can be evoked by attending safeguarding training?

> How could you ensure staff feel supported following their attendance at safeguarding training?

There are on-line safeguarding packages available, however, these do not allow practitioners to discuss safeguarding within a multi-agency forum as recommended by the guidance within *Working Together to Safeguard Children* (Department for Children, Schools and Families 2010). Attending multi-agency training offers practitioners the opportunity to gain increased understanding of different organizations and individual roles and responsibilities. In addition, it also offers the opportunity to early years practitioners to inform colleagues of their role and responsibilities.

Leading safer recruitment procedures

The requirement for anyone responsible for, or involved in, the recruitment of volunteers or practitioners working with children and young people to follow safer recruitment processes and to have attended safer recruitment training came into place following the deaths of Holly Wells and Jessica Chapman in 2002. Ian Huntley, the caretaker at Soham Village College, the school the girls attended, was convicted of their murders in 2003. It became clear, following his conviction, that he had been known to authorities over a period of four years in relation to allegations of eight sexual offences which had not been identified through the recruitment process for the role of caretaker at the school in 2001. The then Home Secretary, the Right Honourable David Blunkett MP asked Sir Michal Bichard to lead an independent inquiry into child protection measures, record keeping, vetting and information sharing in Humberside Police and Cambridgeshire Constabulary. Following the recommendations made by Sir Michael Bichard, it became a legal requirement in 2010 that recruitment panels appointing paid and voluntary staff to the children and young people's workforce should include at least one person who had been trained in safer recruitment. Ofsted include in their inspection a requirement to request evidence that each recruitment panel meet this requirement.

In 2009, the Children's Workforce Development Council (CWDC) issued guidance and training in safer recruitment processes. These gave information on best practice in relation to recruiting people to work with children and young people in non-school or further education settings. The Department for Children Schools and Families (DCSF) produced a separate guidance, *Safeguarding Children and Safer Recruitment in Education* (DfES 2006a) for schools. The CWDC and the DCSF guidance both focused on the processes involved in recruiting safely. The CWDC guidance applies not only to those practitioners who are regularly in contact with children but also those in a support function who are likely to be seen as a safe and trustworthy person because of their regular presence in a setting. The CWDC guidance details 12 steps to ensure safer recruitment processes are followed.

Before the post is released

Step 1: Ensure an up-to-date recruitment and selection policy describes the process and roles in place before the recruitment process begins.

Points to consider

The process should be clear and transparent and offer equality of recruitment. Roles should not be related to individual people but to the roles that need to be completed.

Step 2: Ensure that there is a safeguarding policy in place and that a statement about the setting's commitment to safeguarding is included in all recruitment and selection materials.

Points to consider

A setting's safeguarding policy should include reference to safer recruitment and that all recruitment will be undertaken in line with the policy.

Step 3: Ensure that there are up-to-date job description and person specifications for the role(s) that are to be recruited to, and that they have been agreed with the person responsible for recruitment.

Points to consider

Every role within an organization should have an associated job description and person specification. Offers of employment should be made to the applicant who meets the most requirements outlined in the person specification, through application and interview.

Step 4: Ensure that there is an appropriate advertisement prepared that contains all the necessary information about the role, timetables for recruitment and the setting's commitment to safeguarding.

Points to consider

The advertisement should include information on the post and be accessible to as wide a range of applicants as possible. The inclusion of the setting's commitment to safeguarding can be a deterrent to applicants who may be inappropriate for the role.

Step 5: Ensure that a suitable candidate information pack is available to applicants that contains all the required information about the setting, role, recruitment timetable, safeguarding policy/statement and application form.

Points to consider

All applicants should receive the same information pack and this needs to clearly state that CVs alone will not be acceptable and that the application form will need to be completed in order for the applicant to be considered for the role.

Before interviews

Step 6: Ensure that each application received is scrutinized in a systematic way by a short-listing panel in order to agree your shortlist before sending invitations to interview.

Points to consider

The short-listing panel should be the panel who will then interview the applicants short-listed. It is best practice to grade applicants against the requirements for the role as detailed in the person specification. Those meeting the most essential and desirable criteria are then short-listed for interview.

Step 7: Ensure that all appropriate checks have been undertaken in respect of the short-listed candidates.

Points to consider

Applicants should be given the choice, at application, to request that referees are contacted either before or after interview. However, an offer of employment should be subject to at least two suitable references being received.

Step 8: Ensure that all short-listed applicants receive the same letter of invitation to interview which gives all the necessary information.

> **Points to consider**
>
> A standard letter that is sent to short-listed applicants, that contains all the relevant information, is the most effective way of doing this.

Step 9: Ensure that a face-to-face interview is conducted for all short-listed applicants, based on an objective assessment of the candidate's ability to meet the person specification and job description.

> **Points to consider**
>
> All candidates should be asked the same questions, that is not to say that probing or additional questions cannot be asked, but equality of questions that have been agreed in advance will allow for the correct assessment of candidates based on the criteria contained in the person specification.
>
> Interviews should not be conducted by just one person, a minimum of two people from the organization should interview each applicant.

Step 10: Ensure that all specific questions designed to gain the required information about each candidate's suitability are asked, including those needed to address gaps in information supplied on the application from.

> **Points to consider**
>
> If there are any gaps in employment history on the application form, this should be explored at interview, as this can be an indication that the applicant does not want to declare an employment or has another specific reason why they have had a break in employment.

Before an appointment is made

Step 11: Ensure that a confident selection of a preferred candidate is based upon their demonstration that they are suitable for the role.

Points to consider

Consider using a scoring system that is based on the essential and desirable criteria as detailed in the person specification. By doing this, a comprehensive assessment based on the candidate's suitability for the role can be made.

Step 12: Ensure that the preferred candidate is informed that the offer of employment, including voluntary positions, is conditional on receiving satisfactory information from all necessary checks, including references.

Points to consider

Until you have received the outcomes of all the required checks including references and the applicant's DBR, no final offer of employment should be made. The successful candidate must be informed clearly that employment is subject to satisfactory information being received on all required checks.

Do acknowledge that following a safer recruitment process does require time and adequate resources in order to carry it out effectively. However, the potential consequences of not following the process need to be remembered. Ensuring that people who may pose a risk to children are prevented from educating and caring for children is an essential element of safeguarding children and young people. By following a safer recruitment process, an early years setting can benefit in many different ways including:

- the most suitable practitioners are recruited into the most suitable roles;
- increased cost effectiveness, the correct recruitment costs less than an inappropriate recruitment;
- young children are educated and cared for by appropriate practitioners who have the skills, experience, qualifications and motivation required for the role they are employed to do.

Reflection 7.9: Recruitment processes

Does your recruitment process meet the safer recruitment criteria above?

How are you involved in the recruitment of new staff and how can you influence the process to ensure it prevents, as far as possible, the recruitment of people who could pose a risk to children?

Inform Ofsted of any allegations of serious harm or abuse by any person at the premises

Any allegation made against a member of staff or parents should be taken seriously, even if you consider the alleged behaviour is not consistent with the person's usual behaviour. As well as contacting and informing Ofsted of any allegation, there is a clear procedure that must be followed. *Working Together to Safeguard Children* (DCSF 2010) states that an allegation may relate to a person who works with children who

- has behaved in a way that has harmed a child, or may have harmed a child;
- has possibly committed a criminal offence against or related to a child;
- has behaved towards a child or children in a way that indicates they may pose a risk of harm to children.

Early Years settings are required to have clear polices that are in line with those of the LSCB which detail the process that must be followed if an allegation is made against a member of staff. The manager of the setting must contact the Local Authority Designated Officer (LADO) in addition to Ofsted. It is the LADO's role to manage and oversee the process, offering advice and guidance to employers and liaising with police and other agencies.

In this situation, consideration will need to be given to the member of staff that the allegation has been made against and the remaining staff. Individuals may question their judgements of people, and staff may feel vulnerable and unsure of how to behave in fear of having an allegation made against them. As an Early Years Teacher it could be your role to support staff in these situations. Your sensitivity to how colleagues are feeling will be critical in supporting them through a very difficult time. However, you will need to ensure that confidentiality is maintained and that staff understand their role in the process. You may also need to consider how staff are going to continue working together if the allegation is found to be true or if proven unfounded.

The EYFS requires employers to offer employees regular supervision to support early years practitioners in their work. In the case of an allegation against a member of staff, increased opportunities for supervision, including group supervision, may be an appropriate forum to support staff.

Reflection 7.10: Staff support following an unfounded allegation

How would you and your colleagues support a staff member back to work following an unfounded allegation against them?

What systems do you have in place already in relation to staff support generally?

Information sharing and working with other professionals

Working Together to Safeguard Children (DCSF 2010) identifies that 'children are best protected when professionals are clear about what is required of them individually and how they need to work together.'

Section 10 of the Children Act 2004 requires each Local Authority to make arrangements to promote co-operation between the authority, each of the authority's relevant partners and such other persons or bodies working with children in the Local Authority area as the authority considers appropriate. The arrangements are to be made with a view to improving the well-being of all children in the authority's area, which includes protection from harm and neglect.

Several local serious case reviews – as above – have indicated that ineffectual information sharing had contributed significantly to the death or serious injury of the individual children. Practitioners can be fearful of sharing information as they are concerned about breaking confidentiality. However, *Working Together to Safeguard Children* (2010) clearly states that:

> No professional should assume that someone else will pass on information which they think may be critical to keeping a child safe. If a professional has concerns about a child's welfare and believes they are suffering or likely to suffer harm, then they should share the information with local authorities' children's social care.

Early years practitioners are supported in their information-sharing responsibilities through the guidance contained within *Information Sharing: Guidance for Practitioners and Managers* (DCSF 2008b). This document offers clarity as to when information can be shared and what information is considered confidential. As an Early Years Teacher, you will be sharing information on a daily basis with parents and colleagues specifically about individual children in relation to their development and their general well-being. When sharing information in relation to safeguarding children, you will need to consider whether or not the information is confidential and, if it is confidential, whether or not it is in the public interest to justify sharing information without consent.

Working with parents

The EYFS (DfE 2012) requires early years practitioners to work in partnership with parents. The Teachers' Standards (Early Years) also support partnership working with parents. Effective and positive relationships with parents will support you in your safeguarding responsibilities. If you have concerns about a child, you should report these first to the designated safeguarding lead within your setting. A decision will then be made as to whether or not further action should be taken. In either situation, parents should be informed and concerns discussed. These situations can be difficult and stressful for both the parents and the practitioner, however, the child must remain central to the reason for the discussion. Difficult conversations are made easier if they are factual and keep to key points. Both parents and practitioners can be supported by a clear and transparent safeguarding policy that parents are aware of. Raising concerns normally results in the child and the family receiving the support that they require at that point in time. Concerns should always be raised with the relevant people in, and external to, the setting even if you are concerned about how the parent is going to react. Remember the child's safety is paramount.

As an Early Years Teacher you may have to consider how you either share concerns with a parent yourself or how you will support colleagues in these situations.

Reflection 7.11: Relationships with parents

What currently supports positive relationships with parents within your setting?

How could you improve relationships with parents to support the safe and open culture within the setting?

Conclusion

This chapter has focused on safeguarding children, the current legislation relating to safeguarding and the role of an Early Years Teacher in meeting the statutory and non-statutory requirements in order to protect children. It is essential, in order to continue to protect children from the possible risk of abuse, that early years practitioners understand and carry out their safeguarding responsibilities both as an individual and as a member of an early years team. Legislation is there to protect children and gives practitioners working with children and young people the framework to work within. The child must remain at the centre of all safeguarding practices and procedures and this can be achieved by promoting and enabling environments where children and adults feel safe and secure, where their voices are heard and their needs met. A safe and open culture where children and adults can speak openly about their concerns, wants and wishes will support and enable practitioners to carry out their safeguarding responsibilities effectively and sensitively.

As an Early Years Teacher you are also a leader and supporter of others. This chapter contains vital information that cannot be forgotten among the other, sometimes more inspiring aspects of learning and teaching. These will always be more effective if the issues of health, safety, welfare and child protection are consistently managed.

Chapter 9 further identifies some specific ways that the key points within this chapter may be addressed within placements and your own settings. Remember, safeguarding is everyone's responsibility.

Reflection 7.12: A safe and open culture

How are you going to ensure that the early years setting you are employed in fosters and supports a safe and open culture for both children and adults?

What needs to change or what needs to be in place to enable this to happen?

8

Early Years Teachers as influential leaders
Joanne McKibbin and Gemma Pawson

Chapter objectives

By the end of this chapter you should be able to:

- identify how you can demonstrate leadership and wider professional responsibilities as an Early Years Teacher;
- reflect on different paradigms of leadership and how these can support ongoing developments within early years provision;
- value your influential role within the wider community;
- influence the ethos of your early years setting, bringing about change with children, families, colleagues and others.

Link with Teachers' Standards (Early Years) 2013

S8

Introduction

This chapter will explore leadership and the wider professional responsibilities that Early Years Teachers (EYTs) will need to demonstrate in order to effectively promote an inclusive and collaborative approach to working with others. The chapter will explore different paradigms of leadership and how these will support future developments in the early years sector. Case studies and activities have been provided to facilitate reflection and to support the development of thinking, ideas and practice. Furthermore, the influential role of EYTs as leaders within the wider community will be considered and how they contribute to the ethos of the early years setting.

The chapter covers:

- leadership paradigms;
- responding to change;
- leadership values and beliefs;
- continuing professional development;
- supervision, appraisal and coaching;
- multi-agency working.

Emerging paradigms

There has been an increase in the literature concerning the 'deconstruction' and 'reconceptualization' of leadership within the early years sector. To construct means to build, create or put something together, therefore, to deconstruct a concept such as leadership involves an honest process of reflective analysis to examine what is effective and what requires removal. The reconceptualization of leadership is about new paradigms that capture the complexity of leading in the early years setting. This is an exciting time to be an EYT as you will be able to contribute to the emergence of new paradigms, ensuring that children and families are central to this model and that leadership is viewed as a shared responsibility within staff teams.

The role of the EYT is multi-faceted; this can be compared to the theory of crystallization, as a crystal has many sides, and this reflects the many different angles, perspectives, cultural and pedagogical beliefs that contribute to the development of a leadership model. Crystallization seeks to produce knowledge about a particular phenomenon through generating a deepened, complex interpretation (Richardson 2000).

Although the theory of crystallization is linked to research methodology, specifically challenging the practice of triangulation, we believe that it can also be applied to the multidimensional workings of leadership within the early years sector. Richardson (2000: 934) states: 'We do not triangulate; we crystallize. We recognize that there are far more than "three sides" from which to approach the world.' Drawing on this analogy, just as a crystal has many sides and can look different, depending upon the context, light, time of day and perspective, so there are different elements of leadership and approaches. It is important that as an EYT you are able to be reflective and cultivate a multidimensional approach to leading, working with children, families and the local community.

Exploring leadership in early years

The concept of leadership is complex and difficult to define. The term 'leadership' is used across many different sectors, including the early years. Leadership can be viewed as a social construct that is shaped and developed by the culture, organization or context in which it is situated. There is a prolific amount of literature concerning the notion of leadership, in business, management, human resources, politics and education. In contrast, however, there is a limited amount of research dedicated to leading in the early years sector (Muijs et al. 2004; Aubrey 2011; Rodd 2012).

As a result, leadership within the early years sector has evolved in an ad-hoc fashion by drawing on traditional models from business such as trait theory, which focuses on specific qualities, skills, and attributes that contribute to being a good leader. Transactional theory explores power and how it is used to drive and motivate staff teams. These traditional models promote a culture whereby there is a clear distinction between the leader and the staff team, where things are 'done to' as opposed to 'done with', though this may not always be intentional. As a result, we believe these approaches are not fit for purpose as the focus is placed on one person as the leader. As an EYT, you will not be working in isolation, on the contrary, you will be working as part of a team. It is clear from the emerging literature (McDowall Clark and Murray 2012) that a shift is taking place whereby new and meaningful paradigms of leadership are being created through reflective dialogue. The complexity of the early years sector requires the emergence of a different type of leadership model as historically early years leadership has been constructed via a 'pick' n mix' approach. This reinforces the importance of developing unique early years leadership paradigms that reflect the complex, diverse areas of practice, thus making it inclusive, rather than following the traditional, exclusive hierarchical business models. This will make it more relevant to early years practice in the twenty-first century and reflect the distinctive identity of the early years community.

Research conducted by Sylva et al. (2004) explores the factors that contributed to effective practice in the early years. The Effective Provision of Pre-School Education (EPPE) project made direct links between strong leadership and how this positively impacts on the quality of provision for children, families and the community. However, the EPPE project places significant emphasis on the leader (singular) rather than focusing on leadership as a shared responsibility.

Further research carried out by Raelin (2004) explores the concept of 'leaderful' practice. We believe that 'leaderful' practice offers an exciting and emancipatory model of leadership that encapsulates elements of practice that reflect the fundamental principles of the early years community. Raelin (2004: 66) identifies the four key elements of 'leaderful' practice:

- *Collective leadership* means that everyone in the group can serve as a leader; the team is not dependent on one individual to take over.

- *Concurrent leadership* means that not only can many members serve as leaders, but also they can do it at the same time. No one, not even a supervisor, has to stand down when any team member is making his or her contribution as a leader.

- *Collaborative leadership* means that everyone is in control of and can speak for the entire team. All members pitch in to accomplish the work of the team. Together, they engage in a mutual dialogue to determine what needs to be done and how to do it.

- *Compassionate leadership* means that team members commit to preserving the dignity of every individual on the team, considering each other when a decision is made or action taken.

Case study 8.1: Te Köpae Piripono Mäori Early Childhood Centre in New Zealand

The notion of 'leaderful' practice influenced the research that was carried out at Te Köpae Piripono Mäori Early Childhood Centre in New Zealand (Tamati et al. 2008) where they sought to explore the concept of leadership with the aim of improving the educational experiences and lives of Mäori children and their families. The research was located within the context of the Mäori culture; they sought to discover how all members of the community contribute to being leaderful. Significantly, Ngä Takohanga e Wha, the four responsibilities, shown below, encapsulate a framework whereby everyone, young and old, is seen as a leader with 'leaderful' qualities. According to Tamati et al. (2008: 26), the four responsibilities are:

1 *Te Whai Takohanga - Having responsibility*: Relates to having designated roles and positions of responsibility.
2 *Te Mouri Takohanga - Being responsible*: Relates to an individual's attitude and actions. Being responsible is about being professional, acting ethically and appropriately, being honest, being positive and open to others and different perspectives.
3 *Te Kawe Takohanga - Taking responsibility*: Is about courage, risk-taking, having a go, taking up the challenge and trying new things.
4 *Te Tuku Takohanga - Sharing responsibility*: Is about sharing power, roles and positions. But more than this, it is about relationships. Sharing responsibility denotes an interaction and engagement with others, being able to listen to others' points of view, acknowledging different perspectives and also asking for and providing assistance.

Having a shared leadership approach is promoted by Whitaker (1993: 74), who offers a concise and realistic definition of the complexity of a leader's work: 'Leadership is concerned with creating the conditions in which all members of the organisation can give of their best in a climate of commitment and challenge. Leadership helps an organisation to work well.'

In Australia, Lewis and Hill (2012) have drawn on extensive research and national consultations to develop an understanding of leadership in the early years that concludes:

- leadership is about identity – it starts from within;
- leadership is about influence (both directly and indirectly) and responsibility, and is therefore potentially open to everyone;
- leadership demonstrates respect as an enactment of ethical commitments;
- leadership is about qualities and values rather than position;
- there is not just one way to enact leadership – it is complex, dynamic, and varies from situation to situation and from culture to culture;
- leadership is about purpose;
- leadership capabilities can be professionally developed.

McDowall Clark and Murray (2012) offer a new paradigm of leadership called *leadership within*. It is interesting that this language has been used as it is similar to that of Lewis and Hill (2012). This emerging paradigm has three key areas:

- *catalytic agency* – signifies the role of the individual to make a difference, while respecting shared accountability for delivering high quality practice. This involves taking responsibility, questioning and challenging in a constructive manner to drive practice forward in a spirit of humility and valuing the process of change;
- *reflective integrity* – is the central component of leadership, it facilitates self-regulation, enabling you as an EYT to make sense of lived experiences, values and beliefs. This contributes to a culture of respect and empathy, laying the foundation for constructive change and open dialogue;
- *relational interdependence* – is an inclusive process that requires a deep commitment which demonstrates the value of others, their experiences, culture and belief systems. To create this shared learning community (Wenger 1998), dialogue needs to be fluid, appreciating that this is an evolving co-construction of ideas and practice.

Reflection 8.1: Catalytic agent

After examining the model of a Catalytic Agent (Figure 8.1 below), start your journey by following each stage. Locate yourself within each statement, and consider the following:

What are the challenges?

How can having an awareness of the Catalytic Agent model impact on your practice, self and others?

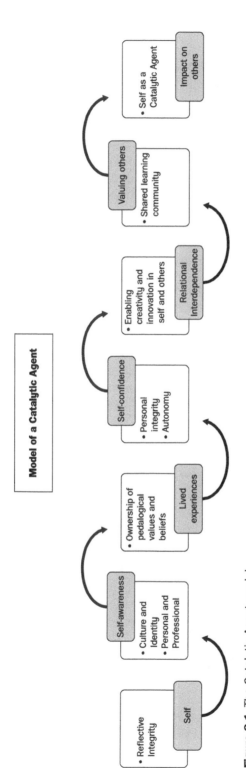

Figure 8.1 The Catalytic Agent model.

Source: adapted from McDowall Clark and Murray (2012).

Responding to change

As Rodd (2012: 182) comments, 'Change is a natural and necessary phenomenon, and one of the few certainties in all aspects of human life.' Gasper (2010) points out that a common reaction to change is to resist it. The stages individuals may go through during change are outlined by Scott and Jaffe (2004) as shock and denial, resistance and exploration, before committing to and accepting the change.

Responding to, as opposed to reacting to (responding is reaction with thought), the latest government agenda and policy shifts requires you as an EYT to be astute, knowledgeable, innovative, creative and poised. While you may not consider yourself to be political, it is essential as an Early Years Teacher that you are aware of the current agenda and the impact that it may have on the services that you offer: 'Mainstream politics – with its particular institutions (government, ministries, parliaments) and processes (general elections, parliamentary votes, budgets, the making and implemen-tation of policy) is the arena where decisions are made that impact on early years' (Dahlberg and Moss 2005:14).

Other policy reforms may directly affect the families that you work with and subsequently, the children who are in your setting. An example of policy impacting upon the early years sector is the introduction of the funding of places for 2-year-olds. From September 2013, Local Authorities will have a statutory duty to provide free early education to disadvantaged 2-year-olds (DfE 2013a). Eligible families will be entitled to 570 hours of free early education for their 2-year-olds. This equates to 15 hours a week over 38 weeks or 11.5 hours per week over 49 weeks. Further expan-sion is due to take place in September 2014 with an estimated 260,000 places required nationally for 2-year-olds.

Case study 8.2: Introduction of funding for places for 2-year-olds

As an EYT, you have been asked to work with Sophie and her team to develop practice and procedures following the introduction of the funding scheme for places for 2-year-olds. The rationale for this is that Sophie and her team need support to make constructive and sustainable change for the benefit of the children, families and prac-titioners within the setting.

The reason development is required

Sophie is the leader of what is traditionally referred to as the 'pre-school' room. She works with a small team of practitioners to provide a welcoming, appropriately chal-lenging, semi-structured environment in which the 3- and 4-year-olds are able to develop positive relationships and learn. Sophie is not aware of the emergent strategy of free funding for 2-year-olds and as a result she was surprised when she was informed that the nursery would be accepting 2-year-olds from September. Collectively the team decides that they will not alter the current provision, instead the 2-year-olds would have to 'fit in' and 'adapt'. Little time or thought was given to the transition of the younger children, who mostly were entering group care for the first time. In line with current practice, the 2-year-olds were not given special consideration with regards to transitional objects, which 3- and 4-year-olds are not permitted to bring into the setting.

As an organization, there are limited opportunities for staff meetings and no formal supervision. As a result, staff consultation is carried out on an 'ad-hoc' informal basis. Sophie's initial reaction to the change was that of resistance, she was negative about the idea and as a result the rest of the pre-school team were opposed also. September arrived and the new cohort of children began, as in previous years, the oldest children started first with a staggered intake for the younger children after this. By the end of September, all the 2-year-old children had attended a number of sessions. Immediately, it was obvious that the dynamics of the classroom had changed with 2-year-olds having differing needs to the 3- and 4-year-olds, that Sophie and the team have been working with. What contributes to the changing dynamics are:

- lower adult/child ratio;
- lack of specific resources and equipment suitable for 2-year-olds;
- different care needs of the younger children;
- different emotional needs to that of 3- and 4-year-olds;
- activities such as story time had not been adapted, with the younger children finding it difficult to concentrate;
- the routine had not been altered to meet the individual needs of the children;
- facilities have not been altered, such as providing sleep spaces;
- unrealistic staff expectations that 2-year-olds will be able to 'fit in' and 'adapt' in an environment that had been developed for older children;
- limited understanding of child development;
- unprepared for the level of support that parents and families accessing the 2-year-old funding may require;
- lack of staff supervision and limited opportunities for meetings;
- limited opportunity for the younger children to develop relationships with the Key Person due to the older children taking precedence over the younger children during the settling-in period;
- limited understanding of the role that transitional objects play during periods of change for younger children.

Sophie and the team have realized that, though they were resistant to change, their reflection of current practice has made them understand that the needs of the children are not being met.

Reflection 8.2: Effectiveness of provision in Case study 8.2

What initial action would you take to make the environment developmentally appropriate for all ages? Consider resources, routine and room layout.

How would you as an EYT develop trusting and meaningful relationships with colleagues?

How would you constructively involve the team in making the changes, why is this important?

How are you going to support the team to cultivate their knowledge and understanding of child development, working effectively with families and feeling confident and able to manage the change more effectively?

Activity 8.1: Action planning

Devise a plan to show the actions that you will take to support Sophie and the staff team in Case study 8.2, considering the time scale and who will be involved.

Leadership values and beliefs

As an EYT, it is important that you critically reflect on your own values and beliefs, being aware of the influence that this can have on you and the way in which you interact with children, families, other professionals and the community in which you are situated. Having an awareness of your pedagogical values is imperative, especially at times when government policy and political agenda are influential in educational 'reform' (see the comment above on the importance of the political agenda).

The Catalytic Agent model (Figure 8.1) considers the importance of values and beliefs within leadership, both individually and collectively. As an EYT, you may work within settings and with practitioners who have different values and belief systems to your own. Bolton (2010: 12) explores values and beliefs in practice, suggesting '[They] are rarely analysed or questioned . . . through reflexive practice professionals realise dissonance between their own values *in* practice and *their* espoused values, or those of their organisation.'

Being a reflective practitioner enables you to become conscious of your position, the tensions that can arise and the impact that you have on the culture and ethos of the organization, staff team, children, families, other professionals and the wider community. Reflective practice is viewed as a useful tool by Bolton (2010) and Goodson (2004), with which to locate oneself in the political and social structures of an organization. Reflexivity, which is a deeper level of reflection, supports the process of finding:

strategies to question our own attitudes, thought processes, values, assumptions, prejudices and habitual actions, to strive to understand our complex roles in relation to others. To be reflexive is to examine, for example, how we – seemingly unwittingly – are involved in creating social or professional structures counter to our own values.

(Cunliffe 2009: 87)

Children and their families now come from an increasingly diverse range of communities, ethnic groups and experiences. To drive practice forward, it is important to not only be aware of but to demonstrate genuine value which incorporates respecting and honouring children and their families.

When considering values and beliefs, this can raise dilemmas and complexities which cannot be ignored. As an EYT, you have an ethical responsibility to explore situations and options, at times through a different lens. Rowson (2006: 19) suggests: 'We generally see ethics as giving us a standpoint from which to decide what is right and wrong and what we ought or ought not to do.'

Activity 8.2: Ethics, values and beliefs

1   Consider how you could use Figure 8.2 to generate discussion points on key themes, areas for development, or to approach challenging situations.

2   This image, or one of your own, could be used to open up dialogue with staff teams.

Figure 8.2 Ethics, values and beliefs.

Continual Professional Development (CPD)

The British Educational Research Association (BERA) (2012: 6) guidance with regards to the quality of research carried out in education suggests it is dependent on the 'expertise of the researchers'. BERA further advocates it is a researcher's responsibility to undertake 'ongoing professional development' to ensure they have the required skills to meet the demands of their role. While BERA guidance focuses on research, the principle is a sound one for EYTs. Creating professional learning communities whereby development of self and others is valued and promoted will facilitate reflective integrity, relational interdependence, enable creativity and innovation, and generate opportunities for open dialogue with colleagues. Furthermore, research carried out by the Organisation for Economic Co-operation and Development (OECD 2008) recognizes that where teachers are deeply engaged in their own learning, there will be improved outcomes for children. Lambert (1998: 18) talks about leadership as being 'the reciprocal learning processes that enable participants in a community to construct meaning toward a shared purpose'.

Professional learning communities

A professional learning community enables practitioners to come together as a group to critically reflect and analyse their practice, knowledge and methods. It is a collaborative and inclusive approach that is learning-orientated, and enables growth and development within an organization and staff team (Stoll and Seashore Louis 2007). Characteristics of a professional learning community are defined by Hord and Sommers (2008) as:

- shared beliefs, values and vision;
- shared and supportive leadership;
- collective learning and its application;
- supportive conditions;
- shared reflective practice.

Activity 8.3: Professional learning community

Explore each of the characteristics above and consider the following:

1   Do you promote a professional learning community in your setting – if yes, how do you do this, if no, why not?
2   What are the benefits for you, the staff, the children and their families if a professional learning community is promoted?
3   What are the challenges and how could you overcome these?
4   Can children and families be involved in a professional learning community?
5   Can you identify commonalities within the model of a Catalytic Agent (Figure 8.1) and would this further the promotion of a professional learning community?

A significant factor when forming professional learning communities is the development of trusting relationships and environments. Frowe (2005) makes direct links between trust and security, which he suggests are key factors when promoting constructive learning environments. J. Roberts (2011: 695) points out that 'relation-ships of trust are central to the provision of public services', and this appears to assume there is a common criterion with regards to the understanding and expectation of trust. The expectation of trust is explored by Groundwater-Smith and Sachs (2002: 343) who consider that 'at its best, trust assumes that promises will be kept and relationships will be dependable'. With the emphasis on partnership between parents and early years settings becoming more significant, the establishment of positive relationships becomes more meaningful. The issue of trust is advocated within the EYFS (DfE 2012), which connects trust to the knowledge and skills of the workforce. The relationship between trust and professionalism is made by Brock (2012) who interestingly makes direct links between professional knowledge and establishing trust; this is particularly pertinent regarding the role you play in your setting.

Professional development of self and others

It is important to continue to develop as an individual by facilitating an attitude that encourages the deconstruction of ideas and welcomes new paradigms of thinking. Professional development is not just about you as an EYT, its sphere of influence is far greater and should impact upon the environment and your work with children, their families and the local community. Thus, professional development is not a selfish pursuit but rather an essential element that is necessary to develop a community that values the learning process. Constructing an environment which values and respects the active pursuit of discovering new knowledge, taking innovative approaches to problem solving and developing creative models of practice encapsulates a deeper dimension of learning. Settings that engage in research, both formal and informal, will cultivate the sense of curiosity and creativity in children and staff teams. Rodd (2012: 210) states that 'effective leaders need to embrace a research orientation'. By creating a culture and an environment in which the cycle of action research is acknowledged, valued and nurtured, there will be many benefits, including:

- developing a reflective community;
- respect for theory but able to explore beyond;
- curiosity;
- shared learning and knowledge;
- active agent in a research community;
- co-researcher with children, families and co-workers;
- enriching practice and improving outcomes;
- creating and evolving practice, thinking and concepts.

The Reggio Emilia approach has been influential in redefining the image of the child (Rinaldi 2012). Early years practitioners can draw inspiration from the Reggio Emilia approach, which views the child as an active participant (researcher) in their own learning, the learning of others and within their community. Your image of the child will determine your pedagogical practice and how you perceive your role as an EYT.

Brownlee (2004) identifies that the 'constructivist approach' is one that does not see children, families, co-workers or the wider community as empty vessels to be filled but rather as active and creative beings who construct their own knowledge. Olsson (2009: 11) describes the practitioner as someone who:

> has the role of listening carefully to children as well as arranging situations where children can work with their questions and problems . . . [so that] children, together with their peers and teachers, can be engaged in the collective construction of knowledge and values.

Rinaldi (2012: 245) discusses how innovation and research act as a stimulus to challenge practice. She states: 'They shake up our frames of reference because they force us to look at the world through new eyes . . . yet only searching and researching are guaranteed to lead us to that which is new, that which moves us forward.'

Supervision, appraisals and coaching

Supervision and appraisals are often perceived to have the same purpose, however, there are distinctions between the two.

Definition of terms

Supervision is planned and structured time between a supervisor and a supervisee. It provides the supervisee with the opportunity to explore issues by critically reflecting on practice, knowledge, self and others. The practice of supervision values staff members, enabling them to be listened to in a non-threatening, constructive environment which enables the supervisee to move forward and develop their knowledge and practice.

An appraisal is an annual meeting (which is ideally reviewed at six months) between a staff member and their line manager. It is an opportunity to review practice over the last year and identify areas of strength and those areas that would benefit from development. However, the appraisal should not raise practice issues or concerns that have not been previously discussed and addressed in supervision. The procedure of an appraisal enables aims and objectives to be set for the next 12 months in line with the organization's expectations. This is an opportunity to outline professional development and plan ahead by setting focused and realistic targets.

The Serious Case Review of Nursery Z (Plymouth Safeguarding Children Board 2010) identified that lack of staff supervision contributed to an environment where practitioners felt silenced, protocols and practice were unchallenged, and reflective practice was minimal. As a result, professional dialogue did not take place and an abusive environment was allowed to fester. The recommendations from the Serious Case Review influenced aspects of the revised EYFS (DfE 2012: 17), with supervision becoming a *statutory* requirement for all early years staff:

- Providers must put appropriate arrangements in place for the supervision of staff who have contact with children and families. Effective supervision provides support, coaching and training for the practitioner and promotes the interests of children.

- Supervision should foster a culture of mutual support, teamwork and continuous improvement which encourages the confidential discussion of sensitive issues.
- Supervision should provide opportunities for staff to do the following:
  - discuss any issues – particularly concerning children's development or well-being;
  - identify solutions to address issues as they arise;
  - receive coaching to improve their personal effectiveness.

Figure 8.3 shows the benefits of effective supervision.

Coaching

The process of coaching is different from supervision and appraisal. Coaching can take place on a day-to-day basis and involves supporting individuals and teams to move forward in their practice. Coaching involves asking questions, listening, supporting, advising, guiding and making suggestions to enable progression. Coaching is a facilitative approach that seeks to enable the individual to take responsibility, question their practice and make appropriate changes with the support of a skilled and experienced practitioner.

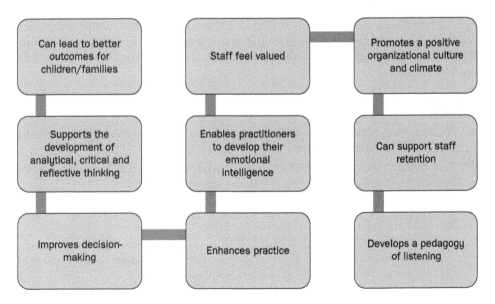

Figure 8.3 Benefits of effective supervision.

Source: Adapted from Maclean (2012).

Concept of multi-agency working

The concept and practice of multi-professional working is not new, with the Children Act 1989 establishing a statutory requirement for agencies to work in collaboration and to find ways to 'work together better' (Cheminais 2009: 1). However, there has been an increased emphasis on its importance in recent years with the Children Act 2004 placing a direct duty on Local Authorities to promote co-operation between agencies with the expectation that professionals will work together in order to promote children's well-being.

As an Early Years Teacher you may work with professionals from a diverse range of agencies such as:

- Health – health visitors, community nursery nurse, speech and language therapist, doctors (GPs), school nurses, occupational therapists (OTs), physiotherapists, nutritionists, children and adolescent mental health services (CAMHS).
- Social Care – social worker, contact facilitator, outreach workers, foster Carers.
- Education – Early Years Teacher, Early Years Educator, Key Stages 1 and 2 Teachers, Head Teacher, Education Welfare Officer, teaching assistants, administration team, wrap around care staff team, mid-day meal supervisors, education psychologists.
- Housing – housing officer.
- Voluntary Sector – Citizen Advice Bureau, portage workers, play link, charitable organizations.

This list is not exhaustive and roles may be interchangeable between services, for instance, outreach workers cross a range of service areas. They may work within a children's centre with families or in a social care setting facilitating family contact sessions or working within the voluntary sector.

The benefits of multi-agency working is that it provides opportunities for professionals to enter into dialogue which improves understanding and awareness of roles, needs, services and enhances positive outcomes, thus enriching provision for children and their families.

Benefits

- Promotes a holistic approach across agencies to develop services that meet the needs of children and families.
- Provides opportunities for dialogue across agencies, finding a common language with no dominant discourse controlling the agenda.
- Reduces the number of services that children and families need to access to support their needs.
- Provides continuity of care across services.
- Various professionals offer different perspectives, which can develop creative approaches to meet the needs of children and families.
- Develops a sustainable approach to leadership.
- Promotes the voice of the child.
- Promotes the voice of the child's families and carers.

- Captures the wider community by drawing on expert local knowledge from the different professionals.

While government rhetoric advocates multi-agency working as an area of high importance, the potential difficulties in achieving success are not always acknowledged. The complexities of multi-agency working are explored by Duffy and Marshall (2009: 111) who argue that 'multi-agency working takes time. Teams need time to come together to develop shared vision and understanding in their roles'. While there are many benefits, there can also be challenges that can create boundaries and restrictions.

Challenges

- Different organizations have different policies, procedures and agendas.
- Varied values and belief systems of organisations.
- Building trust between professionals who have different qualifications, approaches to practice and professional identities.
- Challenges of finding space and time to develop new group dynamics.
- Challenges of differing priorities with regards to workload, commitments and expectations of organizations.
- Lack of confidence in own professional identity.
- Lack of understanding of other professionals' roles and responsibilities.
- Limited communication which draws on exclusive language – excluding rather than including all participants.

Being aware of the challenges that you may encounter, and acknowledging that multi-agency working can be complex, multi-faceted and requires perseverance, will enable you to identify strategies to effectively approach this area of work.

Case study 8.3: Multi-professional practice

As an EYT, you have been asked to work with Tasmina and her team to develop their knowledge and understanding of the benefits and challenges of multi-professional practice. Tasmina and her team are increasingly supporting children and families who are accessing services provided by other professionals. However, their knowledge and understanding of this area of work is limited, impacting on practice.

Why development is required

Tasmina is the leader of what is traditionally referred to as the 'toddler' room. She works with a team of four practitioners to provide a welcoming, caring and stimulating environment for children aged 18–30 months. Many of the children and families that the team work with are either known to or are directly accessing services provided by a wide range of external professionals. Tasmina is aware of the benefits of building constructive relationships with other professionals to support the children and families she works with. However, she has limited experience of multi-agency work and lacks confidence, thinking other professionals are more knowledgeable than she is. Tasmina's lack of confidence is having an impact on the team as a whole. You have recently over-heard two members of the team saying external professionals do not value them as 'they are only early years practitioners, so why should they make an effort?'

Reflection 8.3: Leading practice within a multi-professional community

What initial action will you take to reassure Tasmina and the team that they are valuable members of the wider multi-professional community?

How will you facilitate the development of respectful working relationships with other professionals?

How will you help Tasmina and the team to develop their knowledge and understanding of multi-professional work (the benefits and challenges)?

Can you identify any relevant training opportunities the staff team might access to support their development?

What procedures will you put in place to monitor the team's progression so they confidently interact with other professionals and fully support the children and families they work with?

Conclusion

This chapter has explored a range of leadership paradigms and approaches that are pertinent to the early years sector. The chapter has highlighted the important role you have as an EYT in shaping change and developing provision to ensure positive and sustainable outcomes for children and families. Leadership does not exist in isolation but is about co-constructing an environment where everyone has a voice and feels they are a valued part of the community. As a leader you need to be aware of your own values and beliefs and how you perceive yourself, as this will impact on others. Using the Catalytic Agent model (Figure 8.1) as a stimulus, position yourself within this to deepen your awareness enabling you to become a creative and innovative leader. As a leader, you need to be confident, bold and courageous in moving practice and thinking forward, thus contributing to emerging leadership paradigms. Building shared learning communities which are inclusive rather than exclusive will contribute to sustainable leadership as children, families, practitioners, other professionals and members of the wider community will be active participants. As McDowall Clark and Murray (2012: 36) argue, 'Being proprietorial and not letting others in has no part in leadership and shows a lack of confidence in needing to claim the glory.'

9

A unique Early Years Teacher
Presenting my evidence for assessment
Jessica Johnson

Nobody cares how much you know until they know how much you care.

Theodore Roosevelt

Chapter objectives

By the end of this chapter you should be able to:

- acknowledge your own professional identity, holistically, as an Early Years Teacher with babies and young children;
- demonstrate how your knowledge and understanding, as a specialist of child development from birth, impacts on your leadership and support of high quality care and education;
- submit sound sources of evidence from personal practice with babies and young children, to competently address each of the eight Teachers' Standards (Early Years) (NCTL 2013b);
- engage confidently in the assessment process to gain Early Years Teacher Status (EYTS).

Link with Teachers' Standards (Early Years) 2013

S1, S2, S3, S4, S5, S6, S7, S8

Introduction

As an Early Years Teacher, consider Roosevelt's statement above in relation to your specific role with babies, young children, colleagues and families. You are, as stated at the end of Chapter 1, in a privileged position of continually combining care and knowledge (education) throughout all your provision. When you are preparing your evidence for assessment for Early Years Teacher Status, you need, quite rightly, to present your graduate-level knowledge. However, as will be highlighted throughout this chapter, you will also be demonstrating how you care for the ever-changing needs of individuals and groups – whether babies, toddlers, young children, staff or families – and provide learning opportunities throughout. Observation of your practice, as well as written tasks and portfolio building, are likely to provide sources of evidence for this expertise, as selected by your Early Years Initial Teacher Training (EYITT) provider. In this way, you will own the uniqueness of your Early Years Teacher Status, while being aware of the range of early years provision where you could be employed, which requires collaboration and flexibility.

So how are this uniqueness and the diversity across private, voluntary, independent and maintained sectors acknowledged nationally? The National College for Teaching and Leadership (NCTL) awards Early Years Teacher Status (EYTS) on behalf of the Department for Education (DfE). From the beginning of your training you will have your own unique DfE/NCTL EYTS number which will stay with you for life – so keep it safe. Employers, certainly in the maintained sector, will request it. Your Early Years Initial Teacher Training (EYITT) provider is contracted by the National College for Teaching and Leadership (NCTL) to organize an assessment process that addresses the requirements of providing evidence against the Teachers Standards (Early Years) (NCTL 2013b). This is likely to draw on the range of formative and summative assessment procedures (see Chapter 6) developed nationwide for Early Years Professional Status (EYPS) 2006, and subsequently extended through eight Prime Organisations for EYPS and Early Years Teacher 2012. However, there will also be key differences, as with your entry requirements, to correlate with assessment for Primary Initial Teacher Training. If you have colleagues and mentors who can already call themselves Early Years Teachers, having gained EYPS or EYTS from a 2012 programme, do value their Status as equivalent to yours while sharing developments in the assessment process with them from the start (DfE 2013f).

So what makes Early Years Teacher Status different from other Early Years Teacher positions, for example, those with Qualified Teacher Status or Montessori Teaching Diplomas? Look at the following Preamble for the Teachers' Standards (Early Years):

Early Years Teachers make the education and care of babies and children their first concern. They are accountable for achieving the highest possible standards in their professional practice and conduct. Early Years Teacher Status is awarded to graduates who are leading education and care and who have been judged to have met all of the standards in practice from birth to the end of the Early Years Foundation Stage (EYFS).

Early Years Teachers act with integrity and honesty. They have strong early development knowledge, keep their knowledge and skills up-to-date and are self-critical. Early Years Teachers recognize that the Key Stage 1 and Key Stage 2 curricula follow the EYFS in a continuum. They forge positive professional relationships and work with parents and/or carers in the best interests of babies and children.

(NCTL 2013b)

You are required to be a blender of care and education from the start, so build that in to your vision of personal practice and leadership. Then think critically about how you are seen by babies and young children, colleagues, parents and other professionals. What do they call you? What would they think your 'first concern' was if they shadowed you for a day? Revisit Chapter 1 to position yourself within the ongoing debate about professionalism in early years. You will be practising your professionalism from the time you apply for, and start, the programme. Often it is the programme administrators who identify lack of professional conduct, when course requirements such as punctual attendance, placement procedure and deadlines are disregarded, so develop positive, respectful behaviour with all staff and peers throughout your training. You are being observed and heard!

Activity 9.1: Personal profile

1   Highlight key words in the Preamble above, such as 'leading education and care.'
2   Using up to 400 words, write a profile of your career to date and current role to identify how you meet the demands of these key words.
3   Then, note which key words have not been addressed and how you may explore them further.
4   Update this profile throughout your programme as you gradually cover all the key words.

Case study 9.1: Early Years Professional/Teacher Profile

Now compare your profile with the profile of Sue, an Early Years Professional.

I began my career in childcare working with children aged 3–5 years; this soon extended to children from 0–5, many of whom had additional needs. I mainly worked in crèches, playgroups and school settings, increasing my knowledge and development at each stage of my career.

Seven years ago I moved to take on managing a children's centre based in a multicultural area of an East London borough. Here I have worked with a wide range of families and supported them and their children through the transitions of life such as home to nursery or nursery to primary school. I also support and lead practitioners to provide a stimulating environment following the EYFS 2012 curriculum as well as other government legislation such as the SEN Code of Practice. It was here that I decided to research for my own professional development and decided to complete my Foundation Degree leading to successfully gaining my BA (Hons) in Children's Special Needs and Inclusive Education (S8.3). I decided to complement this qualification by following on with the Early Years Professional pathway.

I aim to provide a friendly and welcoming environment where all children can learn and develop through play. I feel that I lead, support and model good practice to 11 practitioners, helping them to plan and develop a range of differentiated activities for all the children attending my setting. I complete regular supervisions and actively take part in Team around the Child, Child Protection, and Looked after Children meetings, supporting the families and working with other professionals, such as speech and language therapists, physiotherapists and health visitors making sure the children have access and are included in all activities in the setting.

I have led practitioners through changes such as the merging of the 2–3s and 3–5s group rooms into a 2–5s room, to be able to implement further spaces for the 2-year-old Free Early Education Entitlement, and further changes are about to happen with the setting joining the school to became an academy.

With these changes I will have a further opportunity to make a difference in the early years environment by taking up a position to work closer with the families and children with additional needs.

In the future I would like to continue my studies by completing a Master's qualification in Multi-Professional Practice.

The Preamble and the Personal Profile enable you to see the holistic vision of the role of Early Years Teacher. Share your profile with others on your programme and identify the range of job role titles and responsibilities you, or staff in your placement, have. Very few, at the time of writing, are likely to be known as Early Years Teacher, but you will be among those who make this title familiar across early years provision.

Employer links

EYITT providers and early years employers are required to work together to support routes towards EYTS. Depending on your selected pathway, you will be working with employers and managers as you provide evidence for assessment.

While on the Graduate Entry (Mainstream) full-time or Undergraduate Entry route, you have responsibility within each placement to engage with the specific policies, procedures and expectations of the employers and managers. Your programme tutors/placement liaison tutors will also be working with these placement staff to ensure you have a mentor or supervisor, who may or may not be the employer. Value the differences between settings as you extend your own experience and ensure you have opportunities to engage with the whole age range sufficiently to evidence your understanding of child development from birth to age 5. You are likely to be observed within each setting as part of the assessment process so your role in building these relationships demonstrates collaborative skills (Standard 7).

As a graduate on the Graduate Entry (employment-based or assessment-only) routes you will already be an experienced early years practitioner, and possibly the employer of yourself and others. Each EYITT will need to work with your setting to ensure quality provision for children and families is maintained, while you are released to attend training sessions and additional placements as well as being 'out-of-ratio' for assessment purposes when required.

Personal practice record

In order to demonstrate delivery of high quality care and education across provision for birth to 5-year-olds, you will be expected to provide evidence of working – or having a placement – in at least two different early years settings. Your EYITT is likely to have a template to record your hours of practice, but if you create your own template, ensure it covers the timing of each session, the age group in months of the babies and children, the specific context (e.g. baby room, sessional pre-school, nursery class) and is signed by the manager.

In addition, you are required to spend a minimum of 10 days in a Key Stage 1 setting to observe practice and to 'recognize that the Key Stage 1 and Key Stage 2 curricula follow the EYFS in a continuum' (NCTL 2013b). Again, it is important to keep a record, signed by the teacher, of these hours.

Graduate knowledge and understanding of early years care and education

As you will be aware, early years group provision, unlike the expectation mainly for primary and secondary education to have graduates, requires the manager to 'hold at least a full and relevant level 3 qualification and at least half of all other staff . . . at least a full and relevant level 2 qualification' (DfE 2012: 18). Then, in relation to staff:child ratios, each group for under-twos and 2-year-olds requires at least one individual with a full and relevant level 3 and experience of the specific age group (DfE 2012: 19). It is not until consideration of children aged 3 and over that recognition of Qualified Teacher Status, Early Years Professional Status or another suitable level 6 qualification (which is full and relevant) appears within the Early Years Foundation Stage statutory framework (DfE 2012). Here the implication is in relation to being able to have 1:13 as opposed to 1:8 staff:child ratio, so it may be deemed to be cost effective, but how is it supported by theoretical underpinning of practice considering the content of Chapters 2 and 3? Here is a dilemma for your consideration.

Activity 9.2: 'Graduateness' in early years provision

1   You may be having part of your assessment for EYTS in a setting where, quite justifiably, other experienced leaders and staff have level 3 qualifications or are studying hard towards the new Level 3 Early Years Educator or a Foundation Degree/BA(Honours) Early Years while they work. Look for ways to constructively value/support these studies.

2   You are expected to be 'leading education and care', so how do you collaboratively share your knowledge of child development, legislation, theories and current research about practice, for example, from Chapters 2 and 3, constructively with others?

Graduate level 6 work acknowledges that:

- you have up-to-date knowledge and understanding of relevant material and how key concepts relate to one another;

- you acknowledge ambiguity, a sense of the uncertainty or the contradictory nature of materials;

- you can take a critical approach to your work, using a range of evidence, reasoned argument and reflection;

- you have a level of independence/autonomy to solving problems;

- you are willing to innovate or experiment and explore new ideas, being creative;

- you are able to present evidence in clear, accurate English, with good academic practice of citation and referencing.

Some of you may also be taking Master's level 7 modules, further enhancing your critical analysis, reflection and research skills. Do make use of the Reference section at the end of the book as an initial source to search areas of interest arising from previous chapters. Your training provider is likely to have links to e-books and e-journals for ease of access.

Written essays enable you to show your ability to research an area related to child development, demonstrate current knowledge and understanding and state why you are choosing to develop certain practices. Practitioner research takes that a step further to show you are able to follow the selected action through with others, including children, able to evaluate and reflect so that you are activating change. It is the practice that will show your competencies in relation to each Standard, so your evidence needs to directly relate to what you have done/are doing, writing as 'I . . .'

When producing assessment materials at these academic writing levels, you are also seeking to provide high quality care and education, so your role is unique because of your ability to relate theory to practice. You may be doing, or have just done, specific practitioner research that can provide evidence against a combination of Standards. Chapter 8 explores reflective cycles and reflexivity, along with the type of leadership skills that can help you link knowledge and understanding with providing evidence from practice. Use those as you now identify how you can provide specific evidence against each individual standard. The supporting statements in each Standard, rather than being a direct check list, are there to help you identify the range of evidence you can draw together to show your competency against the Standard, especially when you are collecting examples from a range of practice. Most aspects of your practice will show evidence from more than one Standard, so look for the strongest links between practice and competencies when placing evidence alongside a Standard.

Portfolio evidence enables you to collect specific examples authenticated by colleagues, staff, tutors or parents, directly linked to Standards or across several, from practice throughout your programme. Maybe we yet have to explore how children can justify your practice. Your EYITT tutors, and possibly placement mentors, will guide you on selecting evidence. This is a crucial time to check the guidelines provided for 'Ethics and confidentiality of evidence' as you will be involving children and adults in your contributions.

Activity 9.3: Ethics and confidentiality of evidence

Consider yourself as a participant in the practitioner research project below. Read through what you will be doing, as if you were submitting this evidence within your portfolio for assessment towards gaining EYTS. List ethical issues arising in relation to confidentiality.

> Early Years Professionals undertaking pathways towards EYPS and 3–4-year-olds in their settings were involved in research to see if they could effectively integrate children's perspectives into a setting's approach to improving quality across a range of early years provision (Coleyshaw et al. 2012). Clark's Mosaic Approach (Clark and Moss 2011) was used to discover the children's likes and dislikes about their nursery, posing five questions:
>
> 1   Tell me about your photos of your favourite places.
> 2   Are there rules about the use of (photo image)?
> 3   If all the children are doing something and you want to do something different, what happens?
> 4   If child has not mentioned activities such as role play, singing/music, circle time, cooking, etc. ask what activities they like doing.
> 5   Are there any parts of the nursery you don't like?
>
> (Coleyshaw et al. 2012: 31)

Look at your list and check your concerns against your EYITT providers Ethical Guidelines for submitting content that involves:

- a setting;
- 3- and 4-year-old children;
- co-researchers;
- photographic evidence;
- children's documentation.

Now ask yourself:

- What steps can you take to include some supportive evidence?
- What materials may need to be archived (seen by a tutor, signed off and kept in a secure place until completion of assessment, when destroyed), or remain within the setting?
- Is there an opportunity for you to present this evidence through another medium than written research or your portfolio, for example, during an observation within your setting?

Checking competencies against each Standard

In the remainder of this chapter we consider each of the individual Standards in turn and you may like to create your own check list table for each (if your EYITT provider does not provide one for you) showing the following:

Knowledge and understanding	Evidence to date	Action, if needed

As you approach each Standard, take time to break down the vocabulary and critically analyse what is being asked for in the way of evidence. Consider how you can respond in the first person, using specific examples from your own daily practice, working across the age range. Then consider who you are collaborating with to achieve your evidence, finding examples that display different goals relevant to the different expectations across the age range birth to age 5. So let's get started and explore which competencies are required to be evidenced for each Standard, interspersed with activities to support you in your thinking.

Standard 1 Set high expectations which inspire, motivate and challenge all children

1.1 Establish and sustain a safe and stimulating environment where children feel confident and are able to learn and develop.

1.2 Set goals that stretch and challenge children of all backgrounds, abilities and dispositions.

1.3 Demonstrate and model the positive values, attitudes and behaviours expected of children.

As you analyse what is required for Standard 1, start thinking about the diversity of your early years provision, identifying examples where you have extended learning opportunities for 'children of all backgrounds, abilities and dispositions.' Link theory from Chapters 2 and 3, and practice examples of Chapter 5 to your own opportunities.

You are likely to be able to present your knowledge, understanding and skills for this Standard throughout the different types of assessment – written essays, specific portfolio examples, organized routines and activities, and as you are being observed within a setting. So, as you go about your daily practice, highlight when and where you are demonstrating competency.

One outcome noted within the research project above was that co-construction opportunities enabled children to develop the language to express their views and negotiate ownership of aspects of the nursery and improvements to provision. Thinking critically was supported through the provision of safe spaces and the language to do so. Older children acted as models with, therefore, no differentiation by age or ability (Coleyshaw et al. 2012: 20).

So, with evidence provided for babies, children, staff and parents as they settle in an enabling, inclusive emotional environment, with expectations of challenging learning opportunities, what comes next?

Standard 2 Promote good progress and outcomes by children

2.1 Be accountable for children's progress, attainment and outcomes.

2.2 Demonstrate knowledge and understanding of how babies and children learn and develop.

2.3 Know and understand attachment theories, their significance and how effectively to promote secure attachments.

2.4 Lead and model effective strategies to develop and extend children's learning and thinking, including sustained shared thinking.

2.5 Communicate effectively with children from birth to age five, listening and responding sensitively.

2.6 Develop children's confidence, social and communication skills through group learning.

2.7 Understand the important influence of parents and/or carers, working in partnership with them to support the child's well-being, learning and development.

Activity 9.4: Identify the type of evidence that is required

Listed below are verbs/action requirements for this Standard. Against each, note how you can best provide evidence, e.g. assessor observation of you with children or parents, own observation – and if so, what type (Chapter 6), written assignment . . .

Action	Type of evidence
Know and understand	
Demonstrate	
Promote	
Communicate effectively	
Listen and respond sensitively	
Be accountable for	
Develop	
Lead and model	
Work in partnership	
Support	

Chapters 2 and 3 again provide background theories to underpin the choices you make here with practice. The supportive statements can be used to analyse what you are doing within your practice. Remember as a graduate leader you are not doing all of these all the time in every situation. This Standard really gives you a chance to show your reflective practitioner skills (Chapter 8).

Now identify a range of examples to show differentiation here and acknowledge the extent of your expertise:

- why, when, where and how you have used group learning to develop children's confidence, social and communication skills;
- why, when, where and how you have listened and responded sensitively to individual babies and children;
- how you best record evidence of sustained, shared thinking, and how you lead and role model opportunities . . . or are you confident enough to set up learning opportunities for practice observation (Chapter 4)?

Standard 3 Demonstrate good knowledge of early learning and EYFS

3.1 Have a secure knowledge of early childhood development and how that leads to successful learning and development at school.

3.2 Demonstrate a clear understanding of how to widen children's experience and raise their expectations.

3.3 Demonstrate a critical understanding of the EYFS areas of learning and development and engage with the educational continuum of expectations, curricula and teaching of Key Stages 1 and 2.

3.4 Demonstrate a clear understanding of systematic synthetic phonics in the teaching of early reading.

3.5 Demonstrate a clear understanding of appropriate strategies in the teaching of early mathematics.

The verb 'demonstrate' dominates the competencies required here, so take your time to look at other key words. 'Clear understanding of . . .' is different from an expectation that you will be sole deliverer of systematic synthetic phonics or early mathematics programmes. See Chapter 4 for ways to value what you are doing and identify how they link to these programmes, or are a preferred way to address individual learning needs.

However, this Standard can clearly be evidenced when you visit a Key Stage 1 classroom for 10 days. You can place yourself in the observer role, acknowledging ethical guidelines.

Activity 9.5: Observations in Key Stage 1

You will be visiting a KS1 classroom for 10 days during your programme:

1   Create three different observation templates that you can use to record evidence that will help your understanding of:
   1   the educational continuum of expectations, curricula and teaching of Key Stages 1 and 2, following on from EYFS
   2   systematic synthetic phonics in the teaching of early reading.
   3   appropriate strategies in the teaching of early mathematics.

2   In your templates you may like to have a box where you can identify connections between learning experiences for children within EYFS and KS1 and KS2.
3   Complete your own templates during your visit.
4   Share your results with peers, and critically reflect on your understanding of this 'continuum'.
5   These results may be able to become portfolio evidence for S3.
6   Then, also think how you can share your knowledge and understanding through developments within your own practice.

Standard 4 Plan education and care taking account of the needs of all children

4.1 Observe and assess children's development and learning, using this to plan next steps.

4.2 Plan balanced and flexible activities and educational programmes that take into account the stage of development, circumstances and interests of children.

4.3 Promote a love of learning and stimulate children's intellectual curiosity in partnership with parents and/or carers.

4.4 Use a variety of teaching approaches to lead group activities appropriate to the age range and ability of children.

4.5 Reflect on the effectiveness of teaching activities and educational programmes to support the continuous improvement of provision.

Activity 9.6: Presenting written evidence

The extensive excerpt below is from one of Karen's EYPS summative assessments. She is employed in a nursery class, so has undertaken 60 hours placement in full day care provision to gain experience with babies. She has already explained underpinning theories in detail, so now is describing what she has done.

As you read through her description, note at the end of each paragraph different aspects of Standard 4, as well as other Standards you have already encountered. Also note PP for personal practice, and LS if evidence provided for leading and supporting. A sample is provided at the end of paragraph one.

First, I carefully considered the age and stage of all children within the baby room regarding their independent play, their different stage of development, how they engaged with others and everyday routines. To achieve this I spent time observing and recording the babies' different interests, abilities and liaised closely with the children's Key Persons and parents regarding any fears, allergies, developmental and cultural concerns that the nursery might be aware of, to build up an accurate picture of the unique child. (4.1, 4.3) (PP, LS)

When assessing my observations and engaging with Key Persons and parents I discovered that all babies within the nursery setting are stimulated and interested in exploring and investigating using different sensory experiences. I also recognized that they are active learners, therefore I need to provide the correct environment and adult support to encourage their natural curiosity and creativity. I also observed that all babies are communicating at different levels, for example; the younger ones through sounds, such as crying, babbling, squealing, facial expressions, eye contact, smiling, grimacing and body movements, moving legs in excitement or distress, and gestures like pointing, while others are using basic key words such as, ball, bye bye and go.

Taking all this into consideration, I decided to plan a sensory activity to challenge them to think and engage with their senses as well as reinforcing and building upon previous sensory-motor experiances.

I will achieve this by creating age-appropriate sensory bags. To create this resource, I will place some hair gel or liquid soap in a strong transparent zipper bag, and place some small items which have a stimulating sparkly visual effect and other small objects that reflected the babies' interests, such as fish, brightly coloured buttons and lentils. Taking into consideration the health and safety of all babies, I will reinforce the zipper seal with some extra strong tape to ensure no small objects or gel/soap escapes from the bag. I will then secure these on an age- and height-appropriate table for added security as this will prevent the babies from putting the sensory bags into their mouths.

Although the majority of the babies are able to walk securely on their feet, there is one baby who is still developing his gross motor skills. He is currently moving around the environment by crawling and pulling himself up on furniture to a standing position to support his balancing, then using it to support him walking around until he is able to observe and communicate with his peers independently. Therefore, when leading this activity, I will position myself close enough to this child to provide extra support to prevent him from falling but also giving him the space and independence that he will require to independently discover new experiences alongside his peers whilst developing his gross motor skills.

When setting the activity up, I will display the sensory bags in an interesting and inviting way on a table that is a suitable height for all babies to access independently. I will also set the activity up while the babies are in the outdoor learning environment so they will be able independently to discover and participate in the activity upon entering the room.

During this tabletop activity I will encourage social skills, language and physical development. This will be achieved by providing the babies with the opportunity to explore a sensory experience while developing their own thoughts and ideas, leading to them making original discoveries. My role throughout the activity will be to observe and reinforce and introduce language to help develop the babies' language acquisition. I will identify the names of specific objects within the sensory bag as well as reinforcing descriptive words, such as shiny, pretty, soft, and smooth, therefore, facilitating the babies' ability to associate words with objects. As this is a new sensory experience for all the babies, I will model how to interact with the bag by pressing my finger on it and moving it around, repeating in an excited but soft voice the key vocabulary. I will also reinforce language with encouraging facial expressions and body language. I will position myself on the floor in a kneeling position so I am able to interact with all babies at their level. This will also encourage social skills, and physical development that are linked to the EYFS 2012 Development matters prime areas.

Throughout this activity I encouraged all six babies to explore and investigate through play and freedom of choice as outlined by the EYFS 2012. I led and supported this child-centred, age-appropriate activity with the correct ratio of 1:3.Therefore, throughout the activity I also led and supported the interaction of another practitioner.

I independently set up the activity when no babies were present. This enabled me to ensure that all medical records were checked for allergies such as soap or sensitive skin. I also ensured that all health and safety requirements and policies were adhered to, enabling me to provide a safe environment for all to learn and develop in. For example; though the gel that was used was child-safe and non-toxic, it is not fit for consumption and should not be encouraged to go in the mouth. I ensured that all sensory bags were entirely secured to the age-/stage-appropriate table to prevent them from being put into their small investigating mouths and to avoid leakage. This ensured that all babies had the opportunity to learn by actively investigating them within a safe environment.

To support the other practitioners in the room before I led the activity, I provided each of them with an activity plan. This enabled me to discuss the aims and objectives of the activity and the key vocabulary with them. I identified that though the majority of the babies were able to toddle around their environment, the youngest baby is still developing his walking skills, therefore we had to be thoughtful when supporting his balancing skills but we also had to ensure that he was able to take manageable risks to encourage his continuous development. I also led and supported the role of other practitioners by modelling the correct body language and vocabulary throughout the activity. By using this approach I was able to lead and support all staff to achieve the aims and objectives of the activity.

Throughout my planned activity I observed all the babies exploring the sensory bags very closely with their fingers and banging them with their hands, this promoted hand–eye coordination. The babies were also engaged in a sustained way because of their fascination with the shimmering objects within the sensory bag. I supported this by allowing them time to become completely absorbed in their discovery and providing them with the time and space to experiment with the knowledge and skills that they already have.

When leading the activity I also supported a particular child when standing at the activity, ensuring that I was close enough to protect him from becoming unbalanced, while also ensuring that he had the space and independence that he required to independently discover and explore new experiences.

When leading and supporting this activity, I observed that their concentration levels were particularly high as the babies were fascinated with what they were doing. I also observed them focusing and sustaining attention throughout the activity. All babies stayed engaged at the activity for up to five minutes at a time and when they had left the table, they independently returned and continued to investigate and explore different types of sensory bags.

All babies gained pleasure by discovering things for themselves; this was displayed in their facial expressions and by their vocalizations. They were also able to explore the activity by using a trial and error method, for example, one baby demonstrated a lot of curiosity regarding the different objects in the bag and tried to pick the objects up with a small pincer grasp. When they discovered that they were unable to achieve this, they then used their fingers to push the objects around to gain a better view of them. This enabled them to experience first-hand concepts such as texture, shape and mobility. Two of the older babies also began to imitate and approximate the sounds and words which I modelled throughout the activity by referring and pointing to the sensory bag containing the fish as 'ish, ish'.

Through leading this activity I was also able to support all babies in developing their social interaction with their peers. For example, I encouraged all babies to observe their peers by pointing and speaking to them when exploring the sensory bags; this led to them imitating each other and displaying a strong motivation to get involved.

Upon reflection, I believe that the activity was successful, this was because it was a short activity which the babies could leave and return to independently. I also believe that the activity was appropriate for their age and beneficial for building solid motor foundations in a baby.

When leading and supporting this activity again, I would extend it by attaching the sensory bags at different levels around their environment, for example, on the wall or on a reflective mirror at eye level, as this would create a different visual angle. I would also suggest securely placing them on a large tuff spot tray in the outdoor environment as this will enable the babies to concentrate solely on the activity as some have just learnt to walk and stand, so a lot of their thought process is focusing on controlling their balance. Additionally this would encourage them to develop other gross motor skills such as shoulders and upper arm strength. I would also recommend leaving the bags in a fridge or freezer overnight so the babies have the opportunity of experiencing different temperatures; this can also be extended further by placing cooked pasta or tomatoes in a sensory bag to create an experience that is more tactile.

I also felt that the liquid soap did not have the same consistency as the gel, so I would only use gel in the future. I would also recommend that different coloured gel could be used to provide a different visual effect for each bag.

This example, from placement experience, highlights extensive learning for the trainee with babies. Consider how this activity could be further endorsed, maybe through feedback from a colleague, mentor or tutor who had observed the process . . . or visual documentation collected for a display for parents.

Standard 5 Adapt education and care to respond to the strengths and needs of all children

5.1 Have a secure understanding of how a range of factors can inhibit children's learning and development and how best to address these.

5.2 Demonstrate an awareness of the physical, emotional, social, intellectual development and communication needs of babies and children, and know how to adapt education and care to support children at different stages of development.

5.3 Demonstrate a clear understanding of the needs of all children, including those with special educational needs and disabilities, and be able to use and evaluate distinctive approaches to engage and support them.

5.4 Support children through a range of transitions.

5.5 Know when a child is in need of additional support and how this can be accessed, working in partnership with parents and/or carers and other professionals.

Chapter 5 has taken a slightly different slant than the others by using interview techniques with a range of professionals. Hopefully this will encourage you to do likewise, you can certainly use the interview questions as a base.

A unique aspect of the role of Early Years Teacher is the requirement, as confirmed in Chapter 2, to build relationships with parents and/or carers. Each of you will have different ways of doing this, with the opportunity to demonstrate what you do . . . and why that specific way is your choice.

Again, break up the vocabulary within the support statements for Standard 5 and you will note the difference with terms like 'support'. You will be required to show how you work with children, families and colleagues through a 'range' of transitions – vertical and horizontal (Dunlop and Fabian 2007).

In this chapter, different approaches are being taken to each Standard which can be applied to all. The competencies to be evidenced in Standard 6 are likely to have been identified already, but read it critically now and identify key words that may challenge evidence you have to date.

Standard 6 Make accurate and productive use of assessment

6.1 Understand and lead assessment within the EYFS framework, including statutory assessment requirements.

6.2 Engage effectively with parents and/or carers and other professionals in the on-going assessment and provision for each child.

6.3 Give regular feedback to children and parents and/or carers to help children progress towards their goals.

Chapter 6 has focused specifically on this Standard, linked to Standard 4. Exemplars of different ways to observe lead directly into looking at assessment and Sutherland and Maxey have clarified formative and summative assessment for you.

Activity 9.7: Statutory assessment requirements within the EYFS framework

1   Read carefully through the Early Years Foundation Stage Statutory Assessment Guidance as specified for Standard 6 (NCTL Teachers' Standards (Early Years) 2013b: 6–8).
   1   Critically compare and contrast the overview of assessment (p. 6) with the recommendations in Chapter 6.
   2   What do you do now that is similar . . . and why?
2   Read through the requirements for the progress check at age 2 (p. 6).
   1   What evidence do you have of your role in relation to the two-year progress check?
   2   Looking at Chapter 6, what else do you need to do now?
3   Read through the requirements for the Early Years Foundation Stage Profile (EYFSP).
   1   As above, what evidence do you have of your role in relation to the EYFSP?

Visit the following key websites that keep early years providers up-to-date with potential tools available to support assessment. Critically analyse the materials in relation to your own context and professional development.

Key websites

DfE Profile exemplification materials
http://www.education.gov.uk/schools/teachingandlearning/assessment/eyfs/b00217443/eyfs-exemplification

Foundation Years organization
http://www.foundationyears.org.uk/new-eyfs/

National Children's Bureau
http://www.ncb.org.uk/

Select specific documentation that can be shared with colleagues and parents to promote collaboration in the assessment process.

Standard 7 Safeguard and promote the welfare of children, and provide a safe learning environment

7.1 Know and act upon the legal requirements and guidance on health and safety, safeguarding and promoting the welfare of the child.

7.2 Establish and sustain a safe environment and employ practices that promote children's health and safety.

7.3 Know and understand child protection policies and procedures, recognize when a child is in danger or at risk of abuse, and know how to act to protect them.

With Standard 7, key terminology relating to safeguarding and child protection needs to be clearly defined and owned as you produce evidence of your competency to meet all supporting statements here.

Activity 9.8: Define key terms for safeguarding and child protection

1   Using the detail from Chapter 7, create your own definitions that will be understood within your setting/placement for:
   1 Health and safety
   2 Safeguarding
   3 Welfare
   4 Child protection
   5 Policies
   6 Procedures
   7 Abuse.

> 2   How can you use these definitions to collect evidence that will demonstrate your ability to know, recognize, act on, promote, establish and sustain a range of requirements essential within early years provision? Do include details, as this Standard requires personal practice and leadership and support for the benefits of the children, families and colleagues in your care.

Finally, but underpinning all the others, is a Standard recognizing the importance of you. Use 'How can I . . .?' as you read through the competencies required for Standard 8 and supportive statements.

Standard 8 Fulfil wider professional responsibilities

8.1 Promote equality of opportunity and anti-discriminatory practice.

8.2 Make a positive contribution to the wider life and ethos of the setting.

8.3 Take a lead in establishing a culture of cooperative working between colleagues, parents and/or carers and other professionals.

8.4 Model and implement effective education and care, and support and lead other practitioners including Early Years Educators.

8.5 Take responsibility for leading practice through appropriate professional development for self and colleagues.

8.6 Reflect on and evaluate the effectiveness of provision, and shape and support good practice.

8.7 Understand the importance of and contribute to multi-agency team working.

In Chapter 8, McKibbin and Pawson present a range of 'windows' for you to explore your own continuing professional development. If you haven't started already, do keep a personal journal/reflective log and record your experiences throughout your pathway in relation to each of the above.

As you complete your programme, read back and be surprised at how much you have covered. One of the main benefits candidates and trainees have expressed as a result of these programmes is the increase in confidence in bringing about change within early years provision, whatever the setting. See two comments below, from graduates entering early years through the programme:

Rheanne Bernard graduated from Business Management at Kingston before taking up her EYPS place:

> I am not set back at all by not having studied early years before now. We spend so much time on placements, we can use the knowledge we get in the classroom and take it straight into a nursery to put into practice. I have now decided to complete a Master's in Professional Studies in Education and the EYPS course actually covers the first part, so I am halfway there.

Michael Cowley had a good IT career, but decided to follow in his parents' footsteps and run his own nursery:

> I am the only man on the course this year, and it's still hard to get taken seriously in the early years environment. The benefit of this course is that it gives me more credibility with the parents, and being able to say you are a teacher instils more confidence with them than the term nursery nurse.

Keep track of your journey, and reflect on where you would like your career to develop, hopefully within early years.

Final reflection: professional identity

A local network of Early Years Professionals who had gained Early Years Professional Status between 2007 and 2013 shared their job titles:

Education Co-ordinator/Tea maker	Full day care provision
Early Years Teacher/SENCO	Nursery setting
Early Years Professional	
Lead Practitioner for 2.15 provision	Children's Centre with nursery
Toy Library Co-ordinator	
Sessional worker	Pre-school
Childminder (with assistant)	
Operations Manager	Nursery chain
Nursery Nurse	Maintained nursery
Early Years Educator/Key Worker	Nursery
Flexi-educator/SEN support	

- How do you describe your professional identity now?
- How do you see your role developing when you have gained Early Years Teacher Status?
- What next step can you take to achieve your long-term vision for early years provision?

Together, there is the opportunity to really be graduate leaders that babies, young children, families, colleagues and other professionals recognize as inspirational blenders of care and education.

Appendix

Teachers' Standards (Early Years) 2013 (NCTL 2013b)

Preamble

Early Years Teachers make the education and care of babies and children their first concern. They are accountable for achieving the highest possible standards in their professional practice and conduct. Early Years Teacher Status is awarded to graduates who are leading education and care and who have been judged to have met all of the standards in practice from birth to the end of the Early Years Foundation Stage (EYFS).

Early Years Teachers act with integrity and honesty. They have strong early development knowledge, keep their knowledge and skills up-to-date and are self-critical. Early Years Teachers recognize that the Key Stage 1 and Key Stage 2 curricula follow the EYFS in a continuum. They forge positive professional relationships and work with parents and/or carers in the best interests of babies and children.

Standard 1 Set high expectations which inspire, motivate and challenge all children

1.1 Establish and sustain a safe and stimulating environment where children feel confident and are able to learn and develop.

1.2 Set goals that stretch and challenge children of all backgrounds, abilities and dispositions.

1.3 Demonstrate and model the positive values, attitudes and behaviours expected of children

Standard 2 Promote good progress and outcomes by children

2.1 Be accountable for children's progress, attainment and outcomes.

2.2 Demonstrate knowledge and understanding of how babies and children learn and develop.

2.3 Know and understand attachment theories, their significance and how effectively to promote secure attachments.

2.4 Lead and model effective strategies to develop and extend children's learning and thinking, including sustained shared thinking.

2.5 Communicate effectively with children from birth to age five, listening and responding sensitively.

2.6 Develop children's confidence, social and communication skills through group learning.

2.7 Understand the important influence of parents and/or carers, working in partnership with them to support the child's well-being, learning and development.

Standard 3 Demonstrate good knowledge of early learning and EYFS

3.1 Have a secure knowledge of early childhood development and how that leads to successful learning and development at school.

3.2 Demonstrate a clear understanding of how to widen children's experience and raise their expectations.

3.3 Demonstrate a critical understanding of the EYFS areas of learning and development and engage with the educational continuum of expectations, curricula and teaching of Key Stages 1 and 2.

3.4 Demonstrate a clear understanding of systematic synthetic phonics in the teaching of early reading.

3.5 Demonstrate a clear understanding of appropriate strategies in the teaching of early mathematics.

Standard 4 Plan education and care taking account of the needs of all children

4.1 Observe and assess children's development and learning, using this to plan next steps.

4.2 Plan balanced and flexible activities and educational programmes that take into account the stage of development, circumstances and interests of children.

4.3 Promote a love of learning and stimulate children's intellectual curiosity in partnership with parents and/or carers.

4.4 Use a variety of teaching approaches to lead group activities appropriate to the age range and ability of children.

4.5 Reflect on the effectiveness of teaching activities and educational programmes to support the continuous improvement of provision.

Standard 5 Adapt education and care to respond to the strengths and needs of all children

5.1 Have a secure understanding of how a range of factors can inhibit children's learning and development and how best to address these.

5.2 Demonstrate an awareness of the physical, emotional, social, intellectual development and communication needs of babies and children, and know how to adapt education and care to support children at different stages of development.

5.3 Demonstrate a clear understanding of the needs of all children, including those with special educational needs and disabilities, and be able to use and evaluate distinctive approaches to engage and support them.

5.4 Support children through a range of transitions.

5.5 Know when a child is in need of additional support and how this can be accessed, working in partnership with parents and/or carers and other professionals.

Standard 6 Make accurate and productive use of assessment

6.1 Understand and lead assessment within the EYFS framework, including statutory assessment requirements (see annex 1).

6.2 Engage effectively with parents and/or carers and other professionals in the on-going assessment and provision for each child.

6.3 Give regular feedback to children and parents and/or carers to help children progress towards their goals.

Standard 7 Safeguard and promote the welfare of children, and provide a safe learning environment

7.1 Know and act upon the legal requirements and guidance on health and safety, safeguarding and promoting the welfare of the child.

7.2 Establish and sustain a safe environment and employ practices that promote children's health and safety.

7.3 Know and understand child protection policies and procedures, recognize when a child is in danger or at risk of abuse, and know how to act to protect them.

Standard 8 Fulfil wider professional responsibilities

8.1 Promote equality of opportunity and anti-discriminatory practice.

8.2 Make a positive contribution to the wider life and ethos of the setting.

8.3 Take a lead in establishing a culture of cooperative working between colleagues, parents and/or carers and other professionals.

8.4 Model and implement effective education and care, and support and lead other practitioners including Early Years Educators.

8.5 Take responsibility for leading practice through appropriate professional development for self and colleagues.

8.6 Reflect on and evaluate the effectiveness of provision, and shape and support good practice.

8.7 Understand the importance of and contribute to multi-agency team working.

References

AAIA (Association for Achievement and Improvement through Assessment) (2013) Assessment Reform Group. Available at: http://www.aaia.org.uk/afl/assessment-reform-group/ (accessed 27 September 2013).

Ainsworth, M.D.S., Blehar, M.C., Waters, E. and Wall, S. (1978) *Patterns of Attachment: A Psychological Study of the Strange Situation*. Hillsdale, NJ: Erlbaum.

Allen, G. (2011) *Early Intervention: The Next Steps*. London. Cabinet Office.

Allingham, A. (2011) *Transitions in the Early Years: A Practical Guide to Supporting Transitions between Early Years Settings and into Key Stage One*. Salisbury: Practical Pre-School Books.

Arnold, A. and Rutter, R. (2011) *Working with Parents: Key Issues*. London: Featherstone Education.

Assessment Reform Group (1999) *Assessment for Learning Beyond the Black Box*. London: Nuffield Foundation.

Aubrey, C. (2011) *Leading and Managing in the Early Years*. London: Sage.

Bain, A. and Barnet, L. (1980) *The Design of a Day Care System in a Nursery Setting for Children under Five*. London: Tavistock Institute for Human Relations.

Ball, S. (1994) *Education Reform: A Critical and Post-structural Approach*. Buckingham: Open University Press.

Bayley, R. and Featherstone, S. (2009) *Smooth Transitions: Ensuring Continuity from the Foundation Stage*. Harlow: Longman.

BERA (2012) *The BERA Charter for Research Staff in Education*. Available at: http://www.bera.ac.uk (accessed 8 August 2013).

Berger, E.H. (1999) Supporting parents with two essential understandings: attachment and brain development, *Early Childhood Education Journal*, 26(4): 267–70.

Black, P., Harrison, C., Lee, C., Marshall, B. and Wiliam, D. (2002) *Working Inside the Black Box*. London: King's College.

Blandford, S. and Knowles, C. (2009) *Developing Professional Practice 0–7*. Harlow: Pearson Education.

Blenheim Playgroup Parents (2012) *Parents Helping Their Children with Early Reading: An Advice Booklet Made by the Parents of Blenheim Playgroup*. Available at: http://www.real-online.group.shef.ac.uk/docs/Blenheim%20Parents%20Advice%20Booklet.pdf (accessed 20 November 2013).

Bodrova, E. (2008) Make-believe play versus academic skills: a Vygotskian approach to today's dilemma of early childhood education, *European Early Childhood Education Research Journal*, 16(3): 357–69.

Bodrova, E. and Leong, D. (2007) *Tools of the Mind*, 2nd edn. Upper Saddle River, NJ: Pearson Prentice Hall.

Bolton, J. (2010) *Reflective Practice: Writing and Professional Development*, 3rd edn. London: Sage.

Bottery, M. (2006) Education and globalization: redefining the role of the educational professional, *Educational Review*, 58(1): 95–113.

Bowlby, J. (1998) *Separation: Anxiety and Anger*. London: Pimlico.

Broadhead, P. and Burt, A. (2012) *Understanding Young Children's Learning Through Play*. London: Routledge.

Brock, A. (2006) Eliciting Early Years Educators' thinking: how do they define and sustain their professionalism? Paper presented to the EECERA Conference, Reykavik, Iceland, 30 August–2 September.

Brock, A. (2012) Building a model of early years professionalism from practitioners' perspectives, *Journal of Early Childhood Research*, 11(1): 27–44.

Brooker, L. (2008) *Supporting Transitions in the Early Years*. Maidenhead: McGraw-Hill Education.

Brownlee, J. (2004) An investigation of teacher education students' epistemological beliefs: developing a relational model of teaching, *Research in Education*, 72: 1–18.

Bruce, T. (1991) *Time to Play in Early Childhood Education*. London: Hodder Education.

Bruce, T. (2004) *Developing Learning in Early Childhood*. London: Sage.

Bruner, J. (1986) *Actual Minds, Possible Worlds*. Cambridge, MA: Harvard College.

Burton, C. and Lyons, M. (2000) When does a teacher teach? The Queensland early childhood profession on trial, in J. Hayden (ed.) *Landscapes in Early Childhood Education*. New York: Peter Lang.

Butler-Sloss, E. (1988) *Report of the Inquiry into Child Abuse in Cleveland 1987*. London: HMSO.

Cambridge University Press (2013) Pupil, in *Advanced Learner's Dictionary*. Available at: www.dictionary.cambridge.org/dictionary/british/pupil_1?q=pupil (accessed 4 February 2014).

Canning, N. (2011) Identifying unique qualities in play, in N. Canning (ed.) *Play and Practice in the Foundation Years*. London: Sage.

Carr, M. (2008) Presentation to Hui Topu: Professional Development for Early Childhood Education, 28 May, Wellington, NZ.

Cheminais, R. (2009) *Effective Multi-Agency Partnerships: Putting Every Child Matters into Practice*. London: Sage.

Clark, A. and Moss, P. (2011) *Listening to Young Children: The Mosaic Approach*, 2nd edn. London: National Children's Bureau Enterprises.

Clarke, K. and French, A. (2007) Collaboration with parents: the role of the multi-agency setting in working with parents, in I. Siraj-Blatchford, K. Clarke and M. Needham (eds) *The Team around the Child: Multi-Agency Working in the Early Years*. Stoke on Trent: Trentham Books.

Coleyshaw, L., Whitmarsh, J., Jopling, M. and Hadfield, M. (2012) *Listening to Children's Perspectives: Improving the Quality of Provision in Early Years Settings. Part of the Longitudinal Study of Early Years Professional Status DFE-RR239b*. London: DfE.

Colley, H. (2006) Learning to labour with feeling: class, gender and emotion in childcare education and training, *Contemporary Issues in Early Childhood*, 7(1): 15–29.

Cooke, G. and Lawton, K. (2008) *For Love or Money? Pay, Progression and Professionalization in the 'Early Years' Workforce*. London: Institute for Public Policy Research.

Craft, A. (2013) Childhood, possibility thinking and wise, humanising educational futures, *International Journal of Educational Research*, 61: 135–51.

Cremin, T., Chappell, K. and Craft, A. (2013) Reciprocity between narrative, questioning and imagination in the early and primary years: examining the role of narrative in possibility thinking, *Thinking Skills and Creativity*, 9: 135–51.

Cunliffe, A. (2009) The philosophical leader: on relationship, ethics and reflexivity – a critical perspective to teaching leadership, *Management Learning*, 40(1): 87–102.

CWDC (Children's Workforce Development Council) (2006) *A Head Start for All: Early Years Professional Status*. Leeds: CWDC.

CWDC (Children's Workforce Development Council) (2007) *The Common Assessment Framework for Children and Young People*. Leeds: CWDC.

CWDC (Children's Workforce Development Council) (2009) *Recruiting Safely: Summary. Safer Recruitment Guidance Helping to Keep Children and Young People Safe*. Leeds: CWDC.

Dahlberg, G. and Moss, P. (2005) *Ethics and Politics in Early Childhood Education*. London: Routledge Falmer.

Dalli, C. and Urban, M. (2008) Editorial, *European Early Childhood Education Research Journal, Special Edition on Professionalism*, 16(2): 131–33.

Day, C. (2004) *A Passion for Teaching*. London: Routledge.

DCSF (Department for Children, Schools and Families) (2008a) *Early Years Foundation Stage (EYFS) Pack*. Nottingham: HMSO.

DCSF (Department for Children, Schools and Families) (2008b) *Information Sharing: Guidance for Practitioners and Managers*. Nottingham: DCSF.

DCSF (Department for Children, Schools and Families) (2008c) *The Assessment for Learning Strategy*. Nottingham: Department for Children, Schools and Families. Available at: www.education.gov.uk/publications/eOrderingDownloading/DCSF-00341-2008.pdf (accessed 29 August 2013).

DCSF (Department for Children, Schools and Families) (2008d) *Practice Guidance for the Early Years Foundation Stage*. Nottingham: DCSF Publications.

DCSF (Department for Children, Schools and Families) (2010) *Working Together to Safeguard Children: A Guide to Inter-Agency Working to Safeguard and Promote the Welfare of Children*. Nottingham: DCSF Publications.

DCSF and CWDC (Department for Children, Schools and Families and Children's Workforce Development Council) (2008) *Early Years Professional Status*. London: HMSO.

Degotardi, S. and Pearson, E. (2009) Relationship theory in the nursery: attachment and beyond, *Contemporary Issues in Early Childhood*, 10(2): 144–55.

Department for Employment and Skills (2000) *Curriculum Guidance for the Foundation Stage*. London: QCA Publications.

DES (Department of Education and Science) (1990) *Starting with Quality*. London: The Stationery Office.

Desforges, C. and Abouchaar, A. (2003) *The Impact of Parental Involvement, Parental Support and Family Education on Pupil Achievement and Adjustment: A Literature Review*. Nottingham: Department of Education and Skills.

DfE (Department for Education) (2011) *The Tickell Review: Early Years Foundation Stage*. London: HMSO.

DfE (Department for Education) (2012) *Statutory Framework for the Early Years Foundation Stage*. Runcorn: DfE.

DfE (Department for Education) (2013a) *Early Education and Childcare: Statutory Guidance for Local Authorities*. Available at: http://education.gov.uk/aboutdfe/statutory/g00209650/code-of-practice-for-las.

DfE (Department for Education) (2013b) *Early Years Outcomes: A Non-Statutory Guide for Practitioners and Inspectors to Help Inform Understanding of Child Development Through the Early Years*. Runcorn: DfE.

DfE (Department for Education) (2013c) *English Programmes of Study: Key Stages 1 and 2. National Curriculum in England*. Runcorn: DfE.

DfE (Department for Education) (2013d) *More Affordable Childcare*. Runcorn: DfE.

DfE (Department for Education) (2013e) *More Great Childcare: Raising Quality and Giving Parents More Choice*. Runcorn: DfE.

DfE (Department for Education) (2013f) *Teachers' Standards*. Available at: https://www.gov.uk/government/uploads/system/uploads/attachment_data/file/208682/Teachers__Standards_2013.pdf (accessed 25 November 2013).

DfE (Department for Education) (2013g) *The National Curriculum in England. Key Stages 1 and 2 Framework Document*. Runcorn: DfE.

DfE (Department for Education) (2013h) *Working Together to Safeguard Children: A Guide to Inter-Agency Working to Safeguard and Promote the Welfare of Children*. Available at: www.education.gov.uk'aboutdfe/statutory.

DfE/DH (Department for Education/Department of Health) (2011) *Supporting Families in the Foundation Years* Runcorn: Department for Education.

DfES (Department for Education and Skills) (2005) *Children's Workforce Strategy*. Nottingham: DfES.

DfES (Department for Education and Skills) (2006a) *Safeguarding Children and Safer Recruitment in Education*. Nottingham: DfES.

DfES (Department for Education and Skills) (2006b) *What to Do If You're Worried a Child Is Being Abused*. Nottingham: TSO.

DfES (Department for Education and Skills) (2006c) *Working Together to Safeguard Children*. Norwich: TSO.

DfES (Department for Education and Skills) (2007) *Letters and Sounds: Principles and Practice of High Quality Phonics. Six-Phase Teaching Programme*. Norwich: DfES.

DH (Department of Health) (1991) *Child Abuse: A Study of Inquiry Reports, 1980–1989*. London: HMSO.

DH/DfEE (Department of Health/Department for Education and Employment) (1999) *Working Together to Safeguard Children: A Guide to Intra-Agency Working to Safeguard and Promote the Welfare of Children*. London: The National Archives.

Donaldson, M. (1978) *Children's Minds*. London: Fontana.

Downie, R.S. (1990) Professions and professionalism, *Journal of Philosophy of Education*, 24(2): 147–59.

Doyle, M.E. and Smith, M.K. (1999) *Born and Bred?: Leadership, Heart and Informal Education*. London: YMCA George Williams College.

Drury, R. (2013) How silent is the 'Silent Period' for young bilinguals in early years settings in England?, *European Early Childhood Education Research Journal*, 21(3): 380–91.

Duffy, B. and Marshall, J. (2009) Leadership in multi-agency work, in I. Siraj-Blatchford, K. Clarke, and M. Needham (eds) *The Team Around the Child: Multi-agency Working in the Early Years*. Stoke on Trent: Trentham Books.

Dunlop, A-W. and Fabian, H. (eds)(2007) *Informing Transitions in the Early Years*. Maidenhead: McGraw-Hill International.

Dunn, J. (1988) *The Beginnings of Social Understanding*. Oxford: Blackwell.

Dunn, M., Harrison, L. and Coombe, K. (2008) In good hands: preparing research skilled graduates for the early childhood profession, *Teaching and Teacher Education*, 24(3): 703–14.

Early, D., Maxwell, K., Burchinal, M., Bender, R., Ebanks, C. and Henry, G. (2007) Teachers' education, classroom quality, and young children's academic skills: results from seven studies of preschool programs, *Child Development*, 78(2): 558–80.

EarlyBird (2013) *EarlyBird training*. Available at: www.autism.org.uk/Earlybird National Autistic Society.

Early Learning Partnership Engagement Group (ELPPEG) (2010) *Principles for Engaging with Families: A Framework for Local Authorities and National Organisations to Evaluate and Improve with Families*. London: National Quality Improvement Network.

EE (Early Education) (2012) *Development Matters in the Early Years Foundation Stage (EYFS)*. London. Early Education. Available at: www.early-education.org.uk (accessed 1 November 2013).

Elfer, P. (1996) Building intimacy in relationships with young children in nurseries, *Early Years*, 16(2): 30–34.

Elfer, P. (2002) *Holding the Baby: The Emotional Demands on Early Years Practitioners Working with Babies and Toddlers*. London: Tavistock and Portman NHS Trust.

Elfer, P., Goldschmied, E. and Selleck, D. (2012) *Key Persons in the Nursery and Reception Classes: Building Relationships for Quality Provision*. London: David Fulton.

Eliot, L. (1999) *Early Intelligence: How the Brain and Mind Develop in the First Five Years of Life*. London: Penguin.

Eraut, M. (1992) Developing the knowledge base: a process perspective on professional education, in R. Barnett (ed.) *Learning to Effect*. London: SRHE/Open University Press.

Fabian, H. and Mould, C. (eds) (2009) *Development and Learning for Very Young Children*. London: Sage.

Farroni, T., Csibra, G., Simion, F. and Johnson, M.H. (2002) Eye contact detection in humans from birth, *Proceedings of the National Academy of Science*, 99: 9602–5.

Featherstone, S. (2011) *Catching Them at It!* London: A. & C. Black Publishers.

Field, F. (2010) *The Foundation Years: Preventing Poor Children Becoming Poor Adults*. London: The Cabinet Office.

Fitzgerald, D. (2004) *Parent Partnerships in the Early Years*. London: Continuum.

Fleer, M. (2010) *Early Learning and Development: Cultural-Historical Concepts in Play*. Cambridge: Cambridge University Press.

Forbes, R. (2004) *Beginning to Play: Young Children from Birth to Three*. Maidenhead: Open University Press.

Friedson, E. (1994) *Professionalism Reborn: Theory, Prophesy and Policy*. Cambridge: Polity Press.

Frowe, I. (2005) Professional trust, *British Journal of Educational Studies*, 53(1): 34–53.

Fukkink, R. and Lont, A. (2007) Does training matter? A meta-analysis and review of caregiver training studies, *Early Childhood Research Quarterly*, 22: 294–311.

Garvey, C. (1991) *Play*, 2nd edn. London: Fontana.

Gasper, M. (2010) *Multi-agency Working in Early Years: Challenges and Opportunities*. London: Sage.

Gerhardt, S. (2004) *Why Love Matters: How Affection Shapes a Baby's Brain*. London: Routledge.

Gerver, R. (2010) *Creating Tomorrow's Schools Today. Education – Our Children – Their Futures*. London: Continuum.

Goldschmied, E. and Jackson, S. (2005) *People Under Three: Young Children in Day Care*. London: Routledge.

Goldschmied, E. and Selleck, D. (1996) *Communication between Babies in their First Year*. London: National Children's Bureau.

Goodson, I. (2004) Representing teachers, *Teaching and Teacher Education*, 13(1): 111–17.

Goouch, K. (2010) Permission to play, in J. Moyles (ed.) *The Excellence of Play*, 3rd edn. London: Routledge.

Gopnik, A., Meltzoff, P. and Kuhl, K. (2001) *How Babies Think*. London: Phoenix.

Greenman, J.T. and Stonehouse, A. (1996) *Prime Times: A Handbook for Excellence in Infant and Toddler Care*. St. Paul, MN: Redleaf Press.

Groundwater-Smith, S. and Sachs, J. (2002) The activist professional and the reinstatement of trust, *Cambridge Journal of Education*, 32(3): 341–58.

Hargreaves, A. (2000) Mixed emotions: teachers' perceptions of their interactions with students, *Teacher and Teacher Education*, 16(2): 811–26.

Harwood, R.L., Miller, J.G. and Irizarry, N.L. (1995) Cross-cultural validity of the strange situation, in R.L. Harwood (ed.) *Culture and Attachment*. New York: The Guildford Press.

Holmes, J. (1993) *John Bowlby and Attachment Theory*. London: Routledge.

Holmes, J. (1999) Ghosts in the consulting room: an attachment perspective on intergenerational transmission, *Attachment and Human Development*, 1(1): 115–31.

Hopkins, J. (1988) Facilitating the development of intimacy between nurses and infants in day nurseries, *Early Child Development and Care*, 33: 99–111.

Hord, S.M. and Sommers, W.A. (2008) *Leading Professional Learning Communities: Voices from Research and Practice*. Thousand Oaks, CA: Corwin Press.

House, R. (2011) *Too Much, Too Soon? Early Learning and the Erosion of Childhood*. Stroud: Hawthorn Press.

Howe, A. (2002) Developing professional attitudes in training: report from the AMEE Berlin professional development workshop, *Medical Teacher*, 24(2): 208–12.

Hutt, C. (1979) Play in the under-fives: form, development and function, in J. Howells (ed.) *Modern Perspectives in the Psychiatry of Infancy*. New York: Brunner/Mazel.

I CAN (2013) *Early Talk 0-5*. Available at: http://www.ican.org.uk/ (accessed 28 October 2013).

Isaacs, S. (1929) *The Nursery Years: The Mind of the Child from Birth to Six Years*. London. Routledge.

Jensen, J.J. and Hansen, H.K. (2003) The Danish pedagogues: a worker for all ages, *Children in Europe*, 5: 6–9.

Johnson, J. (2010) *Positive and Trusting Relationships with Children in Early Years Settings*. Exeter: Learning Matters.

Jones, D. (2013) *Listening* – so much more than *hearing, Educating Young Children: Learning and Teaching in the Early Childhood Years*, 19(1): 27–8.

Katz, L. (2011) Current perspectives on the early childhood curriculum, in R. House (ed.) *Too Much, Too Soon? Early Learning and the Erosion of Childhood*. Stroud: Hawthorn Press.

Kotulak, R. (1996) *Inside the Brain: Revolutionary Discoveries of How the Mind Works*. Kansas: Andrews and McMeel.

Kraemer, S. (1999) Promoting resilience: changing concepts of parenting and childcare, *International Journal of Child Welfare*, 4(3): 273–8.

Kuisma, M. and Sandberg, A. (2008) Pre-school teachers' and students preschool teachers' thoughts about professionalism in Sweden, *European Early Childhood Education Research Journal*, 16(2): 186–95.

Kwon, Y. (2002) Changing curriculum for early childhood education in England, *Early Childhood Research and Practice*, 4(2): 1–15.

Laevers, F., Daems, M., De Bruyckere, G., Declercq, B., Moons, J., Silkens, K., Snoeck, G. and Van Kessel, M. (2005) *Sics (Ziko) Well-being and Involvement in Care: A Process-Oriented Self-Evaluation Instrument for Care Settings*. Leuven: CEGO Publications. Available at: htttp://www.averbode.be/Pub/CEGO-ENG-Catalogue/Free-downloads.hml (accessed 29 October 2013).

Lambert, L. (1998) How to build leadership capacity, *Educational Leadership*, April: 17–19. Association for Supervision and Curriculum Development; EBSCO Publishing.

Laming, Lord, (2003) *The Victoria Climbié Inquiry*. Norwich: HMSO.

Laming, Lord (2009) *The Protection of Children in England: A Progress Report*. London: The Stationery Office.

Lewis, J. and Hill, J. (2012) What does leadership look like in early years childhood settings? *Every Child*, 18(4): 10–11.

Lieberman, A.F. (1995) *Emotional Life of the Toddler*. New York: Simon & Schuster Inc.

Lindon, J. (2006) *Equality in Early Childhood: Linking Theory and Practice*. London: Hodder Arnold.

Lloyd, E. and Hallet, E. (2010) Professionalising the early childhood workforce in England: work in progress or missed opportunity? *Contemporary Issues in Early Childhood*, 11(1): 75–88.

Lumsden, E. (2012) *Early Years professional status: a new professional or a missed opportunity?*, University of Northampton Electronic Collection of Theses and Research.

Lundy, L. (2007) Voice is not enough: conceptualising Article 12 of the United Nations Convention on the Rights of the Child, *British Educational Research Journal*, 33(6): 9–27.

Macdonald, K.M. (1995) *The Sociology of the Professions*. London: Sage.

Maclean, S. (2012) *Effective Supervision*. Lichfield: Kirwin Maclean Associates Ltd.

McDowall Clark, R. and Murray, J. (2012) *Reconceptualizing Leadership in the Early Years*. Maidenhead: Open University Press.

McGregor, B. (2013) What do we mean by number concept? *Educating Young Children; Learning and Teaching in the Early Childhood Years*, 19(1): 18–23.

McInnes, K., Howard, J., Miles, G. and Crowley, K. (2011) Differences in practitioners understanding of play and how this influences pedagogy and children's perceptions of play. *Early Years: An International Journal of Research and Development*, 31(2): 121–33.

McKie, L., Gregory, S. and Bowlby, S. (2002) Shadow times: the temporal and spatial frameworks and experiences of caring and working, *Sociology*, 36(4): 897–924.

Manning-Morton, J. (2006) The personal is the professional: professionalism and the birth to threes practitioner, *Contemporary Issues in Early Childhood*, 7(1): 42–52.

Manning-Morton, J. and Thorp, M. (2003) *Key Times for Play: The First Three Years*. Maidenhead: Open University Press.

May, P. (2010) *Child Development in Practice: Responsive Teaching and Learning from Birth to Five*. Abingdon: Routledge.

Meggitt, C. and Sunderland, G. (2012) *Child Development: An Illustrated Guide*, 3rd edn. London: Heinemann.

Menzie, K. (2013) Using picture books to build the foundations of global citizenship, *Educating Young Children: Learning and Teaching in the Early Childhood Years*, 19(1): 35–7.

Miller, L. and Cable, C. (2011) *Professionalization: Leadership and Management in the Early Years*. London: Sage.

Miller, P.H. (2002) *Theories of Developmental Psychology*. New York: Worth Publishers.

Mindham, C. (2005) Creativity and the young child, *Early Years: An International Journal of Research and Development*, 25(1): 81–4.

Miskin, R. (2013) *Read. Write. Inc.* Oxford: Oxford University Press.

Montague-Smith, A. and Price, A.J. (2012) *Mathematics in Early Years Education*. London: Routledge.

Moss, P. (2006) Structures, understandings and discourses: possibilities for re-envisioning the early childhood worker, *Contemporary Issues in Early Childhood*, 7(1): 30–41.

Moss, P. (2008) The democratic and reflective professional: rethinking and reforming the early years workforce, in L. Miller and C. Cable (eds) *Professionalism in the Early Years*. London: Hodder Education.

Moss, P. (2010) We cannot continue as we are: the educator in an education for survival, *Contemporary Issues in Early Childhood*, 11(1): 8–19.

Moyles, J. (1989) *Just Playing*. Maidenhead: Open University Press.

Moyles, J. (2001) Passion, paradox and professionalism in early years education, *Early Years*, 21(2): 81–95.

Moyles, J., Adams, S. and Musgrove, A. (2002) *SPEEL Study of Pedagogical Effectiveness in Early Learning*, Department for Education and Skills (DfES) Research Report 363. Norwich: HMSO.

Moyles, J. and Papatheodorou, T. (2009) *Learning Together in the Early Years: Exploring Relational Pedagogy*. London: Routledge.

Muijs, D., Aubrey, C., Harris, A. and Briggs, M. (2004) How do they manage? A review of the research on leadership in early childhood, *Journal of Early Childhood Research*, 200(2): 157–60.

Munro, E. (2010) *The Munro Review of Child Protection – Part One: A Systems Analysis*. London: Department of Health.

Musatti, T. and Mayer, S. (2011) Sharing attention and activities among toddlers: the spatial dimension of the setting and the educator's role, *European Early Childhood Education Research Journal*, 19(2): 207–21.

National Strategies (2008) *Every Child a Talker: Guidance for Early Language Lead Practitioners*. Nottingham: DCSF.

NCB (National Children's Bureau) (2012) *A Know How Guide: The EYFS Progress Check at Age Two*. London: NCB.

NCTL (National College for Teaching and Leadership) (2013a) *Early Years Educator (Level 3) Qualifications Criteria*. Available at: https://www.gov.uk/government/publications/early-years-educator-level-3-qualifications-criteria (accessed 25 November 2013).

NCTL (National College for Teaching and Leadership) (2013b) *Teachers' Standards (Early Years) 2013*. Available at: https://www.gov.uk/government/uploads/system/uploads/attachment_data/file/211646/Early_Years_Teachers__Standards.pdf (accessed 25 November 2013).

Neaum, S. (2013) *Child Development for Early Years Students and Practitioners*, 2nd edn. London: Sage.

Nuffield Foundation (2013) *Assessment for Learning 10 Principles*. London: Nuffield Foundation.

Nursery World (2013). Available at:

http://www.nurseryworld.co.uk/nursery-world/other/11403383/interview-dr-jo-van-herwegen-psychologist-kingston-university-london.

Nutbrown, C. (2011) *Threads of Thinking*, 4th edn. London: Sage.

Nutbrown, C. and Bishop, J. (2013) *Raising Early Achievement in Literacy*. Available at: http://www.real-online.group.shef.ac.uk/ (accessed 20 November 2013).

Nutbrown, C. and Clough, P. (2006) *Inclusion in the Early Years*. London: Sage.

Nutbrown, C., Clough, P. and Selbie, P. (2008) *Early Childhood Education: History, Philosophy and Experience*. London: Sage.

Oakeshott, M. (1989) Teaching and learning, in T. Fuller (ed.) *The Voice of Liberal Learning*. New Haven, CT: Yale University Press.

Oberhuemer, P. (2005) Conceptualising the early childhood pedagogue: policy approaches and issues of professionalism, *European Early Childhood Education Research Journal*, 13(1): 5–16.

Oberhuemer, P. and Scheryer, I. (2008) What professional? Aiming high: a professional workforce for the early years, *Children in Europe*, 5: 9–12.

OECD (Organisation for Economic Co-operation and Development) (2001) *Starting Strong: Early Childhood Education and Care*. Paris: OECD.

OECD (Organisation for Economic Co-operation and Development) (2004) *Starting Strong: Curricula and Pedagogies in Early Childhood Education and Care – Five Curriculum Outlines*. Available at: http://www.oecd.org/education/school/31672150.pdf (accessed 29 October 2013).

OECD (Organisation for Economic Co-operation and Development) (2008) *Education at a Glance: OECD Indicators 2008*. Available at: http://www.oecd.org/ document/9/0,3343, en_2649_39263238_41266761_1_1_1,0 0.htm (accessed 12 October 2013).

Ofsted (2008) *Safeguarding Children: The Third Joint Chief Inspectors' Report on Arrangements to Safeguard Children*. London: Crown Publishers.

Ofsted (2012) *The Report of Her Majesty's Chief Inspector of Education, Children's Services and Skills Early Years*. Available at: www.ofsted.gov.uk/resources/120349.

Oliveira-Formosinho, J. and Barros Araujo, S. (2011) Early education for diversity: starting from birth, *European Early Childhood Education Research Journal*, 19(2): 223–5.

Olsson, L.M (2009) Movement and experimentation in young children's learning: Deleuze and Guattari, in *Early Childhood Education*. London: Routledge.

Osgood, J. (2006a) Deconstructing professionalism in early childhood education: resisting the regulatory gaze, *Contemporary Issues in Early Childhood*, 7(1): 5–15.

Osgood, J. (2006b) Professionalism and performativity: the feminist challenge facing early years practitioners, *Early Years*, 26(2): 187–99.

Osgood, J. (2006c) Rethinking 'professionalism' in the early years: perspectives from the United Kingdom, *Contemporary Issues in Early Childhood*, 7(1): 1–4.

Page, J. (2011) Do mothers want professional carers to love their babies? *Journal of Early Childhood Research*, 9(3): 310–23.

Palaiologou, I. (ed.) (2013) *The Early Years Foundation Stage, Theory and Practice*, 2nd edn. London: Sage.

Palaiologou, I. and Male, T. (2013) Historical developments in policy for early years education and care, in I. Palaiologou. (ed.) *The Early Years Foundation Stage: Theory and Practice*, 2nd edn. London: Sage.

Papatheodorou, T. and Potts, D. (2013) Pedagogy of early years, in I. Palaiologou (ed.) *The Early Years Foundation Stage: Theory and Practice*, 2nd edn. London: Sage.

Papatheodorou, T., Luff, P. and Gill, J. (2011) *Child Observation for Learning and Research*. London: Pearson.

Paton, G. (2013) Half of boys' struggle with basic writing at the age of five, *The Telegraph*, 24 October. Available at: www.telegraph.co.uk/education/educationnews/10402096/Half-of-boys-struggle-with-basic-writing-at-the-age-of-five.html (accessed 4 October 2014).

Patterson, C. (2011) *Parenting Matters: Early Years and Social Mobility*. London: CentreForum.

Pen Green Centre for Under Fives and Families (2007) Available at: http://www.daycaretrust.org.uk/pages/working-in-partnership-with-parents.html§hash.BdIMEgPZ.dpuf.

Penn, H. (1999) *Values and Beliefs in Caring for Babies and Toddlers*. London: Institute of Education.

Penn, H. (2000) *Early Childhood Services: Theory, Policy and Practice*. Buckingham: Open University Press.

Plymouth Safeguarding Children Board (2010) *Serious Case Review Overview Report Executive Summary in Respect of Nursery Z*. Plymouth: Plymouth Safeguarding Children Board.

Porter, L.S. and Porter, B.O. (2004) A blended infant massage-parenting enhancement program for recovering substance-abusing mothers, *Pediatric Nursing*, 30(5): 363–401.

Raelin, J. (2004) *Learning to let go*. Available at: http://www.leaderful.org/pdf/RaelinTD.pdf (accessed 9 October 2013).

Richardson, L. (2000) Writing: a method of inquiry, in N.K. Denzin and Y.S. Lincoln (eds) *Handbook of Qualitative Research*, 2nd edn. Thousand Oaks, CA: Sage.

Rinaldi, C. (2012) The pedagogy of listening: the listening perspective from Reggio Emilia, in C. Edwards, L. Gandini and G. Forman (eds) *The Hundred Languages of Children*. Oxford: Praeger.

Roberts, J. (2011) Trust and early years childcare: parents' relationships with private, state and third sector providers in England, *Journal in Social Policy*, 40(4): 695–715.

Roberts, R. (2011) Companionable learning: a mechanism for holistic well-being development from birth, *European Early Childhood Education Research Journal*, 19(2): 195–205.

Roberts-Holmes, G. (2012) 'It's the bread and butter of our practice': experiencing the Early Years Foundation Stage. *International Journal of Early Years Education*, 20(1): 30–42.

Robinson, K.H. and Diaz, C.J. (2006) *Diversity and Difference in Early Childhood Education: Issues for Theory and Practice*. Maidenhead: Open University Press.

Rodd, J. (2012) *Leadership in Early Childhood: The Pathway to Professionalism*, 4th edn. Maidenhead: Open University Press.

Rogers, S. (2011) Play and pedagogy: a conflict of interests? in S. Rogers (ed.) *Rethinking Play and Pedagogy in Early Childhood Education: Concepts, Contexts and Cultures*. London: Routledge.

Roosevelt, T. (2013) Nobody cares how much you know. Available at: BrainyQuote.com, Xplore Inc, http://www.brainyquote.com/quotes/quotes/t/theodorero140484.html (accessed 27 November 2013).

Rose, J. (2006) *An Independent Review of the Teaching of Early Reading: Final Report*. Nottingham: DfES.

Rowson, R. (2006) *Working Ethics: How to Be Fair in a Culturally Complex World*. London: Jessica Kingsley Publishers.

Royal Borough of Kingston Early Years Advisory Team (2012) *Moving On*. Kingston RBK.

Scheiwe, K. and Willekens, H. (2009) *Child-Care and Preschool Development in Europe: Institutional Perspectives*. Basingstoke: Palgrave Macmillan.

Schön, D.A. (1983 edn, 1991 reprint) The crisis of confidence in professional knowledge, in *The Reflective Practitioner*. London: Arena Ashgate.

Scott, C. and Jaffe, D. (2004) *Managing Change at Work: Leading People through Organizational Transitions*, 3rd edn. Boston: Thompson Learning.

Shuttleworth, J. (1989) Psychoanalytic theory and infant development, in L. Miller, M. Rustin and J. Shuttleworth (eds) *Closely Observed Infants*. London: Duckworth.

Siraj-Blatchford, I., Sylva, K., Muttock, S., Gilden, R. and Bell, D. (2002) *Researching Effective Pedagogy in the Early Years*. Norwich: HMSO.

Smith, A. and Langston, A. (1999) *Managing Staff in Early Years Settings*. London: Routledge.

STA (Standards and Testing Agency) (2013) *National Curriculum Assessments:Early Years Foundation Stage Profile Handbook*. Standards and Testing Agency. Available at: https://www.gov.uk/government/uploads/system/uploads/attachment_data/file/249995/Early_years_foundation_stage_profile_handbook_2014.pdf (accessed: 25 October 2013).

Stern, D.N. (1998) *The Interpersonal World of the Infant*. London: Basic Books.

Stoll, L. and Seashore Louis, K. (2007) *Professional Learning Communities: Divergence, Depth and Dilemmas*. Maidenhead: Open University Press.

Stonehouse, A. (1988) *Trusting Toddlers: Planning for One-to-Three-Year Olds in Child Care Centers*. St. Paul, MN: Toys 'n Things Press.

Sylva, K., Melhuish, E., Sammons, P., Siraj-Blatchford, I. and Taggert, B. (2004) *The Effective Provision of Preschool Education (EPPE) Project: Final Report*. Nottingham: DfES Publications.

Taggart, G. (2011) Don't we care?: The ethics and emotional labour of early years professionalism, *Early Years*, 31(1): 85–95.

Tamati, A., Hond-Flavell, E., Korewha, H. and the whānau of Te Kōpae Piripono (2008) *Centre of Innovation Research Report of Te Kōpae Piripono*. Available at: http://www.education-counts.govt.nz/__data/assets/pdf_file/0008/118457/Te Kopae-Piripono-COI-Full-Report.pdf (accessed 2 October 2013).

Taylor, J.B., Branscombe, N.A., Burcham, J.G. and Land, L. (2011) *Beyond Early Literacy: A Balanced Approach to Developing the Whole Child*. London: Routledge.

Tickell, C. (2011) *The Early Years: Foundations for Life, Health and Learning*. Available at: www.education.go.uk.

Trevarthen, C. (2011a) What is it like to be a person who knows nothing? Defining the active intersubjective mind of a newborn human being, *Infant and Child Development*, 20: 119–35.

Trevarthen, C. (2011b) What young children give to their learning: making education work to sustain a community and its culture, *European Early Childhood Education Research Journal*, 19(2): 173–93.

Urban, M. (2008) Dealing with uncertainty: challenges and possibilities for the early childhood profession, *European Early Childhood Education Research Journal*, 16(2): 135–52.

Vanderstraeten, R. (2007) Profession in organisations, professional work in education, *British Journal of Sociology of Education*, 28(5): 621–35.

Vermeer, H.J. and Van Ijzendoorn, M.H. (2006) Children's elevated cortisol levels at daycare: a review and meta-analysis, *Early Childhood Research Quarterly*, 21: 390–401.

Vygotsky, L. (1962) *Thought and Language*. Cambridge, MA: MIT Press.

Wandschneider, S. and Crosbie, S. (2013) Play, think, link, learn: building language skills in the early years of education, *Educating Young Children: Learning and Teaching in the Early Childhood Years*, 19(1): 25–7.

Wenger, E. (1998) *Communities of Learning: Learning, Meaning and Identity*. Cambridge: Cambridge University Press.

Whalley, M. (ed.) (2007) *Involving Parents in Their Children's Learning*, 2nd edn. London: Paul Chapman.

Whalley, M. (2011) *Leading Practice in Early Years Settings*, 2nd edn. Exeter: Learning Matters.

Wheeler, H. and Connor, J. (2009) *Parents, Early Years and Learning: Parents as Partners in the Early Years Foundation Stage – Principles into Practice*. London: NCB.

Whitaker, P. (1993) *Managing Change in Schools*. Buckingham: Open University Press.

Whitbread, D. and Bingham, S. (2011) *School Readiness; A Critical Review of Perspectives and Evidence*. Occasional Paper No. 2. Available at: http://www.tactyc.org.uk/occasional-papers/occasional-paper2.pdf. (accessed 21 October 2013).

Wiliam, D. and Black, P. (1998) *Inside the Black Box*. London: King's College.

Williams, L. (ed.) (2009) *Listening as a Way of Life: Developing a Listening Culture*. London: National Children's Bureau.

Williams, P. (2008) *Independent Review of Mathematics Teaching in Early Years Settings and Primary Schools*. London: Department for Children, Schools and Families.

Winnicott, D.W. (1960) The theory of the parent-infant relationship, *The International Journal of Psychoanalysis*, 41: 585–95.

Wood, E. (2013) *Play, Learning and the Early Childhood Curriculum*. London: Sage.

Index

accountability 6
activity records 95
adapting to strengths and needs 72–3
  Area Special Needs Co-ordinator (SENCO) 73–6
  head teacher of Local Authority-maintained children's centre 84–9
  Local Authority Early Years Adviser 76–8
  nursery managers 79–81
  observe, assess, plan cycle 89–90
  portage worker 81–4
  Standard 5 167–8, 174*a*
adult-led play 26–7
age-related stages, child-centred learning and 22
Allen, G. 42
America 6–7
appraisals, supervision and 148–9
assessment 93–4
  challenges, issues and strategies 106
  definition and types 101–2
  government agendas and initiatives 103–4
  ICT 110
  Mosaic approach 95, 110
  next steps and planning 111–15
  process-oriented monitoring system (POMS) 111
  purpose of 102–3
  of special needs 85
  Standard 6 168, 174a
  of teachers *see* evidence for assessment
  two-year progress check 104–6, 107–10, 112

Association for Achievement and Improvement through Assessment (AAIA) 93
attachment 35–8, 39, 40, 47
Australia 6–7, 8, 62, 139–40

Bain, A. and Barnet, L. 47, 48
Bernard, R. 170
bilingualism 63, 86–7
Black, P. et al. 93
Bodrova, E. 23
  and Leong, D. 24
Bolton, J. 144
Bottery, M. 12
Bowlby, J. 37, 40, 41, 47
brain development 11, 35, 36
British Educational Research Association (BERA) 145–6
Broadhead, P. and Burt, A. 22, 26
Brownlee, J. 148
Bruce, T. 18, 25–6

care and education *see* education and care
catalytic agent model of leadership 140, 141, 144, 152
check lists 95
child-centred learning 22
child-centred practice 120, 122
Childcare Act (2006) 121
childminders 77–8
Children Act
  1989 117–19, 150
  2004 120–1, 124, 125, 134, 150

children in need, definition of 118
Children's Workforce Development Council
    (CWDC) 5, 128
Clark, A. and Moss, P. 110, 159
Clarke, K. and French, A. 41, 43, 44
coaching 149
Coleyshaw, L. et al. 159, 160
communication
    Computer Mediated Communication (CMC)
       110
    see also language
competence-based approach 7–8
    checking against Standards 160–71
confidentiality, ethics and 159
'consciousness of others' 62–3
'containing'/'holding' 40
continual professional development (CPD)
    145–6
Cowley, M. 171
Cunliffe, A. 145
curious engagement 55–60, 70–1

Dahlberg, G. and Moss, P. 142
Dalli, C. and Urban, M. 10
Degotardi, S. and Pearson, E. 39
Department for Children, Schools and
       Families (DCSF) 90, 101, 124, 128,
       133, 134
    and Children's Workforce Development
       Council (CWDC) 5
Department for Education (DfE) 9, 18–19, 22,
       30, 41, 43, 51, 53, 157
    and Department of Health (DH) 42, 43,
       117
    early years outcomes 93
    guidance for Local Authorities 27–8, 142
    KS1 English 68
    safeguarding and welfare requirement 116,
       121–2, 125, 134
    staff supervision requirement 148–9
    Teachers' Standards 31–2
Department for Education and Skills (DfES)
       5–6, 15, 29, 67–8, 120, 125
Department of Health (DH) 42, 43, 117,
    119
Drury, R. 63

Early Education (EE) 50, 51, 62, 93
Early Learning Partnerships Engagement
    Group (ELPPEG) 44, 45

Early Years Foundation Stage (EYFS) 51–5
    and National Curriculum, comparison
       between 51–4, 59–60
Early Years Foundation Stage Profile (EYFSP)
    103
Early Years Initial Teacher Training (EYITT)
    1, 3, 154, 156, 157, 158, 159
Early Years Teacher Status (EYTS) 154
EarlyBird (EB) programme 84
education and care
    adapting (Standard 5) 167–8, 174*a*
    graduate knowledge and understanding of
       157–8
    historical relationship between 10–12
    planning (Standard 4) 163–7, 173*a*
Effective Provision of Pre-School Education
    (EPPE) 40–1, 42, 138
Elfer, P. 42, 46, 48
Eliot, L. 36, 37
emotional abuse 118
employer, evidence for assessment 156
'entry profile' 79
ethics
    and confidentiality 159
    see also values and beliefs
Every Child Matters 120
evidence for assessment 153–6
    case study: teacher profile 155–6
    checking competences against Standards
       160–71
    employer links 156
    ethics and confidentiality 159
    graduate knowledge and understanding of
       care and education 157–8
    personal practice record 157
expectations (Standard 1) 160–1, 172*a*

family structures 44–5
Farroni, T. et al. 35
Field, F. 42
Fleer, M. 26, 27
formative assessment 101
free-flow play 25–6
    and adult-led play 26–7
Friedson, E. 8
Frowe, I. 12, 13–14, 146–7
funding, eligibility for 142–4

Gerhardt, S. 35, 36
Gerver, R. 60

Goldschmied, E. 47
  and Jackson, S. 40
  and Selleck, D. 42
Gopnik, A. et al. 35
Graduate entry 156
Groundwater-Smith, S. and Sachs, J. 147

'hard-to-reach' services 44–5
head teacher perspective 84–9
health care 87–8
'holding'/'containing' 40
Holmes, J. 37, 38, 40
Home Learning Environment (HLE) 42, 43
home/setting approach 42–4
home visits 85, 87
  portage worker 81–4
Hopkins, J. 47
Hord, S.M. and Sommers, W.A. 146
Hutt, C. 26–7

immature to mature play 24–5
Individual Education Plan (IEP) 83
information communication technology (ICT)
    110
information sharing, collaboration and 134,
    150
Isaacs, S. 37

Jones, D. 57, 62

Key Person 38, 41, 46–8, 79, 80, 85
  case study 48–9
  secondary 39
knowledge
  specialist 5–6, 30
  Standard 3 162–3, 173a
  and understanding of care and education
    157–8
Kraemer, S. 34, 36, 48

Lambert, L. 146
Laming, Lord: inquiry and recommendations
    119–20
language 62–5
  bilingualism 63, 86–7
  and literacy 65–8
  case study: parents and children 63–5
  speech and language skill (SENCO) 73, 75
leadership 27–9
  beliefs and values 144–5

case studies
  funding for places for 2-year-olds 143–4
  multi-professional practice 151–2
  Te Köpae Piripono Mäori Early Childhood
    Centre, New Zealand 139
catalytic agent model 140, 141, 144, 152
concepts of 137–40
continual professional development (CPD)
    145–6
emerging paradigms 137, 140
multi-agency working 150–2
planning role 29–32
professional development of self and others
    147–8
professional learning communities 146–7
responding to change 142–4
safeguarding role see staff
supervision, appraisals and coaching 148–9
learning communities, professional 146–7
learning opportunities 60
Lewis, J. and Hill, J. 139–40
Lieberman, A.F. 37
listening, speaking and 62, 67, 68
Lloyd, E. and Hallet, E. 8
Local Authority
  children's centre, head teacher perspective
    84–9
  cooperation and information sharing 134,
    150
  Designated Officer (LADO) 133
  Early Years Adviser 76–8
  eligibility for free early education 142
  and Standards and Testing Agency (STA)
    103
Local Safeguarding Children Boards (LSCB)
    120, 125, 127
Lumsden, E. 1

McDowell Clark, R. and Murray, J. 140, 152
McInnes, K. et al. 20–1
McKie, L. et al. 10–11
Maisy, D. 4
Makaton 83, 87
Manning-Morton, J. 36, 40, 46, 48
  and Thorp, M. 37, 38, 40, 41, 46
mathematics 68–70, 103
mature play, immature to 24–5
Miller, L. and Cable, C. 6–7, 9, 15, 29
Montague-Smith, A. and Price, A.J. 69
Mosaic approach 95, 110, 159

Moss, P. 6, 7–8, 10, 15–16
 Clark, A. and 110, 159
 Dahlberg, G. and 142
Moyles, J. 11, 15, 26–7
 et al. 20, 21
 and Papatheodorou, T. 53
multi-agency working 150–2
Munro, E. 6, 11

National Children's Bureau (NCB) 41, 93
National College for Teaching and Leadership
 (NCTL) 6, 9, 11, 15, 29, 31, 32, 51, 68,
 103
 see also Teachers' Standards (NCTL 2013b)
National Curriculum and EYFS, comparison
 between 51–4, 59–60
Neaum, S. 33
neglect, abuse and 118–19, 124–5
neuroscience/brain development 11, 35, 36
New Zealand: Te Köpae Piripono Mäori Early
 Childhood Centre (case study) 139
nursery managers 79–81
Nutbrown, C.
 and Clough, P. 43, 44
 et al. 18
nutrition 87–8

Oakeshott, M. 7, 13
Oberhuemer, P. 8, 9
observation
 and assessment cycle 93–4
 challenges, issues and strategies 100
 observe, assess, plan cycle 89–90
 purpose of 95–100
 target child 95
 techniques
  comparison between 97–100
  types and 94–5
 tracking 94–5, 98
 written records 94, 96, 97
 see also assessment
OECD 15, 111, 146
Ofsted 6, 7
 allegations of serious harm or abuse 133
 visits 76, 77
Olsson, L.M. 148
Osgood, J. 6, 8, 11, 15

Page, J. 12, 48
Palaiologou, I. 32–3

parenting programmes 42–3
parents
 case study: literacy with parents and
  children 63–5
 of children with additional needs 74, 86–8
  portage worker 81–4
 and home/setting approach 42–4
 partnership with 40–2, 48, 86, 87–8
  safeguarding responsibilities 134–5
 see also relationships
Paton, G. 65–6
Patterson, C. 42–3
Pen Green Centre 42, 43–4, 90
personal, social and emotional development
  (PSED) 60–1
 assessment 102–3
personal practice record 157
personal values see values and beliefs
phonics 67–8
photographs 80, 84–5, 86, 87
physical abuse 118
Piaget, J. 22, 37, 69
planning 29–32
 assessment 111–15
 Standard 4 163–7, 173a
play and play pedagogy 17–18
 case studies
  private day-care setting 30–1
  structured play using approximate
   number system 70
 child- or adult-led 26–7
 definition and components 23
 leadership 27–9
  and planning 29–32
 play-based curriculum 18–20
 specialist knowledge 30
 theoretical perspectives 21–6
 values, beliefs and shared vision 20–1
portage worker 81–4
process-oriented monitoring system (POMS)
  111
professional identity 171
professional learning communities 146–7
professional responsibilities (Standard 8)
  170–1, 174–5a
professionalism 4–7, 15–16
 competence-based approach 7–8
 historical relationship between education
  and care 10–12
 personal values and beliefs 13–14

role of reflection 9–10
  specialist knowledge 5–6
  see also leadership
progress and outcomes (Standard 2) 161,
    172–3*a*

Raelin, J. 138–9
reflection, role of 9–10
reflective practice 29–30, 144–5
Reggio Emilia approach 147
relationships 34–5
  attachment 35–8, 39, 40, 47
  barriers and obstacles 46–8
  being 'tuned in' to separation issues 40
  'hard-to-reach' services 44–5
  see also Key Person; parents
Rinaldi, C. 147, 148
Roberts, J. 147
Roberts-Holmes, G. 70
Robinson, K.H. and Diaz, C.J. 44–5
Rodd, J. 142, 147
Rogers, S. 19, 26
Rose, J. 67
Rumbold Report 29

safeguarding 116–17
  allegations of serious harm or abuse 133
  case study 123
  child-centred practice 120, 122
  childminders 77–8
  and health care 87–8
  information sharing and working with other
      professionals 134
  legislation and associated statutory
      guidance 117–22
  meeting policy requirements 124–5
  and professionalism 11
  safe and open culture 122–4
  welfare and safe environment (Standard 7)
      169–70, 174*a*
  working with parents 134–5
  see also staff
safeguarding officer 125
Schön, D.A. 5, 9
school and pre-school, relationship between
    80
'school readiness' agenda 20
'secure base' 37, 39, 41, 42
Serious Case Review of Nursery Z 148–9
settling-in period 47–8, 79–80, 81

sexual abuse 118
shared thinking (case study) 64–5
shared vision 20–1
Shuttleworth, J. 40
significant harm, definition of 118
socio-cultural theory 23
socio-economic status 43
socio-grams 95
Special Needs Co-ordinator (SENCO) 73–6
specialist knowledge 5–6, 30
speech and language skills 73, 75
speech and listening practice 62, 67, 68
staff 126–7
  allegations of serious harm or abuse
      against 133
  recruitment 128–32
    before appointment is made 131–2
    before post is released 128–31
  training and support 127–8
  see also leadership
Standards and Testing Agency (STA) 103
Stern, D.N. 37
summative assessment 101, 103, 104–6
supervision 148–9
supportive environment 88–9
sustained shared thinking (case study) 64–5

Taggart, G. 11
target child observation 95
Taylor, J.B. et al. 66
Te Kōpae Piripono Mäori Early Childhood
    Centre, New Zealand (case study)
    139
Teachers' Standards (NCTL 2013b) 160–71,
    172–5*a*
  Preamble 154
time samples 99
  and event samples 95
tracking observation 94–5, 98
Trevarthen, C. 53, 55, 62
trust
  professional 12, 146–7
  and 'triangle of trust' 42, 47–8
two-year progress check 104–6, 107–10, 112

Undergraduate entry 156

values and beliefs
  leadership 144–5
  personal and professional 13–14

play and play pedagogy 20–1
  see also ethics
Van Herwegen, J. 65–6, 70
Vanderstraeten, R. 8
visual aids/timetables 83, 87, 88
vocabulary
  development 65–7
  and socio-economic status 43
volcano project (case study) 57–8
Vygotsky, L. 23–5, 35, 69

Wandschneider, S. and Crosbie, S. 65

Whalley, M. 28, 29, 42
Whitaker, P. 139
Whitbread, D. and Bingham, S. 20
William, D. and Black, P. 93
Williams Review 103
Winnicott, D.W. 40
Wood, E. 18, 19, 22, 23, 25
written records 94, 96, 97
  presenting 164–7

'zone of proximal development' (ZPD) 23–4,
  25